SCHOOL *of* HARD KNOTS

A Citizen Sailor Goes to Sea

HENRY THY JR

D1042426

To

Pam
My mother, father, and sisters
Captain Michael T. Greeley USN (1929–2009)
The officers and men of the USS Furse (DD-882)

CONTENTS

Mount 52
Flight Deck
DASH hangar
Highline station
ASROC

Radar Mast
Director
Signal Bridge
Bridge
Torpedo Deck
Mount 51

882

USS *Furse* (DD 882) with major elements labeled

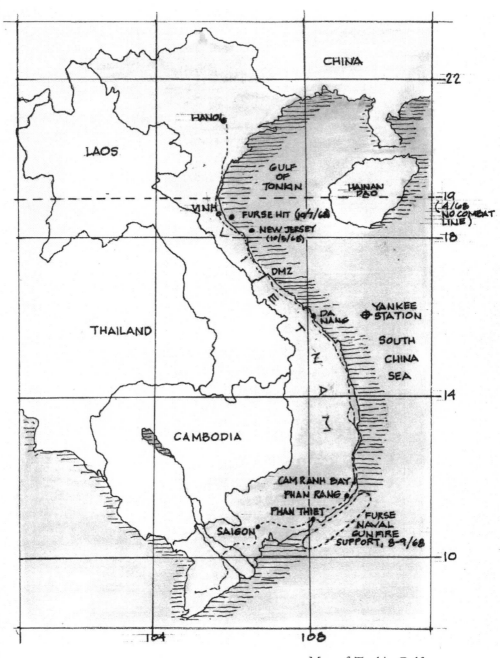

Map of Tonkin Gulf

PREFACE

In the 43 years since I was discharged from the Navy I have raised a family, enjoyed a diverse architectural practice, cofounded a web business, obtained two patents, and run four marathons. The three years I spent on a US Navy destroyer, USS *Furse* (DD-882), from 1966 to 1969, in many ways set the foundation for what I and many citizen sailors like me achieved in later life. Had it not been for the Vietnam War and the draft it is very unlikely that I would have gone into the Navy. But as I look back, I can see with clearer perspective that I learned valuable lessons that have stuck with me all these years:

- Even somebody with no rhythm can learn to march.
- The best alarm clock is someone standing over you and shouting at you to get up.
- When it's dark no one has a problem drinking coffee from the same cup.
- Greasy pork chops are served the first day at sea to make you sick.
- Don't go through the system to get something urgent done.
- Being a bad guy can be a help in getting promoted.
- Good guys sometimes need to act like bad guys.
- Anything you throw overboard is gone for good.

- Don't stand with your hands in your pockets.
- Don't run out of toilet paper.
- An Alka-Seltzer must be taken the night before to prevent a hangover in the morning.
- Navy stories are good for putting your children to sleep.
- A ship has no brakes.
- An aircraft carrier is pretty agile contrary to popular belief.
- The music of the sixties still sounds good.
- If someone takes away the wheel, you can't steer.
- A collision at sea can ruin a man's whole day.
- A murder in port can ruin everybody's day.
- Taking a shower for longer than two minutes still feels like a luxury.
- Living in 90 square feet with three others makes a New York apartment look good.
- A shark nearby makes a good swimmer great.
- Don't choose paint colors at night.
- Be careful what you wish for.

My stint in the Navy also led me to some observations that have helped me in my professional life:

- Good morale is a function of a good leader.
- Thirty to 40 people are about all that can be managed effectively by one person.
- Metrics and formulas should be tempered by experience.
- It takes three years before one can become truly proficient at a new job.
- Trust your experienced people and delegate (do your job; let others do theirs).
- Doing something difficult for the first time has a way of focusing the mind.

- When you get good enough at something you start to like it.
- If something doesn't work, try something else.
- If you keep plugging away things will usually get better.
- A busy person has fewer problems.
- On board, on duty.

The *Furse* was my home from December 1966 to August 1969. Those three years stand out as the most intense and formative of my adult life. Among the events I experienced were running aground, colliding with another ship, being hit by enemy fire, a murder on board, and hurricane-force storms at sea. But many everyday, seemingly insignificant events now loom equally large for what they taught me about myself and about human nature in our tightly packed and tight-knit shipboard community.

I started writing this story in 1970 about a year out of the Navy. It didn't work and I abandoned it. I was just too close to events. I had no perspective on how my three years in the Navy would affect my life. One day in April 2011 I felt compelled to try again. I found that the words and thoughts flowed freely and that time had winnowed out the less significant and memorable events. Time had also blurred the exact sequence of the events from 1966 to 1969 on the *Furse*, but with the aid of the ship's Command Histories as well as selected daily logs obtained from the Naval History & Heritage Command I was able to fill in gaps and reconstruct an accurate timeline. I also benefited greatly from letters saved by my wife and family covering almost every day of this period—a veritable diary that revealed not only the actual events but the spin I put on them at the time. As excerpted here, the text of these letters as well as quotes from Command Histories and daily logs is unedited.

Though there is inevitably some jargon and technical terminology, I have tried to keep these to a minimum. Naval terms are explained in the text, and I have provided a glossary. Notes referenced in the text are found at the end of the book, as is a bibliography.

If you look on the Web for a history of the USS *Furse* (DD-882), you will find that she was commissioned in 1945, had periodic cruises in the Pacific and regular cruises to the Mediterranean and Scandinavia, was decommissioned in 1972, transferred to Spain as the *Gravina*, and scrapped in 1991.[P.1]

What is conspicuously missing from this history is the period 1963 to 1972, when I served on board, including the WestPac (Western Pacific) cruise to Vietnam, one of her most significant deployments and the only time the *Furse* engaged in active combat.

The Command Histories of the *Furse* from its construction in 1945 to its transfer to the Spanish Navy in 1975 are contained in a three-inch-wide file box kept at the History & Archives Division, Naval History & Heritage Command, at the Washington, D.C., Naval Station. They are generally short, factual recordings of major operations with scant information about personnel matters or daily operations. The material contained in them is a function of what the author, usually the Executive Officer (XO), chose to include. There are significant omissions from the 1966–1969 period, such as the change of command in early 1967 and the murder that took place on board in early November 1968. I have started most chapters with the relevant entry from the Command Histories—the official record. Then, as radio commentator Paul Harvey used to say, I give "the rest of the story," at least from my point of view.

This book fills in missing detail and adds color to these events from the perspective of a junior officer. It is both a memoir and a history, infused with observations about the late 1960s and early 1970s, for me a time of transition from a relatively sequestered college life to adulthood. I had been to college to learn facts in a protected atmosphere. The Navy was my School of Hard Knots— real-life lessons learned, often the hard way, from steaming many thousands of nautical miles. (a knot is one nautical mile per hour).

INTRODUCTION

The *Furse* was a modernized World War II destroyer, a sleek sliver of steel carefully designed and fitted out for fighting. It was also a community of men (this was well before women were allowed to serve on ships) living and working together in a very confined space, where divergent personalities interacted for better or worse. It was a veritable laboratory brewing with life churned by ever-changing and often stressful forces both natural and man-made. And the mix was ever evolving as shipmates came and went, all adapting in their own way and all emerging as altered specimens when they departed. Many were not career officers or sailors but volunteered as I had, delaying the start of their civilian careers to serve in this tempestuous time in our history.

The *Furse* was known as a "small combatant" but was, nevertheless, 390 feet long with an allowance—that is, minimum required staff—of 260 to 335 men and 14 to 20 officers. It weighed between 2,500 and 3,500 tons depending on fuel load and could cruise between 5,370 and 6,500 miles at 15 knots (18 mph) on a full load of fuel. Its maximum speed was 34.5 knots (40 mph).[I.1]

The tone of a ship is set by the leader of this community, the captain. The *Furse* had two captains while I was on board, and the contrast could not have been greater in leadership styles and their consequent effect on the ship's morale and performance. The lessons

I learned about leadership were largely forged by observing these two men and by trial and error as a division officer supervising 30 to 40 men myself.

The Navy today is quite different technologically from what it was 40-some years ago, but a ship is still a community, albeit a broader-based one. Today, participation by women on ships has been implemented. "Don't ask, don't tell" has been phased out. And social media have been adopted by the Navy as a way to communicate and to mitigate the effects of long separations from family members. But the basic organizational structure of the officer corps and enlisted ranks is still pretty much the same. There is still an officer candidate school (OCS), and ex-military personnel are still valued by employers for their qualities of leadership and discipline.

Thousands of men (and women when one includes nurses) went through OCS and served as junior officers in the US Naval Reserve before they went on to civilian careers. In fact, since its inception in 1951, this four-month program of basic engineering combined with indoctrination into seamanship, weapons, navigation, and naval justice has supplied more than 50 percent of the junior officers in the Navy, graduating about 3,500 per year.

This is both my personal story and the story of citizen sailors like me. We helped shape the Navy for a few years, but the Navy shaped us for the rest of our lives.

1

EVEN SOMEBODY WITH NO RHYTHM CAN LEARN TO MARCH

Growing Up, Signing On

I was raised as the only boy in a family of six in Wilmington, Delaware. I grew up in neighborhoods that were full of kids. We played touch football and basketball in our backyards and driveways, rode our bikes and climbed trees in a pretty carefree environment. It was a typical suburban life of the 1950s and early 1960s. An early photo of me and my older sister, Janet, shows me in a little sailor's uniform—did my mother know something then?

With four kids, my parents enlisted us in helping around the house. My father and mother instilled a work ethic in all of us. Each of us had his or her own duties. When I was six years old I would mow the lawn with a push mower—no power mowers then. My father was a coin collector and would sometimes pay me with an old coin. This started a lifelong interest in American coins, which I still collect. As I got older I worked most Saturdays with my father on yard and other chores. Both my parents expected jobs to be done with energy and thoroughness, but they were also supportive of our community and sports activities. My mother was a Cub Scout den mother and my father liked to play tennis with us, though he suffered from a bad hip as a result of a childhood football injury. They also placed a high priority on our performance in school. My mother helped type my term papers and my father tried in vain to help me understand chemistry.

My first nautical experience was sailing in the Chesapeake Bay with a childhood friend, Steve Hayes, who lived only one house away from ours. Steve's mother and father were like second parents to me, as mine were to him. I spent several summers with his family in Nags Head, North Carolina, where we swam, fished, and water-skied. We were Cub Scouts and Boy Scouts together and played Little League on the same team; he was the more adventurous of the two of us and would continue to be so when we were in the Navy.

In high school my interests were athletics (running and tennis primarily) and art. I knew I wanted to be an architect as early as junior high school. At Rice University in Houston, Texas, I studied architecture and played intramural sports. I tended to prefer working alone rather than as part of a group on projects in my architecture courses. The Navy would teach me to function in a team environment.

At the time, military service was not even on my radar. Because of my interest in being an architect I never thought of applying to one of the service academies even though, when I was a junior in high school, one of my teachers suggested I consider the military when I graduated after my flippant answer to a question in class suggested I might benefit from a little discipline.

I arrived at Rice at night having never been to the campus or even west of the Mississippi. I was assigned to Weiss College, the most bare-bones building of the four men's colleges, basically a concrete and brick motel structure. The cell-like room assigned to me was on an inside corner without a window and was known as "the handball court." I was later told that my smiling freshman picture made me look like someone who could survive what was considered the worst room in the dorm. Good training for even tighter, more spartan quarters four years later.

When I was a freshman, President Kennedy spoke to us in Rice Stadium about the space program and the goal of putting somebody on the moon. I had no idea then that I would see this vision realized on board a US Navy destroyer seven years later. When the announcement came on the radio that President Kennedy had been shot in Dallas, I was at Rice in the architecture lab. We were working against a deadline and there was not much reaction among the students in my class, who were mostly just listening intently to understand what had happened as the story unfolded. I do remember one student from Houston saying, "He got what he deserved." His was an isolated reaction. Most of us were saddened and bewildered by the events.

Architecture students routinely pulled all-nighters to get our projects done. As morning dawned we had to defend our designs against the scrutiny of our professors in "juries" while we were gaunt with sleeplessness. Stressed-out students often took criticism personally and had to maintain their self-control not to overreact and say something they might regret. Good practice for keeping cool when tired and under pressure on a ship.

These were the years just after the Cuban missile crisis of 1962 and the early years of the Vietnam War (which became official with the Tonkin Gulf Resolution of August 7, 1964). Military service was something to be avoided, deferred, or accepted fatalistically. When I was in my senior year I received my selective service classification of 1A, which made me eligible for the draft. Future presidents, as well as many others, found ways to avoid service in Vietnam, through educational deferments or alternative service in the National Guard. But I was generally supportive of the decision to go to Vietnam, and frankly I was tired of school and visualized serving in the military as a break for some adventure and a chance to reenergize before starting a career.

Therefore, in January of my senior year I decided to face up to military service and went to the local Navy and Air Force recruiting offices to find out more about officer programs. I had had an uncle in the Navy, my only family connection with the military. I remember when he brought me a gift from a cruise he took to the Pacific—a coin encased in lava from Hawaii. I thought of the Navy as somewhat exotic and as providing a chance to see foreign ports.

The Navy recruiter suggested I go to specialized training for the Civil Engineering Corps in line with my architectural background. I asked if I could be on a ship instead—I wanted to experience my vision of the real Navy.

I explained the application process to my girlfriend (now my wife) in a letter dated January 12, 1966:

> I had my physical today. I was in with hundreds of inductees into various services; however, the Navy OCS people (there were 4 of us) got to go through all the lines first. I had prepared myself psychologically enough not to get all nervous for the blood test. However, when the man at "station 5" said, "Go to station 3 where you get your blood drawn," I did begin to have second thoughts. Things were slow but routine until the eye test, which I failed miserably. They are holding my application until I get glasses...

In the succeeding weeks the decision began to sink in, both with me and the girl I had been dating since high school who was concerned but supportive of my decision. My parents were also supportive of my joining the Navy where at least there was less danger if I did have to go to Vietnam. I tried to imagine what life on a ship would be like. For one thing, I knew I would miss running while on a ship, so I found myself running to exhaustion whenever I had the chance, even though it would be six months before I was actually on board. I was sworn in on my birthday, April 20 with orders to report to OCS in August.

After graduation from Rice in early June 1966, I spent the remainder of the summer in Wilmington where I had a job with a local architect and saw as much of my girlfriend as I could. Restless to get started, I tried to keep in shape and periodically went with my friend Steve Hayes on sails in his family's boat.

As the day approached to report to Newport by 11 a.m. on a Saturday late in August, I arranged to spend the night before at my older sister's apartment in New York City and to get up early to complete the drive of about four hours. Though I had planned to get up at 5:30 a.m., the alarm clock didn't go off and I didn't leave until 7:30, already two hours behind schedule. Not a good omen.

OCS

The time I had allowed for the drive up was a little tight with the unexpected late start. There was no bridge across Narragansett Bay at that time and the shortest route was via the Newport ferry. I was fine until I got onto a secondary road leading to the ferry where I started running into a lot of traffic. Eventually the cars in front of me came to a halt. A line of cars, many with hippies on the hoods in tie-dyed shirts strumming guitars, stretched as far as I could see. I asked what was happening and was told it was the weekend of the Newport Folk Festival. I began to get seriously worried that I would not make it to OCS on time.

Thinking I should have priority to report for military duty, I drove what seemed like miles to the head of the line where the police were keeping order. They told me to go back to the end of the line and wait like everyone else. This was not an option since I would be hours late. My only alternative was to drive north around the bay and back down the other side through Providence. OCS was only two miles away as the crow flies, but I would have to drive 50 miles through the densest urban areas of Rhode Island to get there. At least I would be moving. Traffic was heavy, and I really did not know the way (no GPS then). It was a good thing I didn't have any passengers because I used up a month's worth of expletives in that agonizingly slow race to the naval base. And it was hot and humid. And I was low on gas. And I had to be careful not to speed and get stopped by a cop, which would further delay me. I was beyond being mad at myself, just fully focused on shaving every second from the trip.

I finally drove into the base at about 2:30 p.m., three and a half hours late. Not a good way to get started, and it would mark me for weeks to come. Others had arrived the night before; I had tried to squeeze the most out of my remaining civilian hours and had paid for it. I have been a stickler for being on time ever since and have never again depended on just one alarm clock.

The duty officers briefly discussed whether I should be given a haircut right away but decided that I should be taken directly to my assigned barracks. I would have to get the haircut later. Since I had arrived too late to be issued a uniform the staff officer found some items that I could wear until I could get properly fitted. Most critical were the boots. Several used pairs were located and I chose some close to my size.

The barracks was a two-story frame building with dull white clapboard siding and a faded green asphalt shingle roof. It was one in a line of similar structures packed together along a gray concrete roadway with only occasional scattered, scraggly vegetation to relieve their drabness. Even in the summer these buildings were starkly grim, but all of my senses were tuned to obeying instructions, not to aesthetics. Every building was numbered. I was assigned to the barracks for November Company, Section 701 (N 701). November was the month we would graduate. I was now a number as well: 7- - - -6, my service number.

Once inside the building I saw that it was constructed in the most basic way and was without insulation. Wood floors were well worn and coated with many layers of wax. There was no air-conditioning and the rooms were barely heated with antiquated radiators. I hadn't had air-conditioning at Rice (a much hotter environment), so lack of AC didn't really bother me. I would soon learn that these World War II–vintage barracks were aptly known as the splinter barracks in reference to their worn wooden construction. I later learned that there were two newer brick buildings known as King and Nimitz Halls that were fully heated and cooled and fitted with modern windows, toilet facilities, and terrazzo floors. We were envious of the officer candidates who were lucky enough to draw those buildings, though they claimed they were held to higher standards of cleanliness as a result.

To join the rest of my company I was marched down a long, arrow-straight walkway to the mess hall, another old wooden building, by the chief petty officer overseeing our company, Chief Alexander. I did not know how to march so he gave me quick instructions to match his step as I walked beside him. As we approached an officer walking toward us, the chief whispered to me to salute. The only salute I knew was the three-fingered Boy Scout salute so that's what I did. The oncoming officer stopped and said it was the worst salute he had ever seen; the chief apologized and gave me a quick lesson in saluting before he delivered me to section N701 in the mess hall.

I could already feel myself beginning to dissociate mentally from the artificial world I was entering. I was an observer and not really a participant, and I would live in two worlds for the duration and then rejoin the real world when it was over. This defense mechanism deepened in the weeks to come and helped me maintain mental stability. I was reacting to both the loss of control and the sensory deprivation of a colorless, regimented environment that was doubly debilitating to an architect trained to make buildings and their settings attractive and humanizing. This environment was calculated to wipe clean one's old identity so it could be built anew to Navy specifications. Every serviceman and -woman has experienced this to some degree.

When I joined my section in the mess hall I learned that no one was allowed to speak while eating. Almost as soon as I sat down the section got up and filed out on command. I managed only a brief bite. Off we went, two abreast in a column formation, all of the new recruits trying to march in step with one another. I concentrated on trying to fit in. My ill-fitting shoes flopped around on my feet, which further hindered me from staying in step. We were off to get shots administered at the medical building by fluid-injecting guns rather than needles. I had heard stories of needles that were eight inches long being jabbed into the arms of recruits and preferred the guns. I quickly learned that if one did not stay completely still when being shot the injection could sting as it sliced into your flesh. This began a series of evolutions that were programmed for every waking moment of every day for the next 16 weeks. We were on an assembly line to be transformed from civilians into naval officers.

When we got back to the barracks and were finally given a few moments to ourselves I had my first real chance to talk with someone.

"Welcome to OCS," said my new roommate, an ex-chief petty officer. He would be my guide and mentor for the next few weeks. Though he had just arrived at OCS the night before, he was a nine-year veteran of the Navy and had risen to the highest enlisted rank of chief petty officer. He had qualified for the Naval Enlisted Scientific and Education Program (NESEP), which allowed outstanding men from the ranks to go to college and become officers. He was from rural Idaho and had been a member of the Benevolent Paternal Order of the Elks (BPOE). Almost the first day we met he offered to sponsor me as a member and to take me to the local lodge in

Newport. I politely declined. Though our backgrounds were very different I was quick to realize how lucky I was to have such an experienced roommate rather than someone fresh out of college who knew no more than I did.

I stood out from everyone else since I still had all of my hair. Not until late the next day were there a few minutes free for me to be taken for a haircut. And a few minutes is all it took; I was sheared to the skin. I heard stories from others in my section of shoulder-length hair being shorn from a Harvard grad.

Once I got the buzz cut I felt less conspicuous but was still behind. I hadn't mastered the basics of marching, and I was unfamiliar with the uniform and its accoutrements. I got new boonies (boots) and my own uniform in a few days but was still playing catch-up from my late arrival.

An excerpt from an abbreviated letter I wrote to my parents two days after I arrived describes my state of mind:

> Got here late due to Newport Folk Festival traffic— have been paying for it. Haven't had much time to think yet—anyhow, better wait 'til things look a little better to make any judgments.
>
> Discipline is rigid, and marching is a little confusing. It's only been two days, but seems longer.
>
> Each company of about a hundred men was divided into four sections of 20 to 25 each by month of arrival. The men in the oldest section ran the entire company, led by an officer candidate serving as company commander and an assistant company commander. Each section had a section leader and an assistant section leader. The leaders of the newest section to arrive, my section, were selected by the company commander and his assistant, with the chief's approval.

Within a few days of arrival each member of my section was called individually to be interviewed by the company commander, a person who had been there only about 12 weeks himself. At first we were each asked to submit a brief statement of our qualifications to be selected for section leader. I was still catching up and had absolutely no desire to lead anybody at that point, so I submitted a statement declining to be considered.

When I was called in to be interviewed the company commander and assistant company commander told me everyone should want to be the leader. I explained that I had arrived late since I had missed the Newport ferry. This was treated with derision: "You missed the Newport fairy—do you still miss him?" I thought this was pretty sophomoric for a couple of guys who were playing at being leaders themselves; they made me do some push-ups while one of them had his foot on my back to make it harder. I was really dissociating at this point and also plotting revenge if I should ever meet them after OCS in the fleet (I never did). An athletic former all-American swimmer from Ohio State was appointed our section leader.

The daily routine at OCS began with reveille at 5:30 a.m. with the announcement over the hall speakers, "Reveille, reveille. Now all hands heave out and trice up." These announcements were meant to simulate the routine on a ship. It took a leap of faith to equate our old wooden barracks to a ship, though when windy it did creak like sailing vessels of old. There followed a rigidly orchestrated and enforced regimen:

- Make up one's "rack" (bed) with the sheets and blanket tucked in tightly, wipe down all horizontal surfaces, and clip off all "Irish pennants"—loose threads or strings— to make the room for ready for morning inspection.

- Perform 25 minutes of calisthenics in the hallway.

- Rush through washing in the communal bathroom, competing with others for sinks and toilets (known as the three S's: shave, shine, and s--t).

- Report to formation in the courtyard to listen to the plan of the day over the loudspeaker for the regiment, followed by orders for our company.

- March to breakfast in the mess hall with ten minutes for breakfast, then to class.

- Report to classes, usually broken by a short midmorning break.

- Wolf down a quick lunch in the mess hall.

- Break for medical, uniform issue, haircuts, or some other evolution.

- Return to classes, finishing with PT (gym), more calisthenics, or sometimes to the pool to prepare for swimming a mile, a requirement for graduating.

- Go to dinner.

- Study for three hours.

- Hit the rack at about 10:30 p.m., with taps and lights-out and with periodic watches at night.

Result: three to six hours of sleep a night. Repeat the next day.

The first week was a shock to the system. Everyone's internal clock and digestion were thrown into confusion by being awakened with a jolt in the mornings, gulping down meals, the constant regimen of exercise, and the constant sense of uncertainty, not to mention learning a whole new jargon and trying to keep from getting red gigs, points assessed for improper performance, as opposed to blue gigs, points for good performance. It was not uncommon for new recruits to go without a bowel movement for the first week, as happened to most of us.

I wrote to my parents on August 1, 1966, after the first week:

> After a little more than a week here at Newport, I am a little less than enthusiastic. However, now the shouting has ceased somewhat, and we had a good deal of time this weekend.
>
> Classes begin tomorrow, which ought to curtail some of the military influence. We are fairly competent formation marchers, boot and brass polishers and calisthenics doers by now.
>
> The hard part is the realization that I am now in, one way or the other, for at least two years. It is hard to face that if you don't like it you cannot just get out.

One of the missions of OCS was to instill in each person the realization that he (or she, since there was a small contingent of nurses) had to keep going in spite of difficulties. It was not like taking a course in school where you could drop it after a few days and take something else that suited you better. Each person had signed a contract for three years of service, and it was up to each individual to endure this new world as best he could. This self-sufficiency was tested often in the more serious environment on board ship. Failure was not an option.

Every action was calculated to avoid potential red gigs and to make one's life a bit easier. I determined that sleeping on top of the bedcovers would allow me simply to tighten them in the morning without remaking the whole bed. I was discovered in this position at night by the mate of the deck (MOD), who woke me and made me get under them like everyone else. The MOD was an officer candidate from one of the older sections who was on watch at night. All of us had to do this periodically after our first month, which cut into our sleep and trained us for the disruption to the normal diurnal cycle of sleep and wakefulness we would encounter on a ship.

OCS could bring out the sadistic tendencies in those who had them. And like most environments where there are opportunities for hazing, those who were victims are the most likely to become the victimizers. I was made to scrub the floor of one particularly unpleasant "upperclassman" with a toothbrush, admonished gleefully for not getting the corners under the bed sufficiently clean, and awarded a red gig. We all knew this was part of the evolution from being governed to becoming the governors, but since we all knew it was just a game we resented those who seemed to enjoy their power too much. Another person I promised to seek out for retribution later if I ever met him in the fleet, which, again, I never did.

On Friday nights we had schoolwide athletic events where the various companies in the regiment competed against one another. We could volunteer for a sport or be assigned one by the company commander. My preferred sports were running and touch football. The beefier candidates did medicine ball volleyball, and swimmers could compete in the pool. The obstacle course was not something I chose but it turned out to be an unexpected boon to me in gaining some recognition in the company and, more importantly, as a means of canceling out some red gigs.

By September 30 I had collected 15 red gigs—for failing to make my rack perfectly, having a thread dangling from my uniform ("Irish pennant"), a speck of dust found under my rack, or any number of other real or perceived infractions levied by our superiors. This meant that on the weekends I would have to march around the "grinder" (parking lot) for a couple of hours or more to work them off rather than to "go on the beach" (leave the base for "liberty," which one could only do after three weeks and then only in uniform).

Back to the obstacle course. During PT one day our instructor, Chief Murphy, took us to the obstacle course and demonstrated how to go through, around, over, or under each of the obstacles. Then he timed each one of us. Since my last name starts with A, I was one of the first up. When all were finished he announced that my time had set a new OCS course record of 1 minute 55 seconds, beating by three seconds the record established three years earlier.

The next morning at plan-of-the day announcements the martinet company commander who had made me do push-ups announced that I would be awarded three blue (good) gigs for this achievement and would hereafter lead the company obstacle course team at Friday night athletics. This award had been certified by our section leader in a small chit given to me to make it official. It brought me down to twelve red gigs, which meant I would not have to march that weekend and possibly never again if I could keep my count down. I was not eager to change from running to the obstacle course but had no choice and was determined to uphold my new reputation.

Since there were about six companies that competed in the obstacle course I was up against five others each week. It was important to get off to a fast start and take the lead since it was difficult to pass someone on the monkey bars or over the eight-foot wall. The first obstacle was a set of two vertical seven-foot-high steel posts set close together to allow only one person to pass through at a time. The leader through these poles had a real advantage. The second or third week I approached these poles running neck and neck with a very large and athletic black officer candidate. Just as we got to the poles someone from the crowd shouted an unfortunate racial epithet. He heard this and reacted by lashing out at me, nearly knocking me down. I never was able to pass him and came in second that night.

Since we were in the Navy it seemed pretty obvious that we should all know how to swim. I was surprised at how many had trouble with this as well as jumping off the ten-foot platform into the pool. Both were requirements for graduating. There was always an instructor by the side of the pool to rescue those who passed out when they jumped or to cajole those who froze and would not jump. We were also required to swim a mile in a huge pool that could hold about 50 people at a time. The shallow end extended about halfway across the pool, so people would simply walk this part with their bodies bent over as if they were swimming. Nobody seemed to care. I can only speculate that we were needed in the fleet and that strict enforcement of this requirement would wash out or delay too many from commencing their duties.

The weekend started at about 11:30 a.m. on Saturday after a base-wide formation known as Pass in Review (PIR). But before PIR there were inspections of every section conducted by student officers. I had the chance one Saturday to inspect my best friend growing up, Steve Hayes, who had entered OCS two months after I did and was assigned to a different company. I gave him a blue gig on some pretext.

Steve and I would be assigned to different ships and later would just miss each other as my ship was entering Subic Bay in the Philippines and his, USS *Whitfield County* (LST-1169), was leaving. We exchanged a flashing light message regretting that we had missed each other. Steve would go to Swift Boats and earn a bronze star for actions under fire. More on his experiences later.

For PIR we got into a dress uniform including special leggings that bound our uniform pants tightly to our ankles and calves. We also wore our swords and carried an M1 rifle. The whole regiment marched in a formation, with company after company passing in review in front of the base commander, Captain Lemmon. As we marched past we executed an "eyes right" and marched to our assigned position in the formation. Colors were presented and we did various drills with our "pieces" (M1's) and our swords.

I came to enjoy being one small cog in this weekly spectacle and especially marching to the Sousa music of the OCS band. To this day I have Sousa marches on my iPod as I run. The pressure not to mess up during PIR was magnified by our visibility to the crowd of relatives and friends looking on. There was a system of whispered commands by designated monitors to keep everybody lined up. But ultimately each person had to be proficient in such actions as opening and closing his rifle bolt in unison. Random out-of-sequence clicks were penalized by red gigs later.

The M1 rifle was a staple of soldiers in World War II for its durability and reliability. It weighed about ten pounds and had a solid wooden stock and a heavy metal butt plate. Putting it through its motions during drills required arm and upper body strength to maintain tight control, which was a challenge for officer candidates of slight build, such as I. Occasionally we would also fix bayonets, which was a little scary when drilling in close order—we had to be doubly careful not to get too close to our peers for each other's safety. We were amateurs in comparison to the precision drill teams the public sees at military parades.

We also wielded our swords. The sword, when held in the carry position, should be perpendicular from the thigh to a point just touching the bottom of the earlobe. To bring the sword to that position after withdrawing it from the scabbard required a quick flip by the wrist holding the sword at the hilt so it just nicked the ear while the holder's eyes were straight ahead. If a little blood was drawn, all the better to prove one had hit the mark. We were more concerned about putting our eyes out when first learning this action. We also learned the sword salute, which required thrusting and twisting the blade so the flat was facing the person being saluted.

The regimental officer candidates formed in front of everyone else to present the colors to the commanding officer. These were the half-dozen officer candidates who were chosen for their exemplary military bearing. One from this elite group, Roger Guichard, would later serve with me on the *Furse* as a staff officer to the commodore after having served on another destroyer, the USS *Bigelow* (DD-942) as assistant CIC officer. I introduced Roger to my middle sister, Martha, at a ship's party and they eventually married. Roger is multitalented and went on to a career as a development consultant in the Middle East, a scholarly author, a photographer, and an accomplished artist who would produce wonderfully expressive sketches of people in the Middle Eastern countries where he and Martha lived.

Roger and I recently went aboard the battleship *New Jersey* moored as a floating exhibit in Camden, New Jersey. His knowledge of the ship's history far overshadowed that of the tour guide and was an extra bonus for those on our tour.

After three weeks I could finally leave the base on liberty and drive up to Cambridge, just across the Charles River from Boston. Harvard Square was a center of protest and counterculture in the mid-sixties, and since I was required to remain in uniform and had a shaved head I felt very conspicuous but also proud of my new identity. I was happy to be away from OCS for a day no matter what I had to wear. After each weekend there was always someone who had been caught out of uniform, had been picked up drunk and disorderly by the shore patrol, or had committed some other infraction while enjoying his few hours of freedom. We had to be back by dusk on Sunday, and the succeeding five days always seemed a lot longer than a week. Eighteen weeks seemed like it would never end.

As summer turned to autumn the temperature fell and the effects of living in a drafty building with sporadic heat eventually led to colds and worse. For a period of several weeks half of our company had strep throat, with the worst cases sent to the infirmary. This was to be avoided since being out of action for more than two or three days might cause you to be sent back to the class below. So most of us just endured our bad colds, earaches, sore throats, and constant hacking coughs. Those who weren't infected soon became so in those tight quarters.

The worst fate was to be judged unfit to continue at OCS for reason of illness, inability to complete the program, disciplinary action, or any other reason. Then one would be "sent to the fleet," which meant being sent to a duty station as an enlisted man to serve out the remainder of one's time in the Navy, though for two years instead of three. In fact, the rumor was that one's duty would be as a forward air controller in Vietnam, a position with a high mortality rate. This rarely happened, at least from my observation. The closest I saw was a new arrival in our company who was out of shape and just could not deal with physical rigors, wearing his uniform correctly, or being punctual. One time he put on his national defense ribbon and stuck himself in the finger with the prong, which drew blood that got all over his shirt. He was basically such a walking disaster that we started helping rather than harassing him to keep him from being "sent to the fleet." I think he finally made it, though he spent every weekend marching off his red gigs around the grinder.

OCS gave me a greater appreciation for the graduates of the service academies and military schools who lived under this regimen for four years rather than four months. They earned a commission in the "regular Navy" (USN), whereas our commission was in the US Naval Reserve (USNR). No question that Naval Academy grads were far better trained than we were, but the Navy did a pretty good job of teaching us the basics in a short time so that we could hold our own when we graduated. OCS was actually an enhanced version of similar programs in World War II that produced so-called 90-day wonders.

It was an intensive school in subjects such as navigation, "Org" (how the Navy was organized), tactical, engineering, leadership, and seamanship. On certain days we would rise earlier than usual and go out in the bay on the YPs (yard patrol training craft we called Yippees), scaled-down boats that were about 50 feet long with all of the basic components of a larger ship. We learned how to steam in formation, use signal flags, use the radio headsets, and give engine orders. This happened in the last month when we were pretty confident in ourselves and close to reporting to a real ship.

One morning I went to board the bus for the trip to the YPs. As section leader I was required to report to the officer in charge, a nice young LT(jg) who liked to joke with us, that we were all present and ready to go. I didn't salute on approach. I was almost an officer myself and he was so friendly I just dispensed with this formality. I later found out he had given me two red gigs for this oversight. Lesson: Rules are rules.

The event we all approached with a degree of trepidation was damage control training on the USS *Buttercup*. We had heard about this from others almost as soon as we arrived. *Buttercup* was a large steel hull with an upper and lower deck set in a tank of water. We were led on board and told that there were going to be realistic simulations of the ship coming under fire and taking hits that would result in holes in the hull and water pouring in. Our job was to keep the water out and to keep the ship from listing (leaning) more than six degrees.

We were given some basic training about damage control such as how to use wooden shoring members and mattresses to plug the holes. Before the action began, our PT instructor, the feared Chief Murphy, told us that there were two kinds of holes, small holes and big holes. Small holes could be plugged using patches, but big holes needed wood posts and mattresses. "Any questions?" asked the chief. "Yes, chief," said one small voice. "How big is a big hole?" The chief responded with an answer none of us would soon forget: "It's a hole big enough to drive a f--king truck through." This became part of our OCS lore, much like the chief's response when he told us that if stranded on a life raft at sea we could "eat anything that would make a turd," including our shoes.

Our section was the unlucky one sent belowdecks. The explosions and smoke started and holes began to open in the hull. We started trying to plug the holes as the water rushed in. Soon it was up to our waists as the chief was shouting to us above the din to work faster, the ship was sinking. As the water continued to rise we tried to avoid the natural panic of being trapped in a confined space with water rising and our airspace running out, though it never got much above waist-high. Then abruptly everything stopped and the water drained so the next crew could get the experience. Most of the holes we tried to plug were still gaping open. Recognizing the critical importance of damage control, the basic reference manual for enlisted personnel, *The Bluejacket's Manual*, devotes a full chapter to this discipline.

We had similar training in extinguishing various types of fires, donning masks with filters for biological warfare, and basic training on the firing range with M1 rifles. Navy personnel were not expected to have much need for small arms so this training was pretty perfunctory. After a session we would parody the range instructor who had a heavy backcountry drawl: "Reddy on the raht, reddy on the lay-ift, ready on the fahrin' lahn."

As we neared the date when we would graduate and receive our commissions we were given a "dream sheet" to record our preferred, probable, and actual duty after OCS, as well as our nightmare. We were pretty skeptical about this since it was obvious that the Navy was going to assign people where they were needed regardless of their preferences, so we all put down blatantly unattainable requests like shore duty in Hawaii. Those going to submarines, flight school, the Supply Corps, or the Civil Engineering Corps (CEC) had signed up for those prior to OCS and knew where they would be headed. When we got our assignments they were added to our sheets, which were posted so everyone could see the results. My dream sheet read as follows:

Abernathy, Hank

Dream:	Small Non-Combatant, Caribbean
Nightmare:	Fleet Oiler, Pacific, as Engineering Officer
Probable:	Small Combatant, Pacific (Vietnam)
Actual:	U.S.S. Furse (DD 882), H.P. Norfolk
Comments:	East Coast, But I Still May See Vietnam

I was not surprised when I saw that I was assigned to a destroyer, the USS *Furse* (DD-882) out of Norfolk, Virginia. The name was a little funny but it was a destroyer, which was what I wanted. Some were disappointed but tried to rationalize their fate. Norfolk was not really a surprise either since it was the largest destroyer base on the East Coast, though not a place that held any intrinsic appeal for me. I hoped that I would be at sea a lot. Looking back, my comments were pretty prescient.

When I found out I was going to the *Furse* I wrote the executive officer requesting any information he could give me on logistics and reporting. He replied on November 1, 1966, with the upcoming schedule of the ship's movements and informed me that I would become first lieutenant, though my predecessor had already left the ship so I would have no one to relieve. First lieutenant is the officer in charge of deck operations. He ended the letter with a description of Norfolk:

> Although you will be spending three of your first four
> months on board in Boston, you will find Norfolk
> a fine place to live. It is a big-small town, and of
> course a Navy town. I don't know if you are married
> or not, but there are plenty of very nice apartments
> and housing rentals at all price ranges. Prices are
> reasonable for rentals, utilities, food, etc. If married,
> I would advise making no firm plans since you might
> want to move to Boston for three months.

He sounded friendly and helpful, which gave me a good feeling.

That settled, we tried not to screw up in the last couple of weeks. The final day commenced with PIR as usual, attended by family members, after which we assembled in the gym for the ceremony. We were issued new gold ensign bars just prior to marching into the gym, where we were granted our commissions. We threw our hats in the air primarily in relief at being finished as well as for being newly minted "officers and gentlemen." Afterward it was enjoyable to get together with my parents, two of my sisters, my older sister's fiancé, and Steve Hayes's parents, who had also come.

One last obligation remained. We returned to our barracks and each gave our company chief, Chief Alexander, the traditional one dollar and our thanks for getting us through. He gave us our first salute as new officers. OCS was over and we left not only with relief but with nostalgia for the friends we had made in demanding circumstances who were now scattering to their new duty stations. We had only the yearbook (*Seachest 701*) pictures to remember each other in years to come. I never encountered any of my classmates on active duty or in civilian life, but I can still remember many of their faces and names.

By now I was pretty good at marching—I was picking up the rhythm. My civilian psyche was coming to terms with a new framework and new set of skills that no longer seemed alien. I found I fit well in this environment of individual challenge within a context of group discipline. I felt I had regained some measure of control over my life and had accepted the new reality of my military environment. OCS had not destroyed my old identity but had molded it and channeled it in a new direction, at least for the foreseeable future. The prisoner had taken on the psyche of his guards.

Reporting Aboard

Reporting to OCS had been harrowing with my late arrival, but at least I was entering at the same level as everyone else. Reporting to my first duty station was even more unnerving since it was the real Navy, not just a school. This time I was determined to arrive on time and unstressed.

I was able to spend a few days at home before reporting to the *Furse* on December 8. My plan was to drive to Norfolk so I called the ship and asked if there would be a place for me to park since I did not know the layout of the base. Oh, how an innocent question can have unintended consequences! When I did report and was introduced to the other officers in the wardroom they razzed me for requesting a personalized parking space. At least I had reported on time—no repeats of my trip to OCS. Fortunately there was a bridge across the mouth of the Chesapeake Bay.

The Norfolk Naval Base was and still is large. My ship was moored at the destroyer-submarine piers. I parked in a lot of hundreds of cars and walked to the piers, returning salutes as I passed the many men streaming back and forth on this 1,000-foot-long nautical main street lined with ships in nests three or four deep. The *Furse* was at the end of the pier and moored directly adjacent to it. I was both nervous and excited as I approached.

When I first saw the *Furse* hooked up to a forest of pier services I couldn't immediately tell which end was the bow and which the stern among all the visual clutter. I did find the brow, or gangplank, and after saluting the American flag and the officer of the deck I requested permission to come aboard and was led to my stateroom in forward officers' quarters, located in the bow of the ship. If the outside of the ship was confusing, the interior warren of small compartments separated by watertight doors set in bulkheads, or walls, was even more disorienting. The main passageway was periodically interrupted by these doors, requiring a conscious effort to step over the thresholds to avoid tripping while ducking down to avoid bumping one's head. The ship was subdivided into transverse divisions known as frames that were numbered sequentially from fore to aft. Eventually I would learn the frame numbers, which would enable me to pinpoint my position in the ship.

There was a distinctive dead-air smell in the interior from low ventilation levels and lots of people concentrated in tight spaces, as well as warm air coming up from belowdecks, which heated the floor tiles and other surfaces. The odor was not unpleasant and even comforting when the elements outside were harsh. There were slight variations in this odor as one passed the galley, the heads (the shipboard term for toilets), or the engine rooms, which also provided olfactory references to one's location within the passageways.

Within minutes I was met by an energetic young officer from California who served as gunnery assistant and who assumed that I was to be his replacement. He took me under his wing and insisted on showing me all of his spaces—the gun mounts, the ammunition handling rooms, the magazines, the storage areas, the small arms locker, and the fire control director perched atop the ship. I was baffled and disoriented after this blitz. Then he grabbed a football from his stateroom to play catch on the pier next to the ship. This put me at ease and gave those passing by a view of the new ensign who had just reported. I soon met most of the other officers including my new boss, a very able and experienced weapons officer with a somewhat sarcastic manner. I was to be the new first lieutenant (my job designation, not my rank), one of the three division officers in the weapons department.

After I had been aboard for two days I reported my impressions in a letter to my parents,

> In the few minutes I can spare (at 0545) this morning I will write and say hi. I have been aboard now for a couple of days and still feel pretty much like a stranger. However, I can't complain since the whole ship is in a turmoil over their annual Administrative Inspection which I walked into the middle of.

I even got a chance to use my sword this morning at a full dress inspection. I have not assumed my duties yet, and am still learning my way around the ship . . .

All in all, I have gotten a pretty good deal. The living spaces are roomy, since I am in a compartment usually meant for two.

I was lucky not to have a roommate when I first reported; one more would have made my small forward compartment feel claustrophobic rather than roomy as described in my letter. Unlike cruise ships, quarters on naval ships have no portholes. In fact, the majority of the time we spent in our rooms was for sleeping so all that really mattered was that the bed was comfortable. Looking back, I never slept better than when I was rocked to sleep in those bunks. When the weather was stormy we strapped ourselves in so we didn't get tossed out, but even then we slept pretty well as we were periodically levitated off the mattress and shoved back down by the motion of the ship.

I met the ship's captain. The captain of a ship is always designated as such though his actual rank on a destroyer is normally commander. He knew I was not married and told me that in his view I was now married to the ship. He also told me that I would have to ask his permission if I wanted to get married and he would not grant it until I had been on the ship for at least a year. He expected total commitment, and that was about it. I knew this was not a real regulation but wasn't about to say anything but "Yes sir." He fulfilled my image of a captain as absolute master of his realm, and there was no doubt that he was. His intensity was intimidating in a way that left no room for a personal connection of any kind. I would be a cog in his disciplined machine and had better function as expected.

The captain held sway over the wardroom and let it be known that ensigns, in particular, were only to speak when spoken to. At the bottom of the totem pole again! At mealtimes we sat in hierarchical order at the wardroom table, with conversation led by the captain; only a few of the more senior officers had the temerity to initiate new topics. The other officers were clearly cautious of or cowed by this captain, who spoke with a hard, gravelly voice and could be disparaging of someone with whom he disagreed. I was glad I was junior enough not to be worth his attention or ire. That would come later.

Soon I picked up snippets of the history of the ship under the captain from the other officers and crew. He was all Navy and believed in strong discipline, sometimes threatening severe punishments to make his point. I heard him tell a man who had reported back to the ship a few hours late from liberty that in time of war desertion was punishable by death. This captain was all stick and no carrot. In the months I served under him I never heard him compliment or thank anyone for a job well done.

My own opinion would be formed primarily at captain's mast,[1.1] a summary judgment procedure under the Uniform Code of Military Justice (UCMJ) for everyday infractions where the division officer of the man being disciplined would appear on his behalf. The role of the division officer in these proceedings was to act as an advocate for his men, much like a defense attorney. The division officer might mete out discipline internally, but in the face of outside threats he was the protector of his men. I have found that when this principle is violated morale deteriorates and employees have little loyalty. This was especially true of the entry-level enlisted men—seamen apprentice and seamen. Petty officers were expected to know better.

Sometimes I had the sense that the penalties assessed by the captain were really an opportunity to let us know what he expected of his men. A typical penalty for an offense might be a simple reprimand, confinement to the ship for a specified period, reduction in pay, reduction in grade, or some combination. One of the most severe would be "six, six, and a kick," meaning six months' revocation of pay, six months' confinement, and a bad conduct discharge. The latter was assessed for a serious infraction such as an unauthorized absence for a period of days. Really serious breaches could result in a formal court-martial proceeding.

On a previous deployment to the Mediterranean a very respected chief petty officer had come back to the ship drunk one night and thrown all of the captain's clothes into the bay. Some of these articles were fished out but most were lost. The captain, who respected the chiefs more than most of the officers, meted out only token discipline in this case, as reported by those who witnessed the incident. I did not hear specifically what precipitated this action but could imagine his strong personality clashing with that of this particular chief who was revered by the crew and had the confidence to speak his mind.

I was to see later that he could be volatile. I was in CIC, the Combat Information Center, when the captain flew into a red-faced rage over how we were tracking a sonar contact. He smashed down the plotting instruments on the chart table while screaming at all of us for our incompetence. On another occasion he got a grenade to throw at a shark and ran with it through the fully occupied bridge. We hoped he didn't slip.

Many of the officers had living quarters off the base, so after dinner only the officers who lived on the ship or were on watch stayed aboard. Every night in port a movie was shown in the wardroom and it was expected that some of the junior officers would watch it with the captain or command duty officer (CDO) unless either had his wife on board and didn't want company. When the captain chose to stay aboard, a junior officer was designated to watch the movie with him since none would come of his own accord. We would have to make small talk in response to his comments, always awkward sessions. Our captain liked westerns and action films, which were pretty typical of the movies we got anyway. As the most junior officer on the ship and as someone who lived on board I would often get this duty.

At the time I knew nothing about how morale on our ship compared to that on other ships. And who was I, a boot (new, junior) ensign, to question the effect on the crew's spirits of a naval captain with many years' experience and an undeniable passion for his profession? My comment in a letter I wrote home after a couple of weeks on board was, "The Captain is a real disciplinarian and knows the ship inside and out, so jobs better be done strictly by the book." My interest was in learning my job and becoming a productive addition to the ship.

I did see the results of management by intimidation as time progressed. This punitive approach was not conducive to building a cohesive team and was alien to my own style, which tended to be more calm and collaborative. It did make me realize, however, that I needed to be more forceful at times, and the fear factor of incurring the captain's wrath was an incentive to learn my job as quickly as possible. Overall I sensed that the ship was not a happy place.

In the next several weeks I began to get to know my division of about 30 sailors, run by a very salty first class boatswain's (bos'n's) mate known simply as Boats, as was customary for his rate (specialty). Boats, I was told, had some of the most elaborate tattoos of anybody on board, and when I first saw him without a shirt I was not disappointed. Almost every inch of his arms and torso was covered with artwork, with his whole back displaying an eagle with outspread wings and a fearsome beak. When he flexed his muscles the tattoos seemed to come alive.

My introduction to the division for the first time was at "quarters" at 0800 hours (time in the Navy is on a twenty-four-hour clock, with 0800 as 8 a.m. and 2400 as midnight) on the foc's'le (abbreviation for forecastle, or forwardmost part of the main deck of the ship). I was introduced to the men by Boats and at some point answered a question from him with a "Yes sir," to which he shot back, "Don't sir me, I came up through the ranks." He was proud to be enlisted, and even though as a nonofficer he did not merit being called sir, he had earned his position the hard way, rising through six grades to reach first class. As a new officer fresh out of OCS I had not gotten used to being the one called sir. Boats knew how green I was and that he would remain firmly in charge of the division for the foreseeable future.

I was also beginning to form impressions of my fellow officers, known collectively as the wardroom. The wardroom was the name of the officers' combination dining room and lounge, and by extension designated the ship's officers as a group.

Lieutenant Commander (LCDR) K. was an older officer who had a pleasant personality but had to deal directly with a demanding captain and therefore was always under the gun. Often the executive officer is the captain's enforcer, but the captain was his own enforcer, and as a result undermined the XO's authority. I liked him but had little direct contact with him except at captain's mast where he presented the cases for the captain to adjudicate. He would stand in when the captain could not attend.

The department heads—all lieutenants with about five years' experience each—were the backbone of the ship's operations and, in my view, pretty solid.

Lieutenant F. was my direct boss as weapons officer. He was very competent and confident and held his own with the captain. He was a demanding but fair boss, though he could be sarcastic at times. He also had the respect of the enlisted men in his department.

Lieutenant Be. was the engineering officer—tall and imposing but always bent over to avoid hitting his head on the metal frames of the watertight doors. It seemed a cruel twist of fate that he was assigned to a destroyer rather than a larger ship that better fit his size. He had an air of calm assurance and commanded respect by his bearing and knowledge.

Lieutenant Bo. was the operations officer. His somewhat cherubic appearance belied a sharp tongue and quick wit. I had very little contact with him but respected his obvious command of his duties and willingness to mix it up with the captain.

It struck me that these department heads had developed tough personalities to survive in their roles under such a demanding captain. They were all good at their jobs and a real advertisement for the Navy as a place to build character and competence.

Of the junior officers who were division heads, several stand out in my memory. The antisubmarine warfare (ASW) officer, Lieutenant junior grade C. was a former Naval Academy football player. He was pleasant and commanded respect by virtue of his physical condition, but he never seemed very motivated and gave the impression he was just putting in his time. He was in charge of the antisubmarine rocket (ASROC) system, which was the most sophisticated weapons system on the ship and had nuclear weapons capability, which kept him constantly preoccupied with testing and reporting. He was also in charge of the torpedoes and tube launchers. His division was relatively small but highly trained in their specialties.

Ensign B. had reported several months before I had; he was the main propulsion assistant (MPA). Also a Naval Academy grad, he was gung-ho about his job and totally wrapped up in his duties, coming out of the hole, or boiler room, always sweaty and clad in a greasy work uniform. His men seemed devoted to him and he to them, almost more than to his fellow officers.

Ensign C. was the supply officer (pork chop), fairly junior for this important position but smart. Knowledge was power in his case— we were all dependent on him in one way or another. The supply officer was not a line officer and therefore could not stand bridge watches so was subject to some mild resentment (or envy) by the other officers who had to get up at all hours while he slept. But all of us acknowledged his high level of responsibility and tried to stay on his good side since our divisions were dependent on him for supplies.

Lieutenant junior grade L. was the gunnery officer and a typical fun-loving California kid—the one I played catch with on the pier when I first reported. He was getting off of the ship imminently so feeling his oats in his last month aboard. This was too bad for me because he and I had become friends almost from the moment I stepped on board.

Ensign M. was the communications officer and took it upon himself to welcome me and some of the other relatively new arrivals by inviting us to his house occasionally for home cooking. He had a wry but upbeat view of life and tried to give those of us who lived on board some relief from the autocratic atmosphere of the ship. Going to his house was the first opportunity I had to see residential Norfolk. Two years later I would find an apartment with my own wife not too far from his.

All in all, they were a good group of officers, but there was no one I particularly gravitated toward. I sensed that I would only really get to know them when we went to sea and they were away from their families. I was apprehensive about going to sea for the first time. There was just so much equipment to understand, so many new procedures to learn. I would need the help and forbearance of my fellow officers but resisted asking too many questions which would make me seem even more of a neophyte.

My girlfriend, Pam, and my family wrote regularly so I had a good support system even as I gained friends on the ship. In less than a year and a half I would be the only one left on board from this group, and most would leave well before that. And sadly, like those I met at OCS, I would never reconnect with any of them again.

I had been on board about three weeks and had begun to stand quarterdeck watches, which lasted four hours. As the most junior officer I got a disproportionate number of late-night watches, including the midwatch (00-04 a.m.) on New Year's Eve. One of the traditions in the Navy is to write the log for this first watch of the new year in verse. This is delegated to a junior officer. I described this in a letter of January 2, 1967, shortly before we left for Boston:

> Today is New Year's Day and I have stayed aboard to stand a couple of watches. In two days we get underway for Boston . . . I am becoming more settled to ship life and have begun to take on some small responsibilities which will quickly expand. For instance, as junior officer I was called on to write the first entry of the New Year log in verse. . . . I didn't spend much time on it but I think it was well received.

This letter was written before my draft was returned to me by the command duty officer (CDO), who called it "the worst New Year's Day log I have ever read." As I recall the rhyme scheme was pretty loose—almost free verse. I was directed to rewrite it in more traditional verse. I really cannot remember how much of the final version was mine, if any, and how much was the CDO's, but below is the resultant first log entry of the new year 1967, signed by Al Pamplin, the CDO. I can only assume he was the primary author, but I'll take at least some credit as ghost writer:

00-04   In these first few hours of 1967,
The USS FURSE lies in her Norfolk Haven.
She rests in the middle of a three ship nest,
Of which the USS BORIE (DD 704) and
USS GYATT (DD 712) compose the rest.

With standard lines doubled they are tightly moored,
The BORIE to port, the GYATT to starboard.
But the USS FURSE is further protected
With wires fore and aft to the pier connected.

Even in port where attack is not likely
We must maintain some watertight integrity.
Therefore, condition of readiness five has been set
And closures in accordance with Yoke have been met.

At the Destroyer-Submarine piers other ships are quartered
From the Atlantic Fleet and from local waters.
Over them all has SOPA command,
Who at this moment is COMASWFORLANT.

While within our boilers the fires have subsided,
Steam and water from the pier is provided.
Sounding and security reports all secure,
A favorable start toward a Happy New Year.

C.A. Pamplin, Lt(jg), USNR

We were due to get under way in a few weeks for Boston to be re-fitted in the Boston Naval Shipyard in Charlestown where the USS *Constitution*, the oldest active ship in the Navy, was berthed. We left Norfolk in the late evening and transited through the causeway joining the tip of Maryland with Virginia and out to sea. It was early January and very cold. I stood my first underway watch on the port bridge wing that night in my heavy watch coat and was still freezing. Everyone else was stationed inside the bridge, but as the most junior officer I was being initiated as the bridge wing lookout. I steered clear of the captain who was holding court in his chair just inside.

I described this first trip at sea in a letter to my parents:

Being on the bridge underway is quite [an] experience.
All radar contacts must be recorded and tracked.
When they are in visual range they must be followed.
It was foggy off New Jersey [we were about 200

miles off the coast] and cold. It also sleeted part of the time. This meant a constant visual watch out on the exposed flying bridge.

My room is in the bow where the rolling and pitching is accentuated. About ½ the crew were sick when we got out into some of the larger swells. I got sick myself. Most of us quickly recovered.

I remember wondering at the time if I would be able to take three years of this. Anxiety over my first watches at sea, the cold, the ache in my neck from the heaviness of my stiff bridge coat, the mental effort to make sense of all of the instrumentation of the bridge at night, and the proximity of the captain all contributed to my fatigue. But I also liked the invigorating feeling of being out at sea in the raw elements. I was never so relieved to go to my compartment as I was after that first watch, but I was already worrying about the next one. Fortunately there weren't many before we arrived in Boston.

2

DON'T STAND THERE WITH YOUR HANDS IN YOUR POCKETS!

FURSE spent the cold, hard winter of 1967 undergoing her extensive overhaul period in Boston. The bitter cold of Boston's winter compounded the ordinary problems of overhaul and it seemed, at times, that the sub-freezing temperatures would make continuing work impossible. But, by spring, necessary work had been accomplished and FURSE awakened from her winter's nap in the shipyard on May 10, 1967 and headed for Norfolk. *(FURSE Command History of 1967)*

Boston

We arrived at Boston and were hooked up to pier services—water, steam, and electricity. Shortly we were draped with a myriad of hoses and conduits that powered welding machines and compressors and were subjected to a constant din of hammers, sanders, and saws tearing apart and reshaping the ship. My division's job was to keep the decks clean and the ship painted in the midst of this construction.

With fewer watches in port most of the men were free at night to "go on the beach." In spite of being warned of the dangers, many frequented the "Combat Zone" in Boston where the bars and prostitutes were. Some sold blood to get more money to finance their off-ship activities.

Even though we were in the shipyard the pace was intense, as evidenced by a letter I wrote on January 20:

> I am kept going here from 6 AM–6PM and work almost every night trying to keep up. It is an interesting job, with a good deal of variety yet many inherently unpleasant duties to perform. It is extremely cold up here also. Hammering goes on day and night, and many holes cut in the ship make it chilly, so sleep is often a little fitful. However I am not too bothered by this since I am too tired to care at night.

The commodore of our destroyer division, DesDiv 22, was embarked on our ship. The commodore was in charge of operations for our ship and others in the division, to whom the commanding officers of each ship in the division reported. This entitled him to his own stateroom, which was being built as part of our retrofit. Our captain instructed the yard to reduce its size to a minimum on the pretext of watching the budget, but we suspected it was to show who was really the boss on his ship. The commodore was an easygoing four-striper, or captain, who had his own staff officer to coordinate communications between the ships of the division. He did not seem threatened by our commanding officer but was careful not to interfere in our shipboard operations. He seemed to tolerate the captain like a lion tamer tolerates, yet keeps his distance from, a growling cat. His staff officer was equally cautious.

Staff officers were part of the wardroom but not really accepted as part of our group. They needed to stand apart from our daily operations but at the same time get along with us since they lived and ate with us and were frequently with us on the bridge and in CIC. There was always a bit of envy and slight resentment that they did not stand as many late-night watches and had no responsibilities for men or equipment. In port they would often accompany their boss on liberty rather than socialize with us. The few who flaunted their privileged position we derisively referred to as "staff pukes." Those we had on our ship when the commodore was embarked were uniformly friendly and fit well with the culture of our wardroom.

One day I was walking the main deck of the ship inspecting the work of my men who were chipping off old paint in preparation for repainting. I stopped to talk to one of them and asked him for the chipping tool to try it myself. Moments after I started chipping the captain walked by and gave me a tongue-lashing in front of the men, saying that an officer's place was to lead and not to do the work and ending with "Don't let me ever see you doing that again." Tempted as I was to get my hands dirty, this message stuck.

The lesson the captain was teaching is that I didn't have to be able to do everything my men did in order to lead them, and in fact they might have felt that I was diminishing the importance of their work by merely dabbling in it. This went counter to all of my instincts, but I found that the men were proud that they could do their jobs with professionalism. We each had our place and played our roles accordingly. Officers needed to be able to delegate to be effective.

This is very different from the culture of Marine officers who, for instance, are taught to wait until all of their men have eaten before they eat, and even to serve them. Marines embarked on Navy ships find this greater formality between officer and enlisted ranks difficult to get used to. One small formality that is often dispensed with as a matter of practicality, especially at sea, is the requirement of enlisted personnel to salute officers every time they pass.

The exception, however, seemed to be with the engineering officers and crew who operated out of sight belowdecks in a more communal environment. I often saw the main propulsion assistant (MPA) and engineering officer return topside sweaty and stained with oil and grease, obviously from pitching in with repairs to their division's gear. The MPA, as previously described, was a Naval Academy grad respected by officers and men for his diligence and for his willingness to participate in the work. We envied his relative isolation from the prying eyes of higher authority.

I also learned the dangers of being too hands-off. One week I was given a deadline to paint all of the exterior bulkheads of the ship, including carefully cutting around all of the stenciled frame numbers and damage control labels. This meant the men would have to miss liberty and stay on board and work on the weekend. They were determined to finish this job before the weekend and said they could if they used a paint sprayer instead of rollers and brushes. I told them that would be fine as long as the job was done right. They found a sprayer and went to work at night. In the morning the Officer of the Deck (OOD) said the captain wanted to see me.

The men had sprayed over the labels, the equipment, and the rubber gaskets of the watertight doors, which were never to be painted. I was ordered to stay on board until the mess was corrected. I had to get tough and keep everyone on board with me. The men had to see that I would not allow them to get away with sloppy work. The lead boatswain's mate, whose job was to ensure the work was done properly, had let me down and I let him know it. There is a good cop/bad cop routine often played by the division officer (good cop) and the chief or first class petty officer (bad cop) in charge of his division. But sometimes the officer has to be the bad cop.

This hands-on/hands-off dilemma is one I still face as an architect. I much prefer to work on projects than to manage the work of others. Management is a necessary evil for senior-level professionals, but most of us prefer direct involvement in our areas of expertise, whether architecture, engineering, medicine, or law. I would later apply to business school, but in my heart I knew I wanted something more creative. As it turned out I found that I actually gravitated toward managing projects as an architect, though I always sought involvement in the design process.

In addition to our regular duties each officer had a number of collateral duties. One that I inherited was custodian of the ship's vehicle, a fairly banged-up van, which was used for trips around the base to get supplies and run errands. The night I was to take over this responsibility I asked for a ride to verify its condition before I signed for it. The MPA I was relieving took me for a ride in the vehicle in a torrential rain; visibility was a matter of feet. He demonstrated the van's utility by driving fast around the parking lots. At one point he hit something hard that looked like a person. We were both prepared for the worst as we climbed out to see what we had run into. It turned out to be a metal sign about the same height as a person with a round disk on top. Another dent in the fender was hardly noticeable in our relief that we had not injured someone or worse.

The five months in Boston living in a steel shell in cold, noise, and dirt were generally unpleasant, but my memory of a frigid night at sea on the way up from Norfolk tempered my enthusiasm for leaving the relative comfort of the shipyard. In the early spring we conducted a couple of days of sea trials in the waters off Boston Harbor before getting under way for Norfolk en route, ultimately, for Guantánamo Bay, Cuba ("Gitmo"), for intensive refresher training. The captain, full of pent-up energy, was determined to mold his newly refitted ship and its untested crew into a disciplined and efficient team.

One morning just prior to our departure I heard from one of the other officers that we might be delayed because someone had put sand in the reduction gears. These were a set of well-lubricated precision gears that converted the high rotational speeds of the steam turbines to the reduced speeds needed to drive the propeller shafts. Because of their importance, access to them was restricted. Any little bit of sand or grit could foul them to the point of being useless. It turned out that someone had tried to damage them but had not been completely successful—the culprit was never identified but there was speculation that it was one of several disaffected sailors. To me it seemed an isolated incident at the time, but in retrospect it may have been an early indication of the low morale on board.

It also sparked in me a curiosity to learn more about what happened down in the depths occupied by the "snipes," those who worked in the sweltering confines of boilers, steam pipes, panel boards, turbines, and gauges. There were definitely two worlds on a destroyer—those who worked topside and those who worked belowdecks. Each respected the other. In the three years I was on board I never really felt comfortable going below. It always seemed like foreign territory, a sort of Piranesian world into which mortals descended at their own peril. I always remembered what we were told at OCS—that a leak in a superheated steam line could not be seen but could sever a hand or arm that passed in front of it.

The relative remoteness of the boiler and engine rooms also provided cover for things that couldn't happen above decks. After one visit to a foreign port—I don't remember which one—occasional high-pitched barking could be heard in the vicinity of the mess decks. One of the snipes had brought aboard a puppy he had obtained ashore. This new mascot was hidden below decks in the engine room but when discovered made his public appearance to the crew above decks by popular demand. Though he became a mascot for a few days he had to be given up in the next port.

I was beginning to develop a top-down view of the relative importance of departments on the ship based on my own particular vantage point. Those communicating most closely with the captain—the operations department in charge of communications and navigation, located on the upper decks and signal bridge—were at the top. Not only did they have the captain's ear but they dealt with sophisticated communications equipment and coded messages. Those operating the engineering systems belowdecks—steeped in superheated steam and grease—were at the bottom in a sort of satanic environment just above the bilges. The weapons department, including gunnery, ASW (antisubmarine warfare), and deck operations, was in the middle. I was in charge of the "deck apes," a less than complimentary term for the heavily muscled men who manned the lines, did the painting, wrestled with fueling hoses and anchor chains. ASW and gunnery were a little higher in the food chain responsible for complex weapons systems.

Of course this was overly simplistic and, I knew, not always true. The longer I was on the ship the more I realized that every job was both mentally and physically demanding and integral to keeping the organism functioning. If something went wrong belowdecks it often affected the whole ship, not just an isolated system. The main propulsion equipment was highly sophisticated, and its operation required decisiveness to respond to unpredictable orders from the bridge. We tended to take the supply department for granted, except when something like toilet paper ran out. And the "deck apes" manned the bridge watches as well as directed the complex underway replenishments, refueling, and highline transfers.

DASH

I got an eight-week reprieve from the harsh winter weather in Boston with orders to the U.S. Atlantic Fleet Drone Anti-Submarine Helicopter (DASH) Training Center in Dam Neck, Virginia, to learn to fly a remote-controlled helicopter. The school was right on the beach. We lived at the BOQ (bachelor officers' quarters). There I met Tom Reid who was attending gunnery school and would soon become the gunnery officer on *Furse*. Looking back, this was the most enjoyable Navy school I attended, both because of the challenge of learning to fly this exotic machine and the camaraderie of the officers in our group. We were outside much of the time rather than in a stuffy classroom, and we were treated to the always-popular grilled cheese with tomato sandwiches with chips at lunch. Each evening we would go back to the BOQ to do homework, drink, eat, and play Yahtzee. I usually am not a game player but picked up this dice-rolling game when all of the others were doing it; we played for pocket change as I recall.

The DASH could, without being detected, fly out to an enemy submarine picked up on sonar and drop a torpedo directly over the sub before it had a chance to evade. The remote-controlled helicopter had a range of about 10 miles. Its design was unique in that it had two counter-rotating propellers of about 20 feet in diameter positioned about 10 inches above one another. The opposite rotation would cancel out torque without requiring a tail rotor. Therefore the DASH could be stored more easily and required less deck space to take off and land. It was manufactured by a company called Gyrodyne.[2.1] A working version donated by the company can be seen on a destroyer identical to the *Furse*, the USS *Joseph P. Kennedy Jr.* (DD-850), moored at Battleship Cove, Fall River, Massachusetts.

When our class of about eight officers first saw the helo in a hangar we were told that the critical component was the electromechanical rotary actuator, a device that allowed the rotors to spin in opposite directions on a single shaft. They were locked apart until a critical rotational speed was reached. When the lock released they could rotate freely. Once the engine was turned off the lock was automatically reactivated to keep the rotors separated as their speed decreased. If something malfunctioned and they collided while rotating at high speed, lead fragments from their leading edges would fly off like bullets. Thus the operator was provided with a waist-high protective shield to duck behind if this happened.

We all went back to study the manual and memorize the new phrase of the day, "electromechanical rotary actuator." It had been rainy but before long the weather cleared and it was good to fly. We were out in the dunes away from everything, which took some of the pressure off, like learning to drive a car in an empty mall parking lot. The instructors demonstrated and made it look easy. Then they gave each of us a turn at taking the DASH up in the air a foot or two and back down using a joystick and a small wheel called the collective that controlled altitude. I described my first flight in a letter I wrote on February 1, 1967:

> I just finished my first flight, after 3 and ½ hrs. delay. All went well; I made three unassisted take-offs and landings. It is great to finally be flying the drone. My instructor was real pleased with my ability to maneuver the drone without any previous flight experience.

Some got the feel of it faster than others, but after a week everyone could accomplish this basic maneuver. After our first tentative flights we quickly advanced in skill and could fly the drone over the dunes almost out of sight and back. And finally we practiced transferring control to a simulated combat information center (CIC) for flight out of visual range over the water.

We were taught about the paperwork required for regular maintenance and what needed to be filed with the Navy if there was an accident. Off the record, the instructors suggested that it might be better just to ditch a seriously damaged helo over the side since the paperwork would be so onerous otherwise.

I told this story to my father-in-law, Arthur I. Mendolia, about five years later when he was appointed Assistant Secretary of Defense for Logistics and Installations in the Department of Defense and he loved to recount it to his military counterparts as an anecdote of how bureaucracy could drive up costs. He was from industry and had a mission to cut waste in procurement. He had missed service in World War II because he, like my own father, was in the critical chemical industry. He would experience the *Furse* firsthand on one of our family cruises and would later reconnect with our captain at that time, Commander Michael Greeley, when they both were in the Pentagon.

One day we were told that class was canceled. A VIP was visiting and wanted to see the DASH, an object of curiosity since it was relatively new to the fleet. The next day when we went to class there was one less DASH for our practice flights: the Chief of Naval Operations had been offered a chance to fly it and had crashed it in the dunes. All traces had been cleaned up and we speculated that the paperwork would also be taken care of discreetly. A visit by such a distinguished naval officer to our out-of-the-way school made us feel that we were learning something important.

Learning to fly DASH gave me a little more confidence when I rejoined the ship; now I had a special role that only one or two other officers on the ship could fill. And it was an enviable one since the machine was so exotic and obviously required skill to take off and land on our very limited flight deck. We even got to wear a special protective jacket and helmet, though we were careful not to play the role. This lesson—to develop a special skill that makes you indispensable in your business—was not lost on me in the future.

Unlucky 13th

FURSE left Norfolk 29 May for Key West where she was slated to provide services to the Fleet Sonar School. However, while operating in Key West, one day at sea, the unlucky 13th, FURSE grounded on a shoal. Although it was only for a few moments before she wrenched herself back into safe waters, the underwater damage was severe enough to require her to be dry docked again for repairs. This time in Jacksonville. *(FURSE Command History of 1967)*

We continued south from Norfolk to the naval base at Key West, Florida, for a week of training prior to Gitmo. On the way down, to be prepared for what everyone said would be eight weeks of the most rigorous training for ships and their crews in the Navy, we tested our new gear. We had been assigned a few Naval Academy and ROTC students who had come on board for their summer cruises, which they would not soon forget.

On the way down we stopped at the Naval Station at Mayport, Florida, to pick up supplies and fuel. I was tasked with, among other things, restocking the ship with toilet paper. Though this was not a deck division responsibility I was enlisted for this mission and was told it was of vital importance since the ship had only a two-day supply remaining. I dutifully set off to find a source since I knew from my brief experience in Boston that when the need was urgent one could not go through normal channels, and the supply officer seemed busy with his own priorities. I even considered buying some commercially. After a futile search of the base and with time running out, I gave in and told the supply officer that I needed help. After a few strategic calls to his local peers, he had the supplies on board within hours. This time the system worked, but I did wonder why I had been put through all of this in the first place.

Several of the senior officers had invited their wives to meet the ship in Key West to enjoy a week in the sun. We pulled into the harbor on a sunny day and made our approach to the pier, with the wives in their best dresses clustered together at our intended berth. The pressure was on the captain to make a smart approach and show off his seamanship in bringing the ship neatly alongside in front of this audience. My division's job was to get the mooring lines over as soon as we were in range of the pier and follow the bridge's orders for tightening or slacking them to pull the ship in snug to the pier. I was stationed on the fo'c'sle to supervise this operation.

There was a strong tidal current pushing us away from the pier. On the first approach the ship did not get in close enough for us to get the lines across by throwing the bolo (a line with a big knot on the end known as a "monkey fist" that is twirled above one's head before being thrown), and the ship began to drift back out. So the ship backed and approached again. This time we got closer, but the bolo fell short and the ship began to drift out again, so we used the shot line gun to shoot the line over. It made it to the line handlers on the pier, but we were far enough away that the captain could see it would be slow and unseamanlike to be winched in from so far out, so he ordered lines to be retracted. He also sent an angry message down to the fo'c'sle that I was to report to the wardroom as soon as we were alongside and secured.

On his final approach he took no chances and headed straight for the pier at a sharp angle and at high speed. He tried to turn parallel and cut speed sharply but was too late and the bow sliced into the pier, causing the wives standing nearby to beat a hasty retreat to a safe distance. The ship took a neat three-to-four-foot deep by eight-foot-long slice through the wooden guardrail and the white limestone pier as if it had been cut with a sharp knife, which in fact it had been.

Our bow was lined with a plate of steel that narrowed to about a quarter inch at its leading edge. We got the bow, stern, and spring lines over and eventually the ship was secure.

I made my way to the wardroom as directed. I was asked to wait outside while the wives came aboard and were brought to the wardroom. I was let in and the captain lost no time in berating me in front of them for not getting the lines over smartly and contributing to the mooring debacle. I was also told never to stand on deck with my hands in my pockets during the special sea and anchor detail. I was not aware of it, but apparently I had looked like I was taking the situation too casually. Though I felt my men and I had done all we could and were being unfairly singled out as scapegoats, I took to heart his comments and to this day am careful not to stand with my hands in my pockets when being observed by others.

We were all eager to go ashore that night for liberty, but the captain, still angry about the botched mooring, ordered everybody to stay aboard and get the bow and sides repainted and the ship cleaned and prepared for ASW operations the next morning. This went over very poorly with the crew who had already been put through continuous drills on the way down. The next day we got under way early for a full day of exercises and looked forward to going ashore when we got back. That evening we were allowed to go on liberty.

Pent-up frustration led to a lot of drinking and ultimately a brawl by a group of sailors while playing softball with the crew of another ship. Some were put in the naval base brig until they were remanded to our ship. The next day the captain ordered a meeting on the fantail, which only the crew and a few senior officers were allowed to attend while the rest of us were confined to our staterooms. He told the crew that the officers were inexperienced and it was up to the chiefs and senior petty officers to take responsibility for the ship's performance. The officers were confined to the ship for the remainder of the stay while the crew was free to go on liberty.

Our authority as officers had been blatantly and publicly undermined. The captain had openly declared his mistrust of us to the crew. Our reaction was one of uncertainty, and the petty officers felt that they had been put in an equally awkward position. We really did not know what to do except to stick together. Still a very junior officer, I watched this unfold with a sense of incredulity and also of fascination at what the ultimate outcome would be.

That evening the new weapons officer, a friendly and imperturbable person, had gotten permission to get off the ship on the pretext of taking a training course. After we were under way he went to the commanding officer of the naval station and recounted what had happened. He was putting his own career on the line but felt strongly that something needed to be said to higher authority. The ship had already gained some notoriety for taking a slice out of the pier and the belligerence of the crew on liberty.

Shortly after we arrived back from the day's exercises and were moored alongside the pier we heard six bells sound from the quarterdeck and an announcement: "Captain So-and-so arriving." About 15 minutes later, bells again: "Captain So-and-so departing." Messengers were sent to officers' quarters to summon us to the wardroom.

Our captain sat red-faced and seething at the head of the table. He told us that in all of his years in the Navy he had never seen such a sorry group of officers. He told us the base commander had ordered him to let us go ashore and that he was only doing so under duress since in his mind we had committed mutiny. While we were glad to be freed from our confinement we also knew that there would be retribution once we were out at sea again. The midshipmen on board for their summer cruises, who were almost forgotten by us during this drama, were stunned observers of this very unsettling situation.

The next day, Friday, June 13, 1967, we were under way early to steam out to our rendezvous for ASW drills. There were squalls along the way, with heavy rain and, at times, almost zero visibility. I was in my room when I felt a shudder in the ship and knew immediately we must have hit something or had run aground. I ran up the ladder to the fo'c'sle where several boatswain's mates had assembled in the driving rain and confirmed we had run aground. I tried to get communication with the bridge by headphones connected to the 1 MC, the main intercom on the ship, but when I couldn't I ordered the anchor released, thinking I could help prevent the ship from going farther aground. When I established communication with the bridge and reported my action, I was ordered to raise the anchor, which the boatswain's mates did using the anchor windlass.

I described what happened in a letter to my parents a week after it happened:

> The incident was sort of a freak—nobody really knows how it occurred. The Commodore of DESDIV 22 has been riding us from Key West, and conducting his own investigation. I was not on watch at the time, so not drawn in at all [I would later be questioned briefly]. Many things apparently came out in the investigation, such as poor log-keeping, improperly trained lookouts, and bad navigational fixes, which combined left us vulnerable. Actually, as I saw it, it was hard to blame any individual. It was a rainy, foggy day and the sea was choppy.
>
> I was down at my desk in my stateroom when I felt the first vibration. The sides and whole room were shaking in seconds. I ran to the main deck where the rain was whipping across the forecastle. One of my men was already there with a lead line, which he threw over to take depth readings. We were about 8 ft. higher than normal, with about 4' of red hull below the boot topping visible. We immediately made the anchor ready and dropped it—standard procedure for running aground. We hooked by phones to the bridge and got the word to heave up on the anchor, which we did.
>
> We then began to "twist off" by backing one way, then the other; finally we were off, then we hit again. We got off again and headed back to port. This

incident could cause the Captain and the Navigator their jobs. We won't know anything for a week or so.

Reading this now, I see I was clearly speculating about the effect of the investigation as well as stating that dropping anchor was standard operating procedure for running aground. *Knight's Modern Seamanship* advises in its section 12.7, Groundings,[22] that the procedure for grounding on a reef is to drop the anchor to prevent the ship from riding farther up on the reef; the same principle applied here.

The ship's June 13, 1967, log entry for this incident was as follows, with italics in key entries added by me:

12-16 Underway as before. 1202 Sandkey Light bearing 297⁰ PGC. 1215 fog signals and stationed the lookouts in the eyes of the ship. Navigator on the bridge. 1226 c/c 180⁰ PGC. *1229 ship grounded lat 24⁰28.3' N Long 81⁰ 45.9'W. Sounded the collision alarm. Set material condition zebra. Captain at the conn. All engines back emergency full. Maneuvering to clear the reef. Draft reading forward: 6' let go the starboard anchor. 1232 heaved in and housed starboard anchor. 1233 believed to be clear of reef.* 1234 set speed 12 kts course 170⁰ PGC. 1236 c/s 15 kts. 1237 c/s 12 kts. *All engines back emergency full, appear to be momentarily grounded.* 1238 set speed 10 kts. 1242 c/c 200⁰ PGC. 1244 c/c 220⁰ PGC. 1247 visibility increased to 3 miles. Ceased sounding fog signals secured lookouts in the eyes of the ship. An inspection of the ship indicated watertight integrity intact. Set material condition yoke. Secured from collision stations. 1300 visibility decreased to ½ mile due to fog and heavy rain. Commenced sounding fog signals and stationed lookouts in the eyes of the ship. 1321 visibility increased to 7 miles. Ceased sounding fog signals and secured lookouts in the eyes of the ship. *1333 maneuvering at various speeds to test main engine shafts. Tests indicate that due to excessive vibration at speeds above 7 kts the ship is limited to this speed.* 1338 c/c 340⁰ PGC set speed 7 kts. 1339 c/c 320⁰ PGC. 1409 stationed the navigation detail. 1421 c/c 250⁰ PGC. 1432 maneuvering to avoid shipping. 1509 set course 320⁰ PGC speed 7 kts. Stationed the special sea and anchor detail OOD at the conn. Captain and navigator on the bridge. 1511 maneuvering on various courses and at various speeds conforming to Key West Harbor Channel. U.S. Navy Tug 543 came alongside to port. 1537 Captain at the conn. 1542 passed sea buoy to stbd at 100 yds. Entered inland waters.

L.E. Engel, Lt(jg) USN

As we limped back at seven knots we passed another destroyer heading out to sea that sent us a flashing light message: Our commanding officer had been selected for promotion to full four-stripe rank, that is, captain, by his review board. Had this incident been known before his review it would undoubtedly have prevented his selection. He had received a vote of confidence from his peers just in time, which surely reinforced his determination to overcome this setback.

Here is the way Admiral James Stavridis, former Commanding Officer (CO) of the USS *Barry* (DDG-52), describes the consequences to one's ship and career of a grounding:

There are no second chances in shiphandling. When the wind or the current or the fog takes you, and you bounce the ship off the bottom or the buoy or the pier—then you are finished, once and forever, and so is your ship's reputation for a long time.[23]

We had bounced our ship off of both the bottom and the pier—no wonder our reputation suffered, but the selection board had met before these incidents and our CO had been promoted.

When we were back at the pier I went forward to inspect the damage to the storage area in the boatswain's locker, which contained a lot of my division's gear. This is in the most forward part of the ship, and not surprisingly water had infiltrated through a hole in the bow below the waterline. Our watertight integrity was not completely intact. When the bos'n's mate and I went down we found that the compartment two levels below the main deck was partially flooded. This was linked to another compartment that was accessed by a door underwater. I wanted to see how much damage was in that compartment, but the bos'n's mate was not eager to swim underwater and through the submerged door to find out. So I put on my bathing suit, tied a rope held by the bos'n's mate to my waist, and went under. I came up into the air pocket in the adjacent compartment and saw that very little of the gear was still above water. I ducked back under and came back out into the first compartment and up onto the main deck to dry off. The water felt greasy and I found out why when I got curious looks from the seamen on deck—I had been dyed a bright yellow-green from our rescue dye markers that had seeped into the water from the flooding. It took me days of hard scrubbing to get rid of the spectral yellow glow.

Our date with Gitmo was now on hold. Underwater inspections revealed that the sonar dome suspended below the bow was badly damaged and the propeller shafts were bent. We were directed to proceed to dry dock at the Jacksonville Naval Station for repairs. Meanwhile an official investigation into the cause of the grounding was being organized. The captain had not been on the bridge at the actual time we grounded, though he appeared quickly and took the conn. The XO was the navigator and the Ops officer had the deck (the conn) at the time and they would be key witnesses in the investigation, but the captain bore ultimate responsibility.

It was a slow and sullen, two-plus day trip to Jacksonville at seven knots. I could only think what the midshipmen on board would relate to their peers about life on a destroyer. The captain was already pressuring the XO to organize testimony for the ongoing investigation, and the strain showed on him. The XO was generally of a nonconfrontational personality in comparison to our bulldog of a captain. I was also worried that my actions on the foc's'le with the anchor would be found wanting in some way during the investigation, particularly after I had fallen into disfavor with the captain because of the mooring days before.

We were put up on keel blocks in the dry dock and braced on the sides, with pedestrian access across the void via a gangplank. Within hours it seemed the yard workers were swarming below the ship, taking off the damaged sonar dome, and removing the shafts for straightening, a time-consuming and exacting task. Work went on 24/7 with the captain often present on the open floor of the dry dock where the shafts were being repaired. He was urging the yard crew to work faster and similarly driving the XO for the records needed for the investigation. Each day the investigating officers would come on board and interview people in the wardroom.

We were allowed liberty, and with not much else to do in this small port on the far northern edge of Jacksonville we hit the local bars. We would be in dry dock for an estimated two to three weeks. On the second or third day I was returning to the ship one evening when I noticed a crane lifting a wire cage stretcher from the ship to an ambulance next to the dry dock. The XO was strapped into it after reportedly having a seizure reducing him to a catatonic state, unable to walk or talk and with eyes set straight ahead. It seemed as if the strain had finally become too much for him.

This meant that the engineering officer, as the next most senior officer, assumed the duties as executive officer. However, the next night he was apprehended by the shore patrol for fighting in a bar, leaving the weapons officer as the new XO. We began to joke about how long it would be before the ensigns took over the ship.

The XO never rejoined the ship. I happened to see him about a year later when I attended a school at Dam Neck, Virginia, where he had been reassigned to administrative duty. He seemed to have recovered full use of his physical faculties and had a smile on his face. I never went up and spoke to him out of deference to his possible embarrassment.

Finally we were told the investigation was almost over—I was relieved to think I would not be called, but on one of the last days I was. I told my story and apparently it was of no particular interest to the investigators so I was dismissed. There is no mention in the ship's logs of the investigation, or of the transfer of the XO off the ship. The only log entries were "drydocked as before," repeated for each watch. These incidents did not appear in the official log, probably because they were nonoperational in nature, whereas there is a reference to the Engineering Smooth Log and report of results of the investigation of the hull by the "Hull Board."

We were released from dry dock in record time due to, or in spite of, the captain's persistence in pressuring the shipyard. This was a mixed blessing. We were happy to leave the din and dirt of the yards but knew what awaited us with a recharged and possibly vindictive captain. Before we departed, the summer cruise midshipmen left. Then we were off to Gitmo where we arrived and anchored in the bay to begin eight weeks that lived up to everything I had heard.

Gitmo

Following the repair in Jacksonville, FURSE headed further south for refresher training in Guantanamo Bay, Cuba, commencing July 5. (FURSE *Command History of 1967*)

Admiral James Stavridis, USN, in his book *Destroyer Captain, Lessons of a First Command,* describes Gitmo when his ship visited in 1993, 26 years after *Furse*:

> The base is a tiny Navy version of Club Med. It has outdoor movie lyceums; an excellent and large exchange; cheap, duty-free liquor; beautiful beaches and snorkeling, scuba diving, beach volleyball; softball and soccer fields; a nice gym; many interesting small restaurants and clubs. It is a terrific spot for a two-day visit . . . for a quickie, it is a wonderful port, and the crew thoroughly enjoyed themselves.[2.4]

It was an entirely different place in 1967.

The Naval Base at Guantánamo on the southeast end of Cuba is a 45-square-mile enclave cut into Cuba that the United States leases indefinitely. It operates totally independently, including making its own water. It was a pretty grim place in 1967 complete with its big, ugly desalinization plant. If there were recreation areas, we never got to see them.

I wrote my impressions on July 22, 1967:

> Guantanamo is a pretty barren, colorless place. It is strictly Navy. Most of the cars are old and repossessed many times. The base must maintain a posture of alertness and readiness to defend itself, hence conducts continual defense drills. About every fourth day we anchor in the bay as gun fire support ship. We also take our turn at patrolling the area in front of the mouth of the bay to detect invaders.

I was still very green with very little time under way, and all of the exercises I was responsible for organizing and performing were new to me. Each night after we returned from a day of drills exhausted I studied *Knight's Modern Seamanship* and other operational manuals to make a plan for the next day's exercise, including diagrams of each step, what rigging would be required, and safety measures to be employed. Prior to the exercise I briefed key individuals and the petty officers. We rarely had a chance to practice so we had to trust to our preparations. About half of my division had never done most of these drills so I relied heavily on the experienced chiefs and petty officers to pull us through.

Besides the strain of these daily trials we stood watches and kept up with our normal administrative duties. Though there was an officer's club on the base it was understood that we were not to be seen there. We were anchored in the harbor during the first few weeks rather than moored to a pier, which increased our isolation. Watches at night were conducted with extra men who patrolled the deck with rifles vigilant for saboteurs who might swim unseen from communist Cuba and plant a mine on our hull. We were told to shoot and ask questions later if we saw something. I thought sabotage was highly unlikely, but the captain was taking no chances.

The Plan of the Day for Thursday, 13 July 1967, is indicative of the daily routine, which started with reveille at 0445 and ended with crypto training at 2000.

0445	Reveille
0500	Mess gear
0515	Breakfast for the Crew
0605	Station Sea Detail
0635	U/W
0650	Conduct CIC Assistance in Piloting and Low Visibility Piloting Exercise
0720	Complete Piloting exercise

0730	Make BT drop. Brief Gunnery and CIC personnel on Z-1-3-AA, AA Firing Exercise on ASROC Deck
0800	General Quarters
0830	Conduct Z-1-3-AA, AA Firing Exercise. Damage Control Parties and Engineering conduct drills not affecting ship control and remaining clear of Mt. 51 and 52
0945	Secure from General Quarters
1000	General Quarters for Calibration Firing
1030	1230 Conduct Calibration Firing
1030	1100 HM1 Norman conduct on station First Aid instruction of Engineering Department personnel
1100–1130	Instruction for stretcher bearers
1130–1200	Medical representative inventory medical supplies at battle dressing station and post a complete inventory list
1230	Complete Calibration Firing. Secure from General Quarters
1300	Station Gunfire Support Team in CIC, Plot, Director and main Batteries
1330	Commence Z-42-G Gunfire Support Exercise
1500	Muster the Visit and Search, Boarding and Prize Crew. Conduct Tactical Data Maneuvers. Conduct Visit and Search, Boarding and Prize Crew Instruction on the ASROC deck
1700	Station Special Sea Detail
1730	Station the Security Watch IAW note #1
1900	Conduct Collision Drill for Duty Section. Officers briefing in Wardroom
2000	Crypto training for duty Officers and Supply Officer

I reported our routine to my parents in a letter of July 15, 1967:

> We actually get underway from the pier or anchorage at about 0630, which means Reveille at 0500. We get back at 1730 or 1800 (5:30–6 pm), eat, and stay up until 1 or 2 correcting discrepancies from the current day's exercises, and trying to prepare for the next day. I usually get 4–5 hours of sleep per night.
>
> Today, for instance, I had to set up for sending and receiving a personnel transfer rig (Manila highline) and an ammunition transfer rig. Altogether we spent 5 hours during these token replenishment operations while alongside other ships at between 10 and 15 knots. Then I flew DASH, had an Abandon Ship and Man Overboard Exercise, then back in for a night of correcting discrepancies.
>
> I don't know whether the Captain will survive all of the activity, since he is so frustrated by his inability to personally control every detail of shipboard life and training. One of the Fleet Training Group's main recommendations was a separation of powers—keep the Captain from trying to personally control all of the gun fire, anti-submarine, and electronic counter measure exercises.

One upcoming operation that I dreaded was towing another ship using our towing cable. This was one of the most challenging feats of seamanship since it involved getting a half-mile-long cable to another ship and paying, or letting, it out so it did not get fouled in the screws or railings as the conning officer gradually put just the right tension on the cable. We had heard stories of cables parting and lashing back to sever limbs from those in their path.

I huddled with my boatswain's mates the night before to make our plan for laying out the cable, which was a wire rope—steel cable and manila rope intertwined—on the fantail and looping the first couple of hundred feet of cable along the rail outboard of the stanchions attached with small pieces of cordage that would break off as strain was put on them. The other end was led through a bullnose, a chock with a hole in the middle, on the stern and secured to bollards, or stubby steel posts, with a pelican hook, which provides for quick release, in case we needed to release it suddenly. We would shoot a line that was attached to the cable to the towed ship. The towed ship would pull the lines and attached cable through its forward chock and loop it around two large bollards on its fo'c'sle.

As I was instinctively worried whether all of this would actually work the way it was planned,

I insisted on getting everything ready the night before and was glad we did since it took a while to get the cable out of the boatswain's locker and properly "flaked down" (boatswain's mate version of "faked down") and tied off. All went more or less according to plan the next day until our ship pulled forward and stress was put on the cable. It went taut and began to arch out of the water and promptly snapped before we could release the pelican hook. Unlike the stories I had heard, it simply fell back into the water with no backlash. We were then ordered to retrieve the cable and rig the towing hawser, a six-inch nylon line (the measurement refers to circumference—lines larger than five inches are called hawsers).

We had anticipated this possibility but it still required getting this heavy line out of the bos'n's locker and "flaking it down" on the fantail. This nylon line would stretch more than the cable but was less likely to break. When ready, the conning officer took another pass at the ship to be towed, and we sent the line over and repeated previous operations. This time it held. It all took hours, and when it was over I felt like I was over the hump at Gitmo.

We were all extremely tired since the stress was constant and we rarely got more than a few hours of real sleep a night. One day after watch on the bridge I went down to my stateroom and flopped on my bunk fully clothed for a few minutes of rest. Before I had a chance to relax I heard a commotion in the passageway outside. The captain, who was conducting a surprise inspection of the living quarters, barged into my room. By his side was a seaman with a clipboard. The captain asked me what I was doing and before I could give an answer informed me that lying on a bunk with one's shoes on was a violation of Navy regulations. "Never let me see you do this again," he barked. I had heard that before.

Then to my relief he was off to the next room; after a decent interval I took off my shoes and went right down again, always wary in the future of catching a catnap during the daylight hours. The beds we slept in had a fixed bunk on the bottom and one that folded out from the bulkhead on the top. They were made up by the stewards each morning, one of the perks of being an officer. The stewards also laundered our uniforms and served the meals in the wardroom.

The stewards were a special rating (specialty) in the US Navy. Almost all of these men were from the Philippines. Their relationship with the Navy dated from a program started in 1898 by President William McKinley. In his article "From Stewards to Admirals: Filipinos in the U.S. Navy," posted July 21, 2003, in the *Asian Journal*, Ramon J. Farolan writes of the program's appeal:

> For many of our young men, a career in the U.S. Navy was a life-long dream. In a number of communities, joining the U.S. Navy had become a tradition as well as a badge of distinction. The U.S. bases in the Philippines exposed the local people to American wealth, culture and standards of living, generating strong incentive for enlistment. In particular, the

monetary incentive for joining was exceptional—the salary of a raw recruit was a lot higher than many in the towns and villages where they came from. There was also the opportunity to gain permanent residency in the United States and with that, eventual citizenship.

In 1973 stewards were allowed to enter any of the rates for which they were qualified in the US Navy.

I misjudged them as menial workers with little formal education. But one night my simplistic and paternalistic view was changed. I had a transistor radio that had stopped working properly. After fiddling with it I took it to an electrician's mate for diagnosis and repair. He had no clue.

I was again fiddling with it when the steward who had come to get my laundry asked if he could help me. He explained that in the Philippines he had worked in a radio repair shop but could make more money in the US Navy. He would eventually save enough to open his own shop with his family. He took my radio and brought it back the next day fixed. Other stewards had similar stories. Many of them sent most of their pay from their prized Navy jobs to their families.

We all looked forward to R & R having had only a few days off in Key West and Mayport since leaving Boston. As we had learned not to expect anything, we were pleasantly surprised when one day word came that we would be going to Ocho Rios, Jamaica, just southwest of us. As the departure date got closer we wondered if that would really happen. True to form, several days before we were to depart the captain decided we needed the time for training and could not afford the days off. R & R was canceled. As the sailors liked to say sardonically, "Liberty is canceled until morale improves." The tone of this letter suggests I took the change of plans somewhat philosophically:

Life on board the FURSE is a constant surprise. Last week we were told we would be going to Jamaica for one day this coming weekend—today this was cancelled. How hard it was to break the news to my men who had worked so hard for one good weekend of liberty!

. . . I can't really say too much derogatory about our present Captain. He is a naval officer of the old school, and is a fish out of water unless steaming continuously and barking orders. Living conditions contribute toward strained tempers and frequent fights "on the beach" between the men. But, as our XO said, life may be difficult but that is after all a line officer's trade.

I have subsequently taken several trips to Jamaica for vacations with my family but never with quite the anticipation we had for that trip.

On one of our tours patrolling the mouth of the harbor we got word that a Greek merchant ship, the *Apostolos Andrea*, had run aground on a reef north of Jamaica and was experiencing flooding. They had requested assistance from the naval base and we were designated the primary response ship since we were in the area. A Dutch salvage tug had also been dispatched but was much farther away, as was a Jamaican Coast Guard vessel.

When we got close enough to see the ship we made radio contact. Its captain denied wanting help from us except to take members of the crew's families off and back to port. We sent a boat over to talk with him and agreed to provide this level of assistance.

As first lieutenant I was the officer in charge of the motor whaleboat so I went with a few men to assist. We made many trips in choppy waters ferrying the women and children to our ship. It was a challenge to get these people into the boat as it was bouncing in the choppy water. We had to grab the babies and young children from their mothers and take them into the boat, then help the mothers in. The weather was sunny and they were made comfortable on deck. Then back to Gitmo to offload the families at the base. This was a welcome temporary relief from our training.

One of my collateral duties during this period was officer in charge of administering the high school equivalency exams—the GED tests. Several seamen had been studying and were in line to take these tests; it would accelerate their advancement when they passed. I ordered the tests and after they arrived kept them under my control until the day I administered them. It was a very busy day so I left the three sailors to take the tests on the honor system on the mess decks, and after checking a couple of times came back and collected the answer sheets, which I sent in for grading. I was just too busy to sit with them the whole time as a monitor. And I trusted them.

I had forgotten about this when a few weeks later the XO came to me and said he wanted to talk to me about GED exam results. He had been contacted by the agency, which said the answer sheets were all essentially identical—the sailors had cheated by collaborating on the answers. I had to confess that I had not actually been present the whole time they took the test. The XO said this was serious and would result in disciplinary action against each of the sailors and probably a reprimand for me. The latter never happened, but I was temporarily relieved of duty as GED officer. Another lesson learned. As President Reagan said later about the SALT (Strategic Arms Limitation Treaty) Treaty, "Trust but verify."

After ten days the strain was beginning to tell on everyone. I wrote:

> I am really at a low ebb here. This place is all business—no play. Our Captain is slightly maniacal, everybody agrees. He is so uni-directional that you

cannot see him without being bombarded with all sorts of matters that he carefully catalogs in his brain until the next time you run into him. He has alienated many of the Fleet Training Command down here.

The worst part of it all is the reaction of the enlisted people. My division is constantly hard hit by his directions to run and do this, or paint-out that. Three days ago it came to a head when one of my best seamen attempted to cut his wrists. He was taken to a hospital for psychiatric care more than any other reason. Everybody apparently was drunk and just sat by and watched. . . .

The end result of this is that morale is very low on the ship. The training is intense and arduous, usually 18 hrs/day, 6 or 7 days per week. The officers stick together in mutual defense, with only occasional back-biting.

By this time there were already a few changes in the wardroom. Lieutenant E. had replaced Lieutenant F. as weapons officer. He was very calm and seemed to recognize that I was pretty inexperienced. He never raised his voice and was supportive as long as he saw I was trying. I also had the feeling that he did not aspire to be a career naval officer and was fulfilling his commitment with competency if not passion. Occasionally the captain would criticize him for something but he never got rattled. I appreciated his protection as did the other division officers in the weapons department.

There were humorous moments as well. A destroyer escort (DE) that had been given to Taiwan was training at Gitmo with a new Taiwanese crew. When the ship pulled into the pier at the end of the day, often next to us, we cringed. The destroyer escort would come in at some odd angle and then the crew would start running madly along the decks shouting and gesticulating as they tried to get the lines over to us. We had learned to put every fender we had over the side because the ship sometimes looked like it was going to plow into us before the Taiwanese CO somehow managed to slow it enough to avoid serious damage when it made contact. We called this state of confusion a Chinese fire drill, which was the name we gave to this ship. It is considered a somewhat racist term today, but then was new to my lexicon and seemed to fit the situation perfectly.

Surprisingly I don't remember leaving Gitmo, but there was no question that by the time we departed I had gained confidence as a result of being exposed to all aspects of the ship's operation. I had participated in gunnery exercises, refueling, highline transfers, towing, and countless other drills, and I gained experience as a junior officer of the deck standing watches. I learned the necessity of depending on the knowledge and skills of the senior petty officers in my division, especially those who were willing to step up to the daily challenges.

The captain had accomplished his mission of getting the ship up to the required level of readiness to meet our commitments, though with a restive and frayed crew. At the time I did not know if he was typical or atypical of commanding officers or how the morale on our ship compared to that of Navy ships in general. As far as I knew this is the way it would be for the rest of my tour in the Navy. I would soon find out to the contrary.

3

THE VEIL HAS LIFTED

In Port

We returned to port in Norfolk on August 20, 1967. While other junior officers chose to live onshore, I preferred to remain on board and save the money. This could be a mixed blessing, however, when things came up in my area of responsibility that I had to address even though I was technically off duty, especially on weekends. It was also the case with the crew. The operative phrase was "On board, on duty". Nobody liked to hear this but everyone understood it. It could be as simple as providing line handlers to another ship mooring next to ours or helping to load supplies that arrived unexpectedly on the pier. Since we were on board it was our obligation to pitch in.

During the next few months—September through November 1967—we would split our time in port and at sea about fifty-fifty, in increments of 5 to 15 days each. December would be essentially all in port.

Morale, however, remained low, and the ship's reputation for poor appearance and performance persisted. One day shortly after we had returned to Norfolk from Gitmo an officer came on board and many of us were called in for small group sessions with him to discuss why our ship was below par and how we could improve. We were mostly silent or evasive because it seemed pretty obvious that it had to do with leadership and also because, at least in my case, I felt I could have been more effective in holding my division to a higher standard. We all committed to try harder.

The officer said that we were being considered for quarantine to keep our poor morale from infecting other ships. Shades of being restricted to the ship in Key West. Another example of "Liberty is canceled until morale improves." By this time I had gotten to know some of the junior officers on other ships in our destroyer squadron and could see for myself that the low spirits on our ship were not the norm. But no apparent action seemed to come out of this audit.

Now that we were back in port there seemed to be a rash of personnel problems. Sailors separated from their wives, got into financial trouble, or got into incidents in the bars. It was the division officer's duty to provide support by appearing as an advocate at court hearings, counseling the men on financial responsibility, and arranging payment plans to creditors. These distractions were a constant drain on time and energy and disruptive because of their unpredictability. It would be good to get back to sea.

Did You Salute Him?

While in port, watches were stood on the quarterdeck near the brow, or gangplank, to monitor people coming aboard and leaving the ship. A watch consisted of a senior and junior officer or a first class petty officer or chief. There was also an enlisted man called boatswain's mate of the watch (BMOW) who carried a .45 caliber pistol. These four-hour watches could be busy or slow; they were opportunities to get to know the men on watch with you, particularly at night when not much was going on. But one could never tell when there might be unexpected excitement.

On one late-night watch the BMOW with me said he had spotted a rat jumping onto the ship from one of our mooring lines, in spite of our rat guards, the metal cones placed over the lines. I thought he was joking and then I noticed the large shadowy shape scurrying down the deck. The BMOW drew his .45 and was raising it as if to shoot before I stopped him. We searched and couldn't find the rat and could only assume that it had gotten into a hatch or down an air intake into the bowels of the ship.

The next morning we reported the sighting to the XO and the supply officer. Both were very annoyed with us for letting a rat on board—this was a serious matter since it potentially compromised all the food we had stored. The rest of the day the cooks and men in the supply department emptied the food lockers in search of the rat. Likewise, each division was ordered to check all of their living and working spaces. In the end the rat was never found but the episode became much parodied by officers and men alike with gibes like "Did you salute him when he came on board?"

My Name Is Mud

When in port sometimes you tend to forget you are still surrounded by water, which can have quick and unexpected consequences, none of them good.

When I became a lieutenant junior grade I became qualified as a CDO. This was the officer in command of the ship in the captain's absence when in port, often on a weekend. It was normally pretty routine duty since not much would happen on a Saturday or Sunday. The CDO was the keeper of all of the keys including the FZ alarm keys (I don't remember what this stands for) that gave access to the magazine where our ASROC missiles were stored, including at times those with nuclear capability. Only a few need-to-know officers were privy to whether nuclear

71

weapons were on board; I never knew one way or the other even when I had the keys.

One Saturday I had duty as CDO and could not wait to be relieved at 8 a.m. on Sunday morning. I stood at the quarterdeck anxiously waiting for my relief to come aboard so I could brief him and go on liberty. As he approached the ship and started across the brow, on impulse I took the keys out of my pocket and tossed them to him. He reached out and bobbled them and they fell in the water.

I went to get the duty boatswain's mate and asked if there was a magnet we could put on a string and lower over the side where the keys went in. This proved futile; we weren't even sure if any of the keys were magnetic since as we recalled most were brass, copper, or aluminum. I also went to the tender to arrange for divers to go down and search on Monday. They came up and said there was a thick layer of silt and mud that made it impossible to see more than a few feet in front of them. I felt like my name was mud for a few days with the XO. New keys were eventually obtained. I used to tell my kids the story about the princess whose diamond ring fell in the water and she found it again when she was eating the fish that had swallowed it. No such luck in the real world. In fact, no fish could survive in the muck that surrounded our ship.

On the other hand, while at sea I lost only one pair of glasses over the side and never, in three years, my cap, which had to be some kind of record given the stormy conditions we often encountered. We tended to be more careful about objects (and ourselves) going over the side when under way than in port.

School Daze

During extended stays in port many of the officers and crew were sent off the ship to schools. I was scheduled to go to gunfire support school at the nearby amphibious base at Little Creek.

This was a one-week school where we learned the commands and procedures for taking calls for fire from a shore-based spotter. We also learned the exact sequence of firing for the annual qualifications for each destroyer at the firing range at Culebra off the south coast of Puerto Rico. It was like knowing exactly what the road test for a driver's license would be before you got in the car. It was all written on several sheets of paper that we took with us when we left the school.

This school also enabled me to meet my counterparts on other ships and to frequent the Little Creek "O" Club after school, where the music consisted of warmed-over World War II songs such as "Lili Marlene" and "Over There". They even provided song sheets so we could sing along. There were some old-timers at the bar who looked like they were holdovers from the 1940s and '50s. In spite of the music there were always a few officers belting out these songs after they were properly oiled. And there were always a few haggard-looking women at the bar. I found it pretty depressing but the drinks were only 25 cents and it was better than going back to the ship.

The sterile environments, rote learning, and mild hangovers always left me feeling in kind of a daze after these schools, but they were respites from the monotony of shipboard life in port.

Change of Command (September 1, 1967)

Since our captain had been promoted he was due for transfer to another ship and we would be getting a new CO. In my view things could only get better, but sometimes the devil you know is better than the devil you don't know. So when the day came there was much curiosity to see what fate had brought us.

I remember seeing our next captain (then a commander), Michael T. Greeley, for the first time as he was piped aboard for the change of command ceremony. We had heard he was a squared-away Naval

Academy grad who had some previous command experience on destroyers, but otherwise we did not know much about him. The previous captain had not been part of the fraternity of Academy grads since he had received his commission through the ROTC program, a possible factor in his drive to prove himself to his peers.

I learned of Captain Greeley's previous experience from the Change of Command program issued to the crew that day. Michael T. Greeley was born in Columbus, Ohio, on June 20, 1929. He enlisted in the Navy as an aviation electronics technician in 1947 and entered the Naval Academy in 1949 on a fleet appointment. His first assignments were aboard the USS *Seminole* (AKA-104) and USS *Maurice J. Manuel* (DE-3510). He next obtained a master of science degree in electrical engineering from the US Naval Postgraduate School, Monterey, California. He served on the USS *Long Beach* (CGN-9) until May 1963 and subsequently attended the Armed Forces Staff College in Norfolk, Virginia. In 1966 he became the executive officer of USS *Macdonough* (DLG-8) prior to taking command of the USS *Furse*. He was married and had three children.

I saw the new captain banter with the other senior officers taking positions on the hangar deck for the ceremony he was smiling and seemed happy and self-confident. He was about five eight, solidly built, and walked with a spring in his step. I found out later he had been a gymnast at the Naval Academy. He exuded a friendly confidence in his address to his new crew and officers. Though I had yet to meet him, I could feel the veil lifting. He looked like a good guy, but we were still wary.

We were eager to get off on the right foot with the new CO. By this time I felt like a reasonably experienced officer who knew the ship. I had a stronger grasp of my duties and less to fear from a new captain who would be in a learning mode himself for a while. I would, however, have more day-to-day contact with the XO who was relatively new, having replaced Lieutenant Commander K., who had been lifted off the ship so unceremoniously in Jacksonville. He had been a lieutenant when joining the ship shortly before Gitmo, and as a new lieutenant commander was also proving himself.

Good Cop, Bad Cop

The XO was fairly young and gung ho. He could be fun-loving (good cop) but was ready to play the role of enforcer (bad cop) for the new captain. He was an ROTC-trained officer who liked to tell stories of how he and his peers had harassed hippie protesters at his Midwest college campus. The XO could be quick to assert his authority regardless of his jocular manner. He was smart and stayed on top of his shipboard duties as navigator and second in command. He had the aura of someone on the fast track to higher command who was eager to show his abilities and rise above his peers. And indeed, he later achieved flag rank. The combination of a competent, mentoring captain and well-organized, energetic XO was the ideal formula for turning the ship around.

My first real test with the new XO was over something relatively minor but was a lesson in placing one's own priorities over those of one's boss. The XO had picked up on the new captain's penchant for walking the decks and urging the boatswain's mates to "titivate," a new word to me that I learned meant to smarten up all of the little details. The XO likewise became a stickler for the ship's appearance.

He focused especially on the quarterdeck area, which created the first impression for those coming aboard. Besides a couple of ceremonial brass shell casings with a white braided rope spanning them, the most visible object on the quarterdeck was the status board, a three-by-four-inch wooden board with a slot for each officer's name incised on a piece of plastic. These could be slid to a position indicating when an officer was or was not on board. The status board also had white braided cordage attached to it in patterns created by boatswain's mates experienced in fancywork. This was a remnant of the days when seamen were experts in creating spliced loops, monkey's fists, and other ornamental effects, an art that was all but lost by this time.

Our status board was somewhat worn in appearance and the XO let me know soon after he joined the ship that it needed to be refreshed with a new coat of shellac and repairs to the wood, fancywork, and name holders. With so much more critical operational gear to maintain this was low on my list of priorities. Likewise, most of the boatswain's mates mildly resented the spit-and-polish aspect of their jobs versus the "real" work. I finally got the board to our tender (in-port support ship), but in a few days when I returned for it they told me it was a low priority for them as well and required special expertise they did not have.

After a while I got tired of the XO's remarks about it and decided to take things literally into my own hands. I took it to my stateroom in the evenings and attempted repairs myself, but there was little room and I did not have the right tools or materials. It was vexing that I could not find a way to get this relatively simple item repaired. Finally the XO had had enough and told me he would take care of it himself. How he got it done I don't know, but it disappeared from the ship for about a week and looked much better when it was returned—I think he took it to a carpentry shop off the base, but he remained mum. I learned to be more proactive in the future when he wanted something done. I also learned to look at priorities through his eyes and they became my priorities also—a valuable lesson for the future.

The first captain was, by way of training and demonstrated commitment, a dedicated naval officer, while I was a junior officer with a decidedly different temperament and management style and no credentials to judge him. It could be argued that his tough love approach did whip people into shape. I could only contrast him with his successor in terms of the motivation and morale of the ship after the change of command.

In architecture when we want to evaluate the effectiveness of a building we go back after a year or more and observe how people actually use it. Our return visit includes interviewing the occupants to determine if the design has met its intended purpose. We call this evidence-based design. In evaluating the *Furse* after the change of command, the evidence would show that when one primary variable, the commanding officer, was changed there was a noticeable improvement in the ship's morale and performance.

Piano Man?

One immediate difference in the new management of the ship was the camaraderie engendered by the new captain. He was not dictatorial in the wardroom though he did lead the conversation. We felt freer to speak but certainly continued to defer to him. There was more joking and openness among us. This led to a more positive attitude about our own work and a more relaxed relationship with each other. We really wanted to perform for this new captain; morale was measurably improving.

One tangible change in the wardroom was the desserts. The new captain's favorite was deep-dish blueberry pie à la mode. We had this once a week. When for some reason the stewards were not able to supply it, he would pretend to give them a hard time. The conversation always loosened up a bit at dessert time. The captain would ask each of us what our favorite dessert was, though it was clear our favorites would not supplant his on the menu.

One evening after dessert the captain decided we should have some entertainment and asked me to play the piano. Someone had acquired a keyboard. I protested that I did not play the piano, but he insisted he had heard this from a good source. The other officers started egging me on, and I suspected one of them had set me up. The captain wouldn't let it go for weeks afterward and could never quite accept my denials.

It was expected that each officer would arrange to call on a new CO at his house, as I recounted in a letter home about ten days after the change of command:

> Life has eased quite a bit since we are in port and have a new Captain—I paid my call on him a few nights ago along with a few of the other officers. He has a nice house in Virginia Beach, two sons and a daughter, and a French poodle. He is very nice and has a good sense of humor. What a relief for the whole crew.
>
> [Note: I got this wrong; he had two daughters and one son.]

At these get-togethers, the new captain liked to challenge his guests to a game where a person would position himself facedown on the floor supported by his hands and feet while clutching a Coke bottle in each hand to see how far he could stretch without falling while supported by the Coke bottles. Then the person had to return to an upright position without touching the ground, but this time with only one bottle for support, having left the other bottle as far out as one could reach. Your feet had to stay behind the line. You would stretch out supported by the Coke bottles and leave one bottle standing upright, then walk yourself back with the remaining bottle to a point where you could stand up. The secret was being able to do a one-armed push-up. This required great abdominal and arm strength and the captain always won.

Soon we would go to sea for the first time with our new captain— to the North Atlantic, notorious for its unpredictable and often tempestuous seas. I had crossed this stretch of ocean when I was 16 on a cruise ship with my friend Steve Hayes on what we anticipated would be a pleasurable voyage after a summer spent abroad. It was stormy the whole way across and seasickness was the norm among the passengers. That ship, three times as long and far heavier than our destroyer, had been tossed about by the unstable elements, so we could expect the same or worse.

It was immediately obvious as we left the pier that Captain Greeley was a confident and experienced ship handler. This was a good sign for what promised to be a challenging if relatively short deployment. The last time I had sailed north from Norfolk had been on my maiden voyage with *Furse* when she was heading to the shipyard in Boston. I looked back on those days a little less than a year before as a dim memory. Now I felt pretty comfortable standing watches on the bridge, but I still had a lot to learn.

4

NORTH ATLANTIC

After another in-port period in Norfolk, FURSE left
her home port 6 November for CANUS SILEX,
a joint American-Canadian ASW exercise in the
North Atlantic. Following the exercise, FURSE
spent the weekend of the 17th in Halifax, Nova
Scotia, returning to Norfolk 22 November. *(FURSE
Command History of 1967)*

I had heard about destroyers escorting convoys of World War II
merchant ships transiting the North Atlantic and the rough seas they
encountered. I had seen the *Victory at Sea* films with waves washing
over ships that would momentarily vanish under the windblown
swells. I later read letters my uncle Waring Gelzer WTC (water tender
chief) had written from his destroyer, the USS *Swanson* (DD-443),
recounting his experiences protecting the convoy from U-boats
on one such mission. It seemed from all I had read and seen that
conditions there were always rough. This excerpt from the book
on *Destroyer at War!* about the USS *Swanson* (DD-443) describes
conditions on a trip to Iceland:

On 4 November 1941, the SWANSON sailed from Argentia, Newfoundland in company with destroyers, USS BUCK, LUDLOW, COLE, McCORMICK and WOOLSEY, to escort a trans Atlantic convoy to Point MOMP, where the Royal Navy would relieve the U.S. destroyers which would then proceed on to ICELAND. Thus began the real initiation of the SWANSON's officers and men into WW II, and the "Freezing Purgatory" of the North Atlantic. This was the first of three trips made by the SWANSON to ICELAND. From a physical aspect the ICELAND trips were probably the most physically exhausting of any trips made by the SWANSON. The North Atlantic between Newfoundland, Greenland, Iceland and Scotland during the winter months is almost continuously beset by gale winds and mountainous sea. The old sailor axiom about, "One hand for the ship and one hand for yourself!" certainly applied. At times a sailor needed both hands for himself to hold on and prevent being thrown literally through the air as the SWANSON pitched and rolled heavily.[4.1]

Though we were not quite as far east or north as the *Swanson*, we experienced a strong taste of similar conditions. After several days of ever-increasing cold and rough seas we arrived at Halifax, Nova Scotia. We pulled into the harbor with another destroyer early in the morning, and as was the custom First Division lined the foc's'le at attention in dress blues. The temperature was well below freezing and the wind was steady off the bow. Our gloves and coats were no match for the biting cold and wind. It was the coldest I ever remember being before or since.

To gain some small measure of relief we rotated men down to the boatswain's locker for a few minutes to warm up. About the third man to come up out of the hatch had a hot cup of coffee and offered it to the first class boatswain's mate who took a few sips before offering it to someone else. Each had a smile on his face as it was passed around. I sensed something was amiss. Finally the first class went below and emerged with another cup, which he offered to me. One sip confirmed my suspicions—it was laced with rum, forbidden on board. This was a pretty brazen act, offering a "controlled substance" to an officer who by all rights should report those involved. In view of the extreme conditions I took another sip and announced that I had had enough. Lesson: Rules can be overlooked in certain circumstances.

We fired a gun salute and proceeded smartly to our mooring. The line handlers were glad to be able to move about to get warm. The November 18, 1967, Halifax newspaper reported that 4,000 sailors from Canada and the United States were in Halifax that weekend. Our sightseeing was abbreviated because of the inclement weather, but I vowed to return in the future. Although I found myself returning to the Caribbean, I never had the opportunity to revisit Halifax. Perhaps my memories of that bleak visit were enough to deter me.

The North Atlantic deployment was the first time I was involved in a joint operation with another country. We seemed to operate mostly with our own ships, but I am sure on a command level there was a lot of coordination of communications and operational logistics. We did attend a reception on one of the host Canadian ships while in port and had a chance to dance with some of the local women who had been invited. Most of us just wanted to get back to our ship for some rest without being strapped into our bunks before returning to the choppy waters of the North Atlantic.

It was constantly stormy for those two weeks as we chased submarines that were in turn stalking us in a massive ASW exercise.

The sonar was practically useless and generated myriad false contacts. When we did make contact it was because the sub had gotten in close enough to fire a fish, or torpedo, at us. These dummies, which were set to pass just under our hull, generated a distinctive audio signature from the cavitation of their propellers, which all of us with GQ stations in CIC could hear. As the torpedo got closer and the sound louder it was unnerving and a reminder of who ruled these seas.

CIC was tightly packed with heat-producing electronic gear and without outside air ventilation during GQ to simulate possible airborne chemical attack. In that confined and stuffy indoor environment even the saltiest of men got seasick as the ship pitched and rolled. The odor of vomit triggered additional reactions. It was a relief when someone opened the door from the outside which brought in a little fresh air.

We were unable to eat at the wardroom table because the tableware would slide off, so we ate sitting on the carpet, which had been wetted to be less slippery. Still a lot spilled. When going back and forth on the ship we stayed inside as much as possible for safety. Though rails lined the deck the footing remained treacherous as waves washed over us. If someone went overboard in the dark it was unlikely he would be seen by a lookout and difficult to find in the waves even if spotted. It gave me great respect for the men of World War II destroyers like my uncle Waring for whom this was routine duty. Today's destroyers seem to have a higher freeboard (the height of the deck above the waterline), which adds a bit more protection.

This cruise also gave me an opportunity to practice my skills flying our DASH helicopter under rough conditions. We could only do this when the seas had calmed enough for the DASH crew to get the helo out of the hangar and secured on deck for liftoff. The critical periods were getting it away from the stacks and antennas as quickly as possible at liftoff and then bringing it in for landing at the end of the flight. After it was up and well away from the ship, operational control was transferred from manual control on the flight deck to radio control by the assistant DASH officer in CIC,

who vectored it to its target area, dropped the torpedo, and got it back within visual range where control was returned to the officer on the flight deck. The assistant DASH officer and I traded positions on successive flights so each of us stayed in practice flying it manually.

To allow us to land the DASH, the ship steadied on a course into the wind and the DASH was brought to a hover just aft of the flight deck on the port quarter until the bridge cleared it for landing. Then the fun began.

The deck would be moving in three directions and it was important for the two sledlike runners supporting the helo to touch down together, at which time the power was cut to keep it firmly on deck. If one runner hit first it could cause the helo to tip over or start bouncing from one runner to the other until the rotors hit each other or the deck. The flight officer stood behind his waist-high metal shield with the flight console mounted just in front of him. If there was an accident he could duck down for protection from the flying fragments of lead and the splintered rotors.

The best way to accomplish a landing under these conditions was to stand with knees partly bent and to sway gently in sync with the motion of the ship. This motion could be transmitted to the helo through the stick so that as it came down it would be swaying slightly, in sync with the deck, and land flat. This was as much art as science and we all had our close calls, but fortunately we never had an accident or lost a bird. After a successful landing the torpedomen would emerge from the hangar and secure it with tie-downs to the deck. We would walk away as if it had been routine, but we always felt a great sense of relief as we departed the flight deck.

Many DASH helos were lost in the fleet, and this highly engineered but temperamental system was eventually abandoned after limited service as an unmanned aerial platform for cameras called Snoopy used for spotting in Vietnam. When the *Furse* went to Vietnam, the DASH was not aboard and its hangar became a storage area. This helo presaged the fixed-wing drones that were a mainstay of the war in Afghanistan and are increasingly being used for covert actions in other suspected terrorist areas.

The DASH system reminds me of the invention of the Segway PT two-wheeled, self-balancing electric vehicle invented by Dean Kamen. The Segway is an innovative product in search of a use, and it never replaced traditional bicycles as a faster alternative to walking in urban areas, though it is being used in shopping malls and airports by security guards. DASH was designed for ASW but never supplanted the basic torpedo. It never became part of the core ordnance and was ultimately abandoned by the Navy. Some felt that it was seen by the Navy as a threat to naval aviators as an "unmanned aerial vehicle" and quashed as a result (see http://www. gyrodynehelicopters.com/).[21]

5

A SHARK NEARBY MAKES A GOOD SWIMMER GREAT

Springboard

> FURSE (DD 882), departed Norfolk, Virginia, on
> 16 January 1968 for Operation Spring Board in
> the Caribbean. Extensive training and operational
> readiness exercises were accomplished with brief
> visits to San Juan and Ponce, Puerto Rico. *(FURSE
> Command History of 1968)*

After our return to Norfolk we remained in port for December and
the first two weeks of January before we departed for Springboard,
an annual ritual to retrain in ASW operations, engineering drills,
replenishment at sea, and gunnery. And just to shake out the cobwebs
from a winter spent primarily in port. We sailed south to San Juan,
Puerto Rico, which was our home port during Springboard. This
sure beat Halifax in the North Atlantic. As at Key West, wives of the
senior officers came down for part of this period. The daily routine
was almost as intense as Gitmo's, so time ashore was limited. Those
of us without spouses usually headed straight for the O club for a
couple of hours of liquid relief each evening.

On our approach to San Juan Harbor I was junior officer of the deck and had the conn—control of the ship—as we were about to enter the narrow entrance to the harbor. We approached at high speed to make a smart entry. I knew the OOD, the XO or the captain, would take the conn from me at some point since I had no experience bringing the ship into port. As we got closer I was getting nervous as more small craft appeared ahead and the fort known as El Morro, marking the entrance to the harbor, came into sight. Finally the operations officer was directed to take the conn but I felt the captain had been testing me to see how I reacted to this new level of responsibility. This was typical of his willingness to help us grow by pushing us a little beyond the limits of our perceived abilities.

As we approached the harbor entrance a sonar contact was reported and we aborted our entry to investigate. It appeared to be a sub or other object stationed at some depth at the entrance to the harbor. It was obligatory for destroyers to track down any submarine contacts, friendly or otherwise. The captain wanted to verify the depth and called down to the deck crew on the foc's'le to heave the lead line,[5.1] a 20-fathom (120-foot) length of line to which a seven-to-ten-pound lead weight was attached on one end. Strips of leather and canvas in various colors and patterns were attached along its length to mark the depths. This method had been used for centuries. The marks are sung out by the boatswain's mate who hangs out over the edge of the ship with a safety belt reporting the depth as marked on the lead line "by the mark twain, and a half six, by the deep eleven." I loved these old terms and the skill required to throw the line in the direction of the ship's motion so it would reach a vertical position as the ship passed its entry point. It was, however, too deep for us to get a reading since the weight never reached bottom.

The captain decided to let the anchor out to almost its full length to see if we could drag it against the sub. But after slowly dragging it back and forth into the evening we pulled it up and proceeded into the harbor. We had a schedule to meet and it may have simply outwaited us.

Antisubmarine warfare, or ASW, had been a primary mission of destroyers in World War II and continued thereafter even though nuclear subs could now run circles around us. I had been trained only minimally in ASW and was insecure as OOD when the sonarmen reported a contact. Captain's orders were to go to flank speed (about 35 knots) and call him immediately. At first, when this happened on my watch, I would only go to 20 or 25 knots, which seemed fast enough to me since I really had little idea what to do next. After some reprimands I dutifully went to 35 knots, not knowing exactly where I was going but getting there fast.

The daily routine for Springboard was to get under way by about 5:30 or 6 a.m. so we could be in our training area by 8—similar to our schedule at Gitmo. Hangovers from the night before were no excuse. We all had our favorite antidotes but the captain was reported to have a brew almost magical in its powers to banish the effects of overindulgence. He was always perky in the morning even after having consumed as much as we had the night before. He kept his formula a secret, though it reportedly looked like a glass of milk, while we relied on Alka-Seltzer or nothing. I learned that taking an Alka-Seltzer was only effective if taken the night before rather than the morning after when the hangover hit.

Occasionally one of my men would not make it up in the morning or would be so sick he was useless. The chief would make him muster on deck with the rest of the division even if he was miserably sick. Every person was needed for these drills, and one person's absence put an added burden on his shipmates. Sometimes an additional penalty was assessed later as well. We empathized since we had all been there but could show no mercy.

On weekends we would come in early on Saturday and have the day off on Sunday. We had been granted access to the swimming pool at a big hotel, the Caribe Hilton, about a mile from the pier, and could spend the afternoon there. Or we could find our way to one of the local beaches. Once I ventured out as a passenger on the back of a motorcycle with a first class engineman and his division officer. When we changed into our suits in the men's room at the beach I saw tattoos on him in places I never imagined someone would want or be able to get them. He explained he was pretty drunk at the time.

One gunnery exercise I experienced for the first time on Springboard was shooting at a target towed by a plane at the end of a long cable. This anti-air firing exercise gave me insight into another mission of destroyers that operated as picket ships in World War II. The success of hitting a moving target in the air had everything to do with the Mark 1A (Mark One Able) computer and gyroscope mounted in Plot, a secure interior compartment of the ship. This gyroscope established a motion-stable reference no matter how the ship pitched and rolled. The gyro was synched to motors that would constantly raise and lower the gun muzzles and adjust the bearing of the gun mount to compensate for the movement of the ship. Other data had to be entered as well, such as the temperature, humidity, and wind conditions that would affect the flight of the projectile.

The radar in the director—the gimbal-mounted cockpit atop the ship—was operated by a fire control technician (FT) who would acquire the target and attempt to lock on as soon as possible. The FT had to maintain his cool while everyone awaited his announcement "Locked on," which was transmitted to the men in Plot. The radar had to remain locked on target for some seconds to generate a firing solution. The Mark 1A was an analog computer that would project the future position of the target based on its current track. It was temperamental--when it didn't work we called it the Mark Unable computer.

The fuse on the projectile would be set automatically by a fuse-setting device controlled by the computer as it passed from the handling room up to the gun for loading. One type of fuse called a variable time fuse would detonate when the calculated time for it to reach the target expired. We also used proximity fuses, which sent out their own radar signals and detonated when the return signal was strong enough. All of this was automatic once the computer was put in control. The only manual part was loading the projectiles and powder cases into the hoist and placing them in the breech of the gun. The gun captain in the mount controlled when to fire. We could fire up to 20 rounds per minute depending on the effectiveness of the gun crew. Newer destroyers had more highly automated 5"/54 caliber guns, which could fire at a much higher rate but often jammed, particularly in rainy weather.

We had pretty good success in hitting the target sleeve. Sometimes we would sever it from the cable and the radar-controlled shells would follow its descent until cease-fire was called. Occasionally the radar acquired the towing cable itself and started working our rounds back along the cable toward the tow plane. The cable was a mile long to give time for us to break off contact before the rounds got too close to the tow plane. It had to be harrowing, nonetheless, for the tow plane crew to watch our rounds creep ever closer until we ceased fire. They sometimes had to release the cable from the plane if they felt the rounds were getting too close. As the sleeve spiraled down into the water our rounds kept tracking and bursting around it.

A similar exercise was conducted for surface targets called sleds, which were towed behind a boat. Several ships would form into a line, and one after the other would fire at the sled as each entered and exited the designated firing arcs. Hitting the target required firing single shots over and under the target and halving the distance each time in a procedure known as "bracket and halving." When we were on target the order was given to "fire for effect," releasing the gun crews to fire as many rounds as they could until cease-fire was ordered. Many ships started firing for effect immediately in hopes they would be lucky enough to be on target without bracket and halving; they were seldom effective. We consistently scored high by following the prescribed approach.

I finally got my chance to practice what I had learned in school at our scheduled shore-fire bombardment exercise at Culebra. At nearby Roosevelt Roads Naval Station we took on ammo including white phosphorous rounds, commonly called willy peter and star shells, which floated down on little parachutes. I restudied the order of firing that had been issued to all gunnery and bridge personnel. It was just a matter of getting in position in the late afternoon, establishing radio communication with the spotters at the range, and beginning the exercise as they called for fire or set off smoke charges on the beach as targets. We finished when it got dark with the white phosphorous or star shells, which lit up the beach to illuminate the targets. We requalified with an almost perfect score. Most ships did well since it was all scripted in advance.

We were to find out in Vietnam that this training was really not very relevant under conditions of high-speed approaches, dependence on often inexperienced spotters, and difficulty in getting good fixes to establish the ship's position.[5.2]

On the range we also got to be spectators at some pretty impressive night bombing runs by planes with extremely powerful arc lights mounted on the undersides of their fuselages. The brightness of the lights themselves would have had a shock-and-awe effect on anyone below.

Our daily life of long hours of intense training was in sharp contrast to the leisure life of tourists who frequented these islands at this time of year. This was never more apparent to me than the night we conducted a full-power run to test how long we could steam at our top sustained speed of 35 knots (a little less than 40 mph). We would steam continuously for as many hours as the boiler plant would hold out while recording the amount of fuel consumed. The course was a triangle between the islands of Puerto Rico, St. Thomas, and St. Croix. It was a beautiful tropical night with a bright moon and calm waters.

There was nothing much to do except make sure that the straight legs of the course were maintained with as little variation as possible in speed. We knew that contacts picked up by our SPS10 (surface search) radar were most likely small boats. One such contact was plotted to pass very close to us if we both maintained our course and speed. As we got close enough for a visual sighting it was identified as a vessel under sail, which, to our annoyance, automatically had the right-of-way and caused us to alter course slightly, so we cut it as close as we dared. As we passed her I could see that it was a beautiful sloop with a crew in casual clothes enjoying their night sail in the cockpit while we were plowing through the water like a juggernaut. I waved as we went by. They just stared up in curious dismay.

We went to St. Thomas for a few days of R & R. I had tried to get there with the supply officer earlier by plane on a prior weekend without success. When we arrived the captain and commodore got a room in a local hotel so we were able to use the pool. Much to our amusement and that of the other guests, the captain showed his gymnastic skills on the diving board. We wandered through Charlotte Amalie, enjoying being off the ship in a visually rich environment. I missed Pam, now my fiancée, and bought her a bikini, which seemed to be the uniform of the day for the many female tourists—we couldn't help but notice. As with Jamaica, I was able to return in future years as a vacationer to enjoy the island properly.

In spite of the good weather and lively ports, Springboard was exhausting and we were happy when we had completed the training and were on our way home.

Splice the Mainbrace

On February 9th FURSE returned to homeport Norfolk. Preliminary planning for deployment to the

Western Pacific began with an interruption on the
19th and 20th for NASA capsule recovery exercises
in the Virginia Capes area. *(FURSE Command History
of 1968)*

During our in-port period in Norfolk we were called for a
special assignment to be on station for a Gemini space capsule
recovery. These were the early days of spaceflight when astronauts
would descend in small capsules suspended by parachutes. It was
never known precisely where they would come down, so ships were
stationed along the probable recovery corridor. We had to be fitted
with a special rig on the fantail to lift the capsule out of the water
and onto a special cradle.

This required tech reps—technical representatives from the
company that made the gear—to come on board in advance and
make sure all apparatus was ready, including a life-size test capsule
set in the cradle for practice. I remember how precisely every bolt
and piece of gear was set, which was far beyond the tolerances we
were used to for deck-mounted equipment. The more exacting
engineering standards for a spaceflight were impressive. In contrast,
if we needed to repair or replace a damaged or missing part, our
solution was to give it to the machinist mates to turn out on the
lathe, which led to some pretty creative replacement parts. The
machinists prided themselves on their ingenuity; for example, they
made items such as ashtrays from brass shell casings salvaged from
"short charges" used for ceremonial purposes. These brass casings
were sought-after prizes since shell casings for much more prevalent
service rounds were aluminum. I obtained one that we used for years
as an umbrella stand until we lost it during a move.

We departed a day prior to the scheduled space capsule reentry
in order to practice. When we were approximately on station in
the Atlantic, the ship slowed to a stop and the tech reps began the
procedure of putting the practice capsule in the water. We readied

the motor whaleboat with the three seamen elected to go into the water to put the collar onto the capsule for towing to the ship. It was a cold, blustery day with intermittent showers and we didn't envy the swimmers, even though they had wet suits on. I was the boat officer with nothing much to do but watch the proceedings and try to keep dry in the choppy seas.

Everything went slowly as the swimmers tried to get the collar onto the capsule, which was moving erratically. I could just imagine how the astronauts inside would feel and knew it would be almost impossible not to get seasick. Finally, after coaching by the tech rep in the boat, the capsule was snagged and lifted on board. We returned to the ship a little queasy as well as wet to the bone. When all were aboard, the boatswain's pipe was heard over the topside speakers with the announcement: "The boat party to report to the bridge—now splice the main brace." [5.3]

This is an old nautical term that means to break out and administer a shot of rum to individuals who have been out in inclement conditions. Drinking alcohol is strictly forbidden on U.S. Navy ships with this exception. The medical corpsman keeps the rum under lock and key for these occasions. As I had found out in Halifax, some was also kept clandestinely in other locations on the ship. Each of us was poured a small amount of rum when we arrived on the bridge. The swimmers were allowed seconds.

Adjustments were made in the gear and we trained again the next day, this time with more success but no rum as a reward. One precaution when men were in the water was the stationing of shark lookouts and marksmen on the O-1 (upper) deck. We usually didn't see many sharks in cold mid-Atlantic waters, but the sounds made by all of the commotion were sure to draw some. Captain Greeley, one of the best marksmen on the ship, enjoyed shooting at sharks when they did appear.

Sharks were much more of a concern in our Springboard exercises in the Caribbean where the water was warmer. There we had to recover torpedoes that we had shot in exercises. We always encountered sharks when the swimmers went into the water to attach the recovery collars. The captain and gunner's mates peppered away at incoming sharks with their M1 rifles, heavy relics of World War II. I never saw blood actually drawn, since the bullets lost some effect when they penetrated the water and the sharks' skins were thick. But they did back off.

On the day of the splashdown we steamed in our assigned sector. The capsule came down hundreds of miles from us and was picked up by an aircraft carrier. It was all anticlimactic, though we felt we had been part of something big in the relatively young space race, and we had gotten to see an exact replica of the capsule "up close and personal."

We periodically had tech reps or personnel from other Navy agencies visit us on board to help install new equipment or help with maintenance and repair. When the Navy instituted its Preventive Maintenance System (PMS), men came aboard to train us in its use. The system was simple in concept: Maintenance that had to be done on each piece of gear daily, weekly, monthly, or annually was spelled out on a card. All that the men had to do was look at the cards each week and record on them that they had performed the required maintenance. This really was an honor system since, as was frequently done, it was easy to fill out the cards without performing the maintenance completely. This is referred to in the Navy as "gun decking," which loosely translated means falsifying reports. It was up to the petty officers and division officers to do spot checks. Every plan of the day had the preventive maintenance cycle at the top as a reminder.

When something broke down we could look at the cards to see if the PMS had been kept up to date. It was human nature not to keep up with this system and rely on fixing things only when they broke. But the work that had gone into developing the system was pretty impressive, and gradually it was relied on more and more. The beauty of it was that a chief or first class petty officer could give a third class or seaman the card with instructions detailing what needed to be done without having to explain it every time—just tell him to follow the card. This brought consistency and quality to the maintenance process, assuming it was implemented. In our case it was often treated as a necessary evil and just more paperwork.

Later when I worked as an architect with institutions that hired us to renovate their buildings I was struck by the lack of regular maintenance on roofs, windows, and mechanical equipment that could have prolonged their life. My boss at one architectural firm had actually talked to an insurance company to try to persuade them to offer an insurance policy to replace these systems at the end of their useful life. For instance, if a roof was rated at fifteen years, the premiums would cover replacement at that time.

This idea never gained traction; the if-it-ain't-broke-don't-fix-it mentality was too strongly embedded. In our case, if something didn't work properly we would check the PMS records retrospectively and inevitably find deficiencies. Then we would blame the person responsible, when in fact we had all been culpable of treating the PMS system as busywork.

Author next to NASA recovery capsule

NASA capsule recovery training February 19 & 20, 1968

6

BE CAREFUL WHAT YOU WISH FOR

Orders

When I had been aboard for a little over a year I started to think of what I might request when I had the opportunity to change duty for my final year and a half. Midway through a tour, a junior officer got the opportunity to express his preferences, subject to "the needs of the Navy." It was mildly liberating to think that I could actually have a say in my next assignment, unlike filling out a "dream sheet" as I had at OCS knowing what I wrote was just that—a dream. I tried to keep in regular contact with my detailer at BUPERS (Bureau of Naval Personnel) to find out what might be available. If I was in the Washington area I would make it a point to stop by and pay a visit to make sure he knew who I was and could advocate for me if necessary.

One day shortly before I was up for reassignment we got an announcement in the wardroom that an officer was coming to visit and talk about the Navy's Swift Boat program. Swift Boats and river patrol boats were akin to the torpedo boats of World War II—small, fast, shallow-draft boats with automatic weapons mounted fore and aft. Their mission in Vietnam was ferrying troops to rendezvous points, interdicting, or disrupting, enemy supply craft on rivers and canals, and generally denying use of these waterways to the North Vietnamese Army. They were also highly vulnerable, with little protection against mines or fire from the shore. Boat crews often fabricated their own metal screens around the sides to intercept incoming rounds or grenades.

I signed up out of curiosity and attended his presentation with a few others. I remember asking some questions and must have seemed interested. I pretty much forgot about it after that. Three weeks later I got orders to Swift Boat school in San Diego. I told Pam the news. Her reaction was no way! We had both seen enough on TV of combat on the rivers of Vietnam to know this was seriously dangerous duty. As much as I was drawn to the adventure of commanding one of these boats my naturally cautious nature said not to do it. In retrospect I had not been definitive with BUPERS about what I wanted, and my detailer probably took my attendance as an expression of interest. Lesson: Be careful what you wish for (or show interest in).

I went to the captain for his assistance. Fortunately the ship had just received orders to go to the Tonkin Gulf, so the captain said he could have my orders annulled if I would remain on *Furse* for the remainder of my naval obligation. I readily agreed. I liked the captain and saw no reason to leave the ship for Swift Boats or another destroyer where I would have to learn a new culture. I did have a twinge of disappointment in forgoing this unique experience.

My friend Steve Hayes came up for a change in duty shortly after I did. We kept in touch mainly through news transferred between our parents and then relayed to each of us. He was serving on the USS *Whitfield County* (LST-1169) in the Pacific and was encouraged to go into Swift Boats by a friend and fellow officer on his ship. Steve had been away from the US for more than a year and wanted a change of duty from the LST and a chance to get some home leave between duty assignments. Steve had always been the one to go right to the edge of danger when we were kids, and it was a wonder that he survived his childhood. Though he did not choose this duty for the adventure, he was a good match for it and was awarded a Bronze Star when he helped rescue another boat under fire and had his own Swift Boat shot up in the process.

The good news for me was that I would be in substantially less danger in the Tonkin Gulf than patrolling the rivers. The bad news was that my fiancée and I would have to defer our wedding until after this long deployment. My friends on board urged me to get married before we left to become eligible for separation pay as well as combat pay. We decided to wait.

The New Wardroom

The original wardroom had almost completely changed from the days when I had first come on board. By electing to stay on the ship I was inheriting a new group of officers who were rotating to the *Furse* as their new duty station. This gave me a chance to meet new people while still on familiar turf. Whereas in my early days aboard almost all of the officers had been senior to me, now about a third were at my level or junior to me.

As before, the department heads—the lieutenants who had about five years of experience -- were solid and competent. Most had been to Destroyer School in Newport, which had the reputation of being a very rigorous training program in every aspect of destroyer operations and had become a necessary step for advancement to eventual command of a destroyer. Ship handling, including taking the ship in and out of port, a task rarely if ever entrusted to anyone without specific training, was an important part of the school's curriculum. In my three years aboard I was never allowed to pull the ship away from or bring it alongside the pier.

I was lucky to have two very competent and agreeable bosses after the original weapons officer, Lieutenant F., departed shortly after I had reported aboard. Lieutenant E., the officer who had reported to the first captain in Key West, was, as I recall, relieved shortly after we returned from Gitmo. I was sorry to see him leave since I considered him a mentor and friend. His successor, Lieutenant B., was higher energy and quickly became a friend as well. He and his wife had met in France on his previous duty on a spit-and-polish cruiser. They were to live across the street from us after I was married, and my wife and I saw them frequently, often for dinner at one another's apartments. He was energetic both on and off of the ship though our friendship didn't keep him from being a taskmaster on board.

Many of the other junior officers lived out at Virginia Beach in shared houses. Some had steady girlfriends and all enjoyed being near the beach when they were off the ship. Occasionally they would have parties in the fratlike atmosphere of their house. It was a little too free-form for me even if I had not been engaged. They added a lighthearted vibe to the wardroom.

Two of these fun-loving officers became a sort of matched pair throughout the upcoming WestPac deployment. One had gone to the Naval Academy and bemoaned finishing next to last in his class and missing the dollar traditionally given by each classmate to the last-place grad. The other was a boyishly good-looking officer from New Jersey who always seemed to be smiling and not taking anything too seriously.

By contrast, the communications officer had graduated high in his USNA class and was super squared away. He was pleasant but seemed to be on his own track, careful to do his job without becoming engaged in the antics of his more happy-go-lucky peers. He eventually moved on and was replaced by a blond, clean-cut officer from the Midwest who had a mellow, upbeat personality and was always ready for a little fun. Somehow, by happenstance, self-selection, or design, the officers on the ship were all pretty even-keeled and a compatible group. Many now seemed a little green to me since I had put in some pretty intense duty in a short span of time under the previous captain, which aged me more quickly than most of the newcomers.

It promised to be a good group for our upcoming WestPac deployment, and we would pick up a few more along the way. I was also getting a little better acquainted with the group that really ran the ship—the chiefs.

They're Called Chiefs for Good Reason

The Navy relies nearly as much on the chief petty officers (CPOs) as the officers. The chiefs, like the officers, have their own living quarters and mess, or dining hall. On the *Furse* this area was below the main deck in the forward part of the ship. It is an honor to be asked to eat with the chiefs in their mess, one I was accorded only once or twice. They are career Navy personnel, most of whom have served at least ten years, and some many more. They are charged with maintaining discipline and organizing the day's work for their enlisted charges and are looked upon as anchors of experience, judgment, and professionalism. When a chief is present, everyone feels calmer and more secure. The chiefs fill in the gaps in the knowledge and experience of the junior officers. Their uniform is more like an officer's than a sailor's—the cap is essentially the same, with a black strap instead of gold, and their dress uniforms have jackets similar to the officers'.

My first real exposure to the special status of chiefs was at Gitmo where chiefs were the observers and evaluators of each ship's performance. Many of the chiefs were on their last tour of duty and had been selected to pass on their wealth of experience to neophytes like me before the Navy lost them. Their word was law in Gitmo, whether evaluating a seaman, a lieutenant, or a captain.

To call a chief out of chief's quarters when he is off duty was only done with good reason. One night during a storm I heard something banging up on the deck above my stateroom. Since I was ultimately responsible for ensuring that deck equipment was secure in foul weather I knew it was better to address this head-on than go to bed and have somebody call me about it later. My first reaction was to call the chief to take a look and get somebody up to take care of it. But that meant inconveniencing both of us. I decided to go up and take a look first.

I found that a large metal gas cylinder had broken loose from its straps next to the ASROC magazine. It was rolling around on the deck. At about five feet tall and 80 to 100 pounds—about two thirds of my weight at the time—it was an accident in search of a victim. It was dark, rainy, and the ship was pitching and rolling pretty badly. During a short lull I managed to roll it back to the bulkhead and tip it up into the straps but it broke loose before I could secure it and I lurched to get out of the way. On the second try I managed to get it up and secured well enough to last until I could get help. I found two sailors on the main deck who helped strap it in safely for the night.

When I got back down to my room I realized that I had put myself in danger and should have notified the chief who would have gotten help. But I was reluctant to inconvenience him. The next day I told him about it and of course he said I should have called him. The previous captain would not have approved of my taking things into my own hands rather than delegating.

On another occasion one of the most grizzled old chiefs came back with two other chiefs from liberty one night feeling no pain. He came swaggering down the deck as I was approaching from the opposite direction. He was as wide as two men and had a dense, short beard. Before I knew it he grabbed me in a bear hug and pressed his beard into my face while he rubbed it back and forth for the full sandpaper effect. Then he put me down with a laugh and proceeded on to chiefs' quarters with his entourage. I stood stunned as if I had just escaped from the jaws of a lion while others who had seen it were glad they hadn't been in his path. In his own way he was showing me and all watching what this chief thought of junior officers.

My division was led at times by a chief and at times by a first class petty officer. Each had his own particular style. The chiefs tended to impose order by speaking in moderate tones with an air of authority and leaving the first or second class petty officers to make it happen. Their actions were rarely, if ever, second-guessed by their division officers and then only in private. They solved many problems that never came to our attention. Sometimes we would hear about tense situations in the living compartments that they had defused, some involving threats to officers when troublesome sailors came back drunk. A division officer with a good chief had a lot less to worry about. My two chiefs—Chief M. and Chief C.—were excellent.

7

GO WESTPAC, YOUNG MAN

With COMDESDIV TWO TWO on board and
in company with USS LIND (DD 703) and USS
LOWRY (DD 770), FURSE got underway for
Southeast Asia on 9 April.

A WestPac readiness stop was made in San
Diego from 22 April to 25 April. Four days were
spent in Pearl Harbor, Hawaii, from 1 May to 5 May.
On 8 May, FURSE made a fuel stop at Midway and
continued on to Guam for an overnight fuel and
replenishment stop on 15 May. Drills and readiness
inspections were the rule during transit. *(FURSE
Command History of 1968)*

The famous quote "Go West, young man," wrongly attributed
to Horace Greeley,[7.1] was an invitation to adventure and opportunity
in the 1840s just as our orders to the western Pacific—WestPac as
abbreviated by the Navy—provided our opportunity for adventure
under our own Greeley, Captain Michael Greeley.

As the time grew shorter before departure there was some apprehension. I wrote this passage in a letter two weeks before sailing:

> The ship is in an increased state of tension as it finally becomes aware to all of us that in less than 2 weeks we sail. Some of the enlisted men are already getting upset. I sent two to the psychiatrist yesterday from nervous anxiety about going to Vietnam.

When the day eventually came for us to depart for WestPac there was a small brass band on the pier and members of the crew's families waved to us as we pulled out. Most of us were glad to get under way for what promised to be an adventurous deployment.

We had an uneventful transit to the Panama Canal. All I remember was sailing down the coast of Florida where there were essentially no navigational aids. The east coast of Florida is so uniform that few distinguishing features show up on radar. We relied to a large extent on conventional land maps to find structures such as water towers that we could sight for a visual fix. Even depth soundings by sonar were of little help since the depths along the continental shelf varied so little.

The Panama Canal

> A fast transit of the Panama Canal was made 14 April with a short stop for fuel in Rodman, C.Z., the same day. *(FURSE Command History of 1968)*

The Panama Canal is about 51 miles long and is segmented into a series of locks that take a ship up 26 meters above sea level to Gatun Lake, a central freshwater lake, and back down to the Pacific in the bay of Panama.[7.2] I had read accounts of the lives lost in this monumental engineering undertaking and was very curious to see it and to experience the transit through the jungles of Panama. When we arrived at the canal there was a sense of anticipation that the trip was entering a new phase, as hinted in this letter of April 14, 1968:

> We have had real good sailing so far—nobody sick. We are in four section watch, which is real easy to take. On Easter Sunday we will be stopping in Rodman in the Canal Zone for refueling.
>
> Well, tomorrow we get up at 4:45 AM to go through the Panama Canal—and guess who has the watch? I think the distance will seem so much greater when we get into the Pacific.

We stood idle for a brief period outside the entry to the first lock, with scores of other, much larger merchant ships. A pilot came aboard and in short order we were on our way into the first lock with USS *Lowry* (DD-770) accompanying us. It seemed like a pretty snug fit with two ships end to end in one lock; the width of a lock is just over 35 meters and the length about 320 meters, just long enough for two destroyers. Once our lines were secured to the sides of the locks it was a matter of waiting on deck on a hot, humid day for the water to rise and bring us to the next level. This was repeated until we reached the level of Gatun Lake, between the eastern and western locks.

Most every ship that passes through takes advantage of this body of freshwater to break out the fire hoses and give the salt-encrusted ship a complete wash-down. The water was pumped directly from the lake itself. The men made sure to spray themselves as well as the ship to cool off from their exertions. We were ordered to touch up the rust spots on the hull with new paint even before the hull was completely dry. Then into the western locks. The passage took all day and into the late evening before we were disgorged into the Pacific Ocean. *Lowry's* log reported a short fuel stop at the U.S. Naval Station, Rodman. It was a fascinating but tiring day, especially for my division on whose shoulders fell the bulk of the line handling, wash-down, and painting. Our passage through the canal as reported in the history of the *Lowry*, our companion ship, took 12 hours,[7.3] not much in comparison to sailing vessels that had to round the Horn at the southern end of South America, a passage that added weeks if not months to voyages before the building of the canal.

Across the Pacific

We were Atlantic sailors excited to be in the Pacific where the water seemed bluer and the air milder. The next stop up the west coast of Central America and Mexico was the small town of Manzanillo. We cruised at our most efficient speed of about 15 knots—roughly 20 mph—which took us about four days. We anchored next to the Manzanillo fueling station, which was just a single big black hose snaking its way down a hillside from a fuel storage tank on top. The thick oil flowed by gravity rather than being pumped. Other ships lined up to take on fuel, so we had to get in and out quickly. Manzanillo was a notoriously difficult fueling stop for Navy ships,[7.4] requiring us to anchor off the pier with both anchors to hold our position.

During the fueling we were advised that one of the electrical panels had a problem. This panel provided power to our anchor windlass, which raised and lowered the anchors. I was informed that we might have to raise the anchors by another means. Each of our anchors weighed 4,000 pounds. I got together with the chief boatswain's mate to figure out what we could do. We went through scenarios of using a series of block-and-tackle arrangements to pull the anchors up by hand with a large working party, which seemed far-fetched given the time we had available. We really did not have a practical answer and prayed that the electricians would get their gear working.

The captain seemed totally nonplussed until about half an hour before our scheduled departure. Then, miraculously, the electricians came up with a jury-rigged fix that provided just enough power to operate the windlass and carefully raise the anchors. At several points we had to stop while the electricians made adjustments. I was impressed by how cool the captain stayed in this situation. By his calmness he created an atmosphere in which the problem could be solved methodically rather than in a panic. Our previous captain would have micromanaged every move.

We joined *Harwood* and *Lind* proceeding as Task Unit 15.3.2 arriving at San Diego on April 22. Two days were spent outfitting the ship before the Task Unit proceeded to Pearl Harbor.

We steamed out of San Diego at the same time a carrier was leaving port. We were told to keep a watch for small craft from the militant environmental organization Greenpeace who planned to protest the presence of the nuclear-powered carrier; the narrow harbor is advantageous for this kind of protest. The Coast Guard was patrolling in force and we sailed out without incident. Though I somewhat admired the temerity of this group to bring attention to their issues, their confrontational methods forced ships such as ours to adopt a protective posture.

Periodically we needed to be refueled at sea. On one occasion the XO, an avid golfer, decided to try to get the first small "messenger" line over to the oiler by attaching it to a golf ball and hitting it with his driver. He had a rubber mat fitted with a tee and tested various configurations of attaching the line to the ball, finally settling on a cotter pin stuck into a hole drilled into the ball, to which the line was attached. He also tested methods of arranging the line on deck so it could pay out without interference. On a couple of test runs he managed to get it out about a hundred yards.

When the actual moment came the wind was a little strong, and after several tries he had to admit defeat, much to the amusement of those on the oiler and our own crew. But it was a welcome diversion in our daily routine.

Training Means More When You Might Get Shot At

A full regimen of daily training exercises kept us occupied during the potentially tedious long haul to Hawaii. We were now standing 3-section watches, half of which were in the engineering spaces. I have only a dim recollection of these engineering watches, probably because the boiler and engine rooms were foreign territory to me and I was there to gain knowledge through observation rather than direct participation.

In some ways I resented the constant training when we had the opportunity to wind down a little. But we weren't on a pleasure cruise and needed to keep from getting complacent. It was also an opportunity to perform some of the technical calibration procedures on our equipment, such as "shooting the moon"—sighting the moon at night through our gun barrels to check their alignment—that had to be done under stable conditions.

One exercise that we practiced repeatedly and without warning day or night was shooting shells that contained chaff from our two gun mounts. Chaff rounds were filled with small bits of tinfoil and were set to explode almost immediately after they were fired to provide false targets for incoming missiles that might be shot from fast missile boats. An Israeli destroyer, the *Eilat*, had been sunk by missiles from such an Egyptian missile boat in the Mediterranean a year before, which exposed a real weakness in a destroyer's defenses.[7.5]

Our goal was to get to general quarters and fire off the rounds within a minute, which was about as much warning as we would get. It took us many tries before we achieved this goal. The real problem was that the chaff had been packed in the shells too tightly and clumped together rather than dispersing evenly in a cloud, so we were very skeptical that this would actually work.

When we got to Hawaii we had .50-caliber machine guns installed on the two bridge wings to give us some defense against small, fast craft that might go undetected by radar until they got too close or were below the firing arcs of our 5"/38 guns. They were mounted on the bridge wings within curved metal bars acting as stops to prevent them from being fired into the ship itself. The gunner's mates and the captain enjoyed shooting these for practice at boxes thrown over the side. The installation of these guns reminded us that soon enough we would be in the combat zone. I noticed on a recent visit to the USS *Roosevelt* (DDG-80) while in port in New York that similar guns were mounted fore and aft, another indication of heightened awareness of threats even while in friendly waters.

Navigating over this 2,200-nautical-mile expanse of the Pacific was by conventional celestial fixes, sun lines, and "dead reckoning" (originally "deduced reckoning," shortened to "ded" or "dead," according to our navigation instructor at OCS). Dead reckoning was simply determining where we should be by continuously plotting our path from our actual courses and speeds. The problem with this method was that it was not self-correcting, and variations caused by currents, wind, or the mechanical error of the plotter would cause distortions in the path plotted so that it had to be reset after each celestial fix. But it was an interim indicator of position and a valuable fallback when all else failed.

Another means to determine our approximate position was to track commercial planes overhead. We knew the normal flight corridors and could pick up the IFF (identification friend or foe) signals on radar returned from transponders in these planes in reply to our signals. As long as we stayed along this corridor we were essentially on course. Not something the ancient mariners had, but then again we did not have GPS at that time either.

You Can't Steer Without a Wheel

To keep from getting bored on long, uneventful watches at night we liked to play tricks on each other, and on one officer in particular. We called him Junior Jarhead, alluding to his Marine-like appearance.

He had little use for our somewhat juvenile humor, which made it even more fun. We would arrange to have the helmsman unscrew the large brass steering wheel from its spindle on the bridge and pass it back to CIC when this officer wasn't looking. Prior to this we secretly transferred steering control to "after steering," a manual way to steer: A sailor sitting just above the actual rudder in the stern of the ship could steer manually with a small wheel. When the officer of the deck gave an order to the helmsman, the helmsman would say, "Sir, I cannot comply since the wheel has disappeared." The OOD would momentarily panic before the wheel was reattached.

This always unnerving trick was played on all of us, but only when steaming well apart from other ships. Transferring control to after steering was required once during each watch to make sure that the man stationed in that lonely spot was kept alert. It was an emergency fallback, one we never expected to have to utilize in a real situation. In a few short weeks we would put this training to the test.

We were excited to get to Hawaii and enter Pearl Harbor where we moored across the pier from a British destroyer. We were all envious of the crew's more casual and more practical uniform of loose-fitting khaki shorts. They were also allowed to have beer on board, though in moderation. The British sailors looked comfortable and confident in spite of, or maybe because of, this informality. Of course the Brits had a maritime history a lot older than that of the U.S. Navy and had honed their own procedures through centuries of training and practical experience.

The weapons officer and I rented a little open beach car and drove around the island, stopping at some of the famous surfing beaches. I wrote to my fiancée:

> We leave today for the Philippines. Have had a good
> time here, but only wish you and I could have shared
> the beauty of the island. Took a tour of the island
> with Steve Braddish in an Austin Mini Moke as
> shown in the enclosed Polaroid shot.

After taking on supplies and fuel we resumed our long journey of island-hopping across the Pacific to our new home port, Subic Bay in the Philippines. The British destroyer was also heading west, and a rendezvous was arranged to exchange movies and operational material. As we pulled into station beside her we wanted to make a good impression. We were lined up smartly along the deck rails at attention, as were the Brits. My division was amidships on the 01 deck just behind the bridge. I stood in front of the men, and as soon as we were steaming in tandem and facing our counterparts across 80 to120 feet of water I told the men to lock arms and form a kickline like the Rockettes of Radio City Music Hall fame. We were a little rusty, but as soon as our legs went up in the air the Brits broke out laughing and imitated us on their side.

The XO on the bridge deck finally saw what was happening and shouted to us angrily to resume our formation and for me to report immediately to the bridge. I was reprimanded for this breach of maritime etiquette, but the captain seemed to appreciate the show of good spirits and all was soon forgiven. We connected the highline to the king post and transferred the movies. We also gave a few men a trip over and back via highline on the sling used by the Brits, a much simpler method than our metal chair. I had had my initiation in the highline chair earlier on Springboard when I was dipped into the water midway in the journey across—the usual first trip ritual.

Transferring personnel at sea is an inherently dangerous procedure, and unlike transferring supplies is done using a five-inch manila line that will not stretch, unlike a nylon line. And unlike transferring supplies with a winch, which is subject to mechanical malfunction, men are used to maintain a constant tension in the line—like a human spring. The men are stationed on the deck below (or on some ships the hangar deck) out of sight of the highline itself, gripping the rope as in a tug of war while they walk up and back to take up slack or let out the line to compensate for the movements of the two ships. When the ships roll toward each other the line tends to slacken, so the men must move back to take up the slack and vice versa when the ships roll apart, tending to tighten the line. The men on the deck below are directed by hand signals given by an experienced boatswain's mate.

We steamed toward Midway Island, the scene of one of the major battles of World War II that was a turning point in the Pacific war six months after the attack on Pearl Harbor. Military historian John Keegan has called it "the most stunning and decisive blow in the history of naval warfare."[7.6]

En route to Midway I was qualified as an OOD. I wrote this description of some of our training activities, some with curious names like frogex, in transit, on May 7, 1968:

> We are now on our way to Midway Island, about 1000 miles west of Pearl Harbor. We arrive tomorrow morning; we will only [stay] six or seven hours for a fuel stop. Then we go another 1000 miles to Guam.
>
> I was briefly elevated to standing officer of the deck watches. Qualifying for officer of the deck is the goal of a junior officer, and until he qualifies he cannot hope to advance very far. This morning I brought the ship alongside another destroyer during "leapfrog" exercises, which we call a "frogex" to correspond to "iffex" (identification friend or foe exercise), "ecmex" (electronic countermeasures exercise), "gunex" (gunnery exercise), and "pubex" (publications exercise). The Captain asked two of the other Ensigns to take it first. They were new and hadn't seen it done so he turned to me and told me to take it alongside. I had done this twice before. I did a fairly good job—I get a kick out of shiphandling ...

I was the only ensign standing watch as an OOD, in some cases with lieutenant junior grades as JOODs (junior officers of the deck) under me. I was still nervous about unanticipated events on watch, but fortunately we were proceeding with only two other ships in the open sea.

Midway was flat and featureless, but the water looked almost turquoise blue. Some of the men had brought scuba-diving gear and took the opportunity for a brief dive near the ship. I went off on foot with another officer to see the fabled gooney birds.[7.7] Eventually we saw one come in for a comical landing, but we never saw one take off, which they do by running down a dirt strip like a plane leaving a runway.

It felt incredibly luxurious to be off the ship and walking along a beautiful beach, even if in uniform and only for an hour. I knew we had only a fleeting moment before we disembarked to continue our long, slow slog across the Pacific bound for Guam, another hotly contested island in the Pacific war. But this brief respite was enough to recharge our spirits to face the next thousand-mile journey.

On May 13 Task Unit 15.3.2 was dissolved and units under command of Captain Cole became Task Element 70.8.4.2 as part of the Seventh Fleet. We were now at the eastern edge of WestPac which included the Tonkin Gulf on its western edge. It took us another week of steady steaming to reach Guam, in the Marianas chain on May 15, 1968 which was larger than Midway and also pretty featureless. By this time we were all getting a little stir-crazy from being at sea for so long. I was once told by a submariner that after he had been cooped up for almost a month and finally reached port he walked without caring where he went for almost a whole day. Likewise, I was almost desperate to run and didn't much care where. Once off the ship, I was joined by the engineering officer and the weapons officer, himself a runner who had completed several nine-mile Bay to Breakers runs in San Francisco. We didn't know where we were going and eventually lost sight of the ship, but our internal dead-reckoning system got us back.

We ran about six miles and repeated this again before we left. Now we were also beginning to see ships going the other way, returning from their WestPac tours, which increased our sense of anticipation. We got under way and headed west again: next stop, our new home port in the Philippines, Subic Bay. We were joined by the USS *Lowry* (DD-770), which had been moored next to us in Guam. Two days later, on May 18, 1968, we approached the *Lowry* for a highline transfer.

A Collision at Sea Will Ruin a Man's Whole Day

> On 18 May during a high line transfer of observers an engineering casualty caused FURSE to collide with USS LOWRY. Damage was not serious and the ships continued their transit to the Philippines. FURSE arrived in Subic Bay, Republic of the Philippines, on 20 May for tender availability and collision repairs. A fast but effective tender availability with USS AJAX (AR 6) had FURSE underway for Tonkin Gulf Operations as scheduled on 28 May. COMDESDIV 22 lowered his pennant and assumed duties on USS BOSTON (CAG 1). *(FURSE Command History of 1968)*

Yes, we collided with the *Lowry,* and though the damage was superficial the event itself was pretty dramatic. Two days after the collision, I wrote an account to my parents, based on my vantage point amidships:

> Well, I've been through pier collisions, groundings, and now a collision with another destroyer. We made an approach to high-line with the USS *Lowry* (DD 770) for observer transfer.

I was on the second deck (0-1 level) in charge of the high-line detail. We were all in Kapok life jackets. The messenger line had been shot over and we were preparing to "hook up" when all of a sudden we stood agape at the sight of the Lowry steering directly into us from about 80 feet on our starboard side. We were at 12 knots. I yelled for everyone to grab onto something. At that time the collision alarm sounded and then the two 3400-ton ships met.

We both had the same speed indicated, so the relative speed was close to zero. In nautical terminology we "kissed" at an angle of about 20^0. The jolt was not excessive. We "rode up" onto the Lowry. That is, our deck edge (starboard) slid above hers; our starboard anchor was tightly "housed" and caught on stanchions on the deck, ripping them off. Finally the strain on our 2 ton anchor was too great, the chain parted and the anchor fell into the drink. The two ships slid apart; result—no personnel losses and no major holes in either ship.

We had actually veered into the Lowry. We had a boiler casualty and had to secure the boiler to avoid personnel hazard in the engine room (called "high water"). Before the shaft could be restored with steam from the other boiler our port engine had applied a moment which turned us to starboard. We lost steering control simultaneously when the forward switchboard went dead with the loss of auxiliary steam to the generator. It was restored in a matter of seconds, but a switch in emergency steering failed to function so we could not switch to the alternate method. All our drills in transferring control to after steering came to naught when the transfer switch failed.

Even more coincidentally, those being transferred were all members of the engineering department, and were not present below to aid in remedying the situation.

It was sort of frightening to see two ships coming together like that. However, the Captain did the only thing he could—at the last minute he gave a backing bell; perhaps given earlier it would have avoided the collision.

I'm now struck by how much detail I wrote of the causes of this event in the letter, and I remember how concerned we all were to find out what had happened, particularly since I had just started standing OOD watches and realized I could have been on the bridge at the time.

It all seemed to happen in slow motion. We were going the same speed as the *Lowry* when we began to lose speed and steerage—it took measurable seconds to touch after the collision alarm sounded. Time stood still as we all hung on tight to any nearby support while we watched the two ships slide inexorably toward metal-to-metal contact. At the point of collision I was in a perfect position to watch the anchor flukes tearing off stanchions one after the other until finally the anchor chain broke and we disengaged. I don't remember much sound; it was probably drowned out by the continued blaring of the collision alarm. Actual contact was less than a minute (see log below).

The actual log entry reads as follows, with italics added by me:

08-12 Underway as before. 0801 on station alongside portside of USS Lowry. First line over. *0805 bridge lost steering control. After steering ordered to take control. 0806 sounded the collision alarm. Captain took the conn, Starboard bow raked the portside of USS Lowry taking away this ship's starboard anchor, breaking 5 stanchions, and causing minor buckling at the deck edge starboard side from bow to frame 23. 0807 clear of the port side of USS Lowry. 0808 set the hand steering detail in after steering. 0811 shifted control of steering to the bridge.* Officer of the Deck took the conn. Maneuvering on various courses speeds while investigating cause of lost steering control. 0832 secured from General Quarters 0858 mustered the crew on station, absentees: none. 0921 maneuvering to take station 3 of a column formation with USS Lowry, the guide on station 1 and USS W. L. Lind in station 2. [Remainder records various stations and speeds to maintain formation.]

S. D. Braddish Lt. USN

A phrase I remembered from OCS popped into my head: "A collision at sea can ruin your whole day."[7,8] I knew there would be consequences, but first we were all wondering how it had happened.

My immediate thought was to go to the foc's'le to assess the damage. I found that the anchor chain had broken at one of the links, but otherwise the damage did not appear to be more than superficial to our own rails and sides. The *Lowry* sustained a lot more damage. I still have the piece of the anchor chain link that broke, which I retrieved as a memento of this event.

The entry in the Command History gives the impression that this was a mere brush with the *Lowry*, akin to a minor fender-bender between two cars. I guess it depends on whether you were on the giving or receiving end. Here is the matter-of-fact entry from a trip diary kept by a member of the *Lowry*. I hadn't remembered that we had had another close call with them:

> 18 May—At sea, U.S.S. Furse (DD 882) while on highline station collided with us, port side of Lowry. The Furse has Commodore on board.

> 19 May—At sea, transit through the San Bernardino Straits, a ferry cut between the Lowry and the Furse. Almost had a second collision with the Furse.[7.9]

A fuller description of the damage also appears on the *Lowry* website,[7.10] detailing the damage from bow to screw guard as well as providing photos.

Once the damage was assessed and temporary repairs made to the rails we proceeded to the U.S. Naval Reservation, Subic Bay, Republic of the Philippines, where, along with the *Lowry*, we arrived at 1100 hours on May 20. Task Element 70.8.4.2 was dissolved. We had steamed almost 12,000 miles since leaving Norfolk. But there was no time to rest: We had to arrange for our damage to be repaired, and I had to find a new anchor. Apart from the embarrassing appearance of only one anchor on our bow, we were 4,000 pounds heavier on the port side and due to go back out to sea in a matter of days. To put this in perspective, this was two tons out of 3,500 tons, the total weight of the ship, or less than one tenth of a percent, and fuel could be shifted in the tanks to trim the balance.

Subic Bay

Subic Bay was the primary naval base for the Seventh Fleet in the Tonkin Gulf. It was crowded with every type of ship, mostly American but also Australian and British. It had a large supply depot where just about any type of gear could be obtained. I arranged to go by vehicle to the yard area containing the anchors. As I passed through the gates to the main naval base I could not help noticing the ceremonial anchor that marked this entry. It was painted with the name of the base, and it looked surprisingly like ours.

I looked at probably 30 anchors lying in the yard, but none met the specifications of the one we lost, so I proceeded back to the ship. As we drove back through the main entry gates I asked the driver to stop next to the ornamental anchor so I could read the specifications cast into the metal. Sure enough, it was an exact match for our lost anchor. But how could we obtain it?

I reported my failed search to the captain and also the lucky find of the anchor at the gate and suggested he contact the CO of the base to see if we could obtain it. Whether he decided to try or not I don't know, but we did not get that anchor and instead had to order one through normal supply channels. We knew that this could take weeks if not months. But at least I had done everything I could. This was one case where I could not send a boatswain's mate around to another ship to barter for an anchor as if it were a can of paint.

Subic Bay had thousands of sailors and marines starved for contact with the opposite sex. A town on the edge of the base, Olongapo, like the border towns in Mexico across the Rio Grande, fulfilled these needs. All of the sailors were dying for their first visit. In anticipation, a medical specialist came on board and gave a mandatory presentation on the ravages of venereal disease, complete with graphic pictures and descriptions. Seeing these should have been enough to deter anyone but seemed to have little or no effect on the crew and many of the officers who streamed there when liberty call was sounded. It is interesting to read the comment in the Commander Destroyer Two "WestPac Trip Report" 1968 (pages 137–138) on this subject. It seems to reflect the value system of the author about the most common form of venereal disease:

14. General Comments: Gonorrhea is not a serious medical problem, but rather a social and moral one. No man lost a day of work because he had gonorrhea.

The average number of cases per ship for the entire deployment was 22.

The next day the ship was buzzing with stories of barhopping and topless and bottomless bar girls. As officers we also warned the men that many of these women would try to dupe them into promises of marriage in order to become U.S. citizens. Whenever we returned to Subic in the future, the men seemed to reconnect with their favorite "hostesses," and by the time we were ready to return to the United States, sure enough some wanted to get married or claimed they had already gotten married.

On the second or third day in port some of us who had not seen this spectacle decided to take a look. We went in civilian clothes and had to walk across a muddy, foul-smelling field. Lights were visible ahead. At the entry to the town the shore patrol was very much in evidence. We walked down the center of the main street, which was like a western town with bars lining both sides and sailors going in and out of the swinging doors, many raucous and staggering. We poked our heads into a few bars to see clusters of barely clad girls smiling and joking with the sailors in the semidarkness. It was more brazen and filthier than the Mexican border towns I had seen when a student in Texas.

We had gotten to the end of the main street when sirens sounded and the shore patrol came out in force telling all to return to their ships immediately. We knew it would be a madhouse so we tried to get out in front of the exodus. We never found out what the emergency was and guessed this was just a routine way to clear things out and get the men back to their ships before they did too much damage to themselves. It was lightly raining and the mud was becoming more viscous and smelly. I was relieved to be back on the ship and took a long "Hollywood" shower, a shower where one could let the water flow freely since we were hooked up to unlimited pier water.

Where We Fit In

Of course when we went to Vietnam we knew the history up until our arrival but not how the war would evolve. Our mission in the summer of 1968 fit into a bigger picture that I did not fully appreciate then but is clearer with the passage of more than 40 years. A comprehensive history of the Navy's involvement in Vietnam can be found in Edward J. Marolda's *The U.S. Navy in the Vietnam War* (see Bibliography), which I will paraphrase in order to place our service within the overall context of the major events of the war.

United States involvement in Vietnam dated from as early as 1950 and extended to the eventual pullout in 1975 with the fall of South Vietnam. I remember hearing about the French war in Vietnam in Current Events in elementary school in the early fifties (Dien Bien Phu[8.11] was in 1954 when I was ten years old) and how terrible it was going to be when the communists took over. The so-called Tonkin Gulf incidents culminating in the naval engagements by the USS *Maddox* (DD-731) and USS *Turner Joy* (DD-951) with North Vietnamese boats in early August 1964 led to the Tonkin Gulf Resolution of August 7, 1964. Passed unanimously in the House and 88–2 in the Senate, this resolution authorized the president to use U.S. armed forces in the defense of noncommunist nations in Southeast Asia. This became the basis for the support given to the South Vietnamese throughout the war and was the de facto start of the war. Questions were debated about the extent to which these ships were fired upon if at all, and whether this was sufficient basis for going to war, but there was also widespread public acceptance of the domino theory, which presumed that if Vietnam fell it would open the rest of Southeast Asia to the Chinese communists.

By the summer of 1968 the years of heavy combat were beginning to transition to a stage that Marolda writes about in a chapter called "Winding Down the War, 1968–1973." The Tet offensive of February and March 1968, just a few months before we arrived, led to decisions to gradually withdraw troops and to accelerate the "Vietnamization" of the war. Diplomatic talks were begun in Paris. Marolda summarizes the strategy as follows:

> As U.S. forces prepared the South Vietnamese military to assume complete responsibility for the war, they also worked to keep pressure on the enemy. In fact, from 1968 to 1971, the allies exploited the Communists' staggering battlefield losses during the Tet attacks by pushing the enemy's large main force units out of the border areas, extending the government's presence into Viet Cong strongholds, and consolidating control over population centers.[7.11]

The summer of 1968 saw the last great surge of air attacks in Southeast Asia before tapering off just after *Furse* left the Gulf in October of that year. In 1968 ships fired double the number of rounds on the gun line as were subsequently fired in 1969. Cruisers, destroyers, and rocket ships (LSMRs) were attached from other operations to form Naval Gunfire Support Task Unit 70.8.9. There were typically one or two cruisers and two to four destroyers as part of this Task Unit.[7.12]

Furse's service coincided with this final surge to put pressure on the North to gain advantage in the diplomatic talks. The United States was, quite literally, throwing everything it had at the enemy in the air, on the land, and by sea.

Neighborhood kids, with four Abernathys

Sailor in the making with sister Janet

Hank (on rail) and Steve Hayes in Steve's yard. From a painting by Steve's mother, Tua Hayes

Hank and Pam's wedding, from left: Herman (father), Ann (sister), Annie Lou (mother), Hank, Pam, Martha (sister), Janet Robertson (sister), Hugh Robertson

Author getting sea legs on Hayes's boat

Chief Murphy supervises at the obstacle course

Obstacle course

"Your left, your left, your left-right, right-o-left"

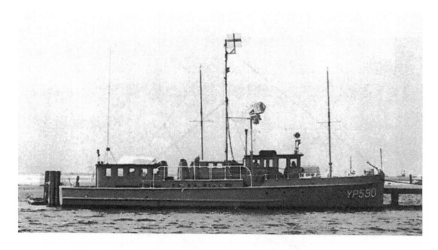

Yard Patrol Craft, a.k.a. YP

An officer and a gentleman

Author on quarterdeck

DASH landing (image from www.gyrodynehelicopters.com)

Uncle Waring Gelzer, Pam, author, and daughter Kate

Entering Gitmo-author on fo'c'sle with seaman

USS SWANSON DD443
Ann Abernathy 4.06
from Photo National Archives.

Drawing of USS *Swanson* (DD 443) by Ann Abernathy

Fleets Are In; 4,000 Sailors Arrive In Port

Some 4,000 Canadian and United States sailors from twenty-two warships and submarines made a friendly invasion of the Halifax - Dartmouth area when the last warship tied-up alongside in HMC Dockyard at the completion of an 11-day anti-submarine warfare exercise in the North Atlantic.

The exercise, which began Nov. 6, involved Canadian and American sea and air anti-submarine forces in the detection of submarines at var-

ious positions in the North Atlantic.

The warships and submarines that are now in Halifax Harbor are:

Canadian: Fleet replenishment ship HMCS Provider, Captain W. J. Stuart, RCN; destroyer escorts HMCS Gatineau, Cdr. W. A. Hughes, RCN; H M C S Restigouche, Cdr. R. A. Evans, RCN; helicopter destroyers HMCS Fraser, Cdr. J. F. Watson, RCN, and HMCS Annapolis, Cdr. D. N. Mainguy, RCN; and the submarine HMCS Ojibwa, Lt.-Cdr. J. C. Wood, RCN.

United States: The destroyers USS Davis, Cdr. E. J. Mountford, USN; USS Blandy, Cdr. J. H. Berry, USN; USS Furse, Cdr. M. T. Greely,

USN; USS Rich, Cdr. E. C. Whelan, USN; USS Beatty, Cdr. F. F. Jewett, USN; USS R. E. Kraus, Cdr. R. L. Buck, USN; the destroyer escorts USS Lester, Lt.-Cdr. W. T. Piotti, USN; USS John Willis, Lt.-Cdr. H. C. Atwood, USN; USS Hartley, Lt.-Cdr. T. R. M. Emery, USN, and USS Vanvoorhis, Lt.-Cdr. J. G. Storms, USN. The submarines USS Irex, Cdr. R. S. Denbagh, USN; USS Cobblar, Lt.-Cdr. A. H. Gilmore, USN; USS Corporal, Lt.-Cdr. W. B. Hubbell, USN; USS Entemedor, ,

Lt.-Cdr. C. D. Fellows, USN; and USS Tusk, Lt.-Cdr. G. D. McCarthy, USN; and the United States Coast Guard Cutter Sebago.

The destroyers carry a complement of 14 officers and 260 men, while the destroyer escorts have 13 officers and 154 men. The submarines Irex and Tusk are of the Tench class and carry a complement of eight officers and 74 men. The other three submarines are of the Balao class and carry eight officers and 72 men each.

Welcome to Halifax, 11-18-67

134

Departing Norfolk, April 9, 1968

Pacific bound, one lock at a time (from WestPac cruisebook)

Helmsman, transfer control to after steering (author is OOD with binoculars—from WestPac cruisebook)

Author takes a break in Hawaii, May 3, 1968

Highline transfer. Note the line of
men on the hangar deck keeping the line taught

Furse and *Lowry* nested at Midway Island, May, 1968 (author with cigar)

Author with beard   Author on bridge wing

Torpedo tubes firing

8

TONKIN GULF YACHT CLUB
(AKA SEVENTH FLEET)

FURSE's initial assignment off Vietnam was plane
guard operations with USS AMERICA (CVA 66).
These duties were disrupted on 6 June with a one day
assignment to Northern Search and Rescue as escort
for USS PREBLE (DLG 15), with an additional day
of ASW exercises on 7 June in the ASW operations
area. Plane guarding was again interrupted with
FURSE assigned to screen ship against the Soviet
trawler BARGRAF on 22 and 23 June. *(FURSE
Command History of 1968)*

Arriving in the Tonkin Gulf during this surge was like joining
a floating boat show because so many were ships conducting
operations in a relatively confined body of water. Several aircraft
carriers with their destroyer escorts conducted flight ops at 25 knots
while cruisers, destroyers, auxiliary craft, and Coast Guard vessels
blanketed the coastal areas. Fleet oilers, ammunition, and refrigerator
ships cruised amid the fleet to keep combatants supplied through
almost continuous underway replenishments. There was hardly ever

a time when we did not have several contacts on the radar. This was in stark contrast to our long and relatively lonely crossing of the Pacific where we rarely saw another ship other than *Lind*, *Lowry*, and *Harwood* who transited with us.

We had three main missions while on duty in the Gulf of Tonkin: plane guard for the aircraft carrier USS *America* (CVA-66); gunfire support for troops ashore; and interdiction of supplies flowing south on boats as part of Operation Sea Dragon. Plane guard involved trailing the carrier to pick up downed pilots and acting as a guide to incoming aircraft. Gunfire support could be simple shore bombardment of enemy territory, called harassment and interdiction (H & I) fire with no specific target, or calls for fire from troops directed toward specific targets. Interdiction of supplies involved tracking contacts and firing on boats that were traveling north to south along coastal areas where this was forbidden by order of the U.S. military command.

We also spent a short amount of time on SAR (search and rescue); PIRAZ (Positive Identification and Radar Advisory Zone); shadowing a Soviet intelligence ship, the *Bargraf*, and ASW operations. By the end of our tour we had fired thousands of rounds from our 5" guns. Most of our gunfire support operations were carried out under port-and-starboard watches: six hours on and six hours off. The hours off did not mean we could sleep because we had our other duties to perform. We averaged about four to six hours of sleep a day.

Yankee Station

Yankee Station was a point in the middle of the Gulf of Tonkin used by U.S. Navy aircraft carriers of Task Force 77, the main battle group of the U.S. Seventh Fleet, to launch strikes against targets in Vietnam (see the enlarged map of the Tonkin Gulf at the beginning of this book). While its official designation was "Point Yankee," it was universally referred to as Yankee Station. Carriers conducting air operations at Yankee Station were said to be "on the line," and statistical summaries were based on days on the line.[8.1]

We probably spent more time on plane guard duty "chasing" carriers (colloquially called bird farms by the sailors) on Yankee Station than on any other assignment. We operated almost exclusively with the USS *America* (*CVA-66*). "The fifth USS *America* (CVA/CV-66) was one of four Kitty Hawk-class carriers built for the United States Navy in the 1960s. Commissioned in 1965, she spent most of her career in the Atlantic and Mediterranean, but did make three Pacific deployments serving in the Vietnam War." (Wikipedia) Her air wing ultimately lost five killed in action and five prisoners of war, two of whom never returned during her Vietnam service.

I summarized my first experience with plane guarding in a letter of May 27, 1968:

> Here we are out at sea on the start of our 30 day stint "chasing the bird farm." The bird farm is the aircraft carrier USS America (CVA 66). It is a totally new experience for me, and I am still standing OOD watches.
>
> We are plane-guarding for the carrier—that is, standing by to recover any planes that crash or people that fall off the flight deck. So far no casualties. The operation is amazing. About 30 planes must be landed and 30 more recovered in the period of 90 minutes. That means a plane takes off or lands every minute and a half. This cycle occurs two or three times a day.
>
> It is pretty awesome to see those big jets roaring in and out; they land in a couple of hundred yards at full power, so if they miss the restraining wire they can take off again. This happened to several today which looked like they would surely run off into the drink.

Our station relative to the carrier was about 20 degrees off of her starboard quarter at about 2,000 yards astern. This position lined up with the flight deck so that as planes prepared to land they could come in over our mast and make a straight approach. This was particularly helpful at night—our masthead light marked our position. We could sometimes see the "ball" on the carrier deck and listen to the controller announcing "call the ball" to the pilot on the carrier's radio net. This is a request to the pilot from the Landing Signal Officer to name the type of plane he is landing so that the LSO can select the pattern of lights that corresponds to the glide slope for that type of aircraft. The pilot lines up vertical and horizontal lights with lines painted on the ship's deck. This multicolored optical landing system shows the pilot the correct approach path so that he can adjust as necessary to hit the flight deck at the right place to pick up the restraining wire with his tail hook.

When the carrier conducted flight ops it would be steaming at high speed—usually about 25-plus knots—heading into the wind. This meant that we had to match her speed and be alert to her turning movements not to be left behind. We were not always signaled in advance. For instance, if the carrier turned to port by 30 degrees we would have to quickly plot our new position and the correct course and speed to get back to our station 20 degrees off her starboard quarter. This was a problem in relative motion that we solved by using a grease pencil to plot the calculated course on the glass display of the SPS 10 (surface search) radar. We had practiced this kind of problem at OCS with what was called a maneuvering board and parallel rulers. Our captain had a shortcut he called the radian rule, which used angular measurement. He was very fast at it and eventually we picked it up.

The new course and speed were calculated both on the bridge by the OOD and in CIC (combat information center, or simply combat). The OOD was usually more confident with his own solution and used combat's solution as a double check. Combat was usually slower at coming to a solution than we could afford without falling behind so it was necessary for the OOD to move to an approximate course at high speed and correct when a final solution was reached. Combat did not have a direct visual connection with the other ships or the same sense of urgency as those on the bridge. Plus they were accustomed to being second-guessed so they wanted to make sure their solution was correct. When I was in combat I did no better. There was something about being disconnected visually from the action in CIC that slowed down its response time. CIC is several levels below the bridge in newer destroyers which effectively eliminates direct contact.

All of us made mistakes and got left miles behind; the captain was always informed of any changes in the carrier's movements. He would usually be in his seat on the bridge or just behind the bridge in his cabin so he was quickly accessible. It was always embarrassing to be caught out of station, but the carrier didn't wait to give us advance warning of her turns. At night the pattern of lights on the carrier could also be confusing—it was not always apparent visually when she had initiated a turn or in what direction. At a distance of only 2,000 yards there was no room for complacency.

I wrote to my parents on June 2, 1968, of getting left in the dust:

> I am still standing OOD watches, which can be hectic. Last night we were chasing the carrier at 27 knots. All of a sudden she slowed and I slowed so as not to get too close. Then she took off without signal and I was left in the dust.

During the daytime we could watch the planes come over and got to know them as much by their sounds as their appearance. Most were powerfully built F4 Phantoms with their turned-down tail fins and high-pitched whine as they passed overhead. The second most prevalent were the bulkier A6 intruders with their big bulging noses.

They were not as sleek but could carry a heavier bomb load. There were also RA-5C Vigilantes and the prop-powered ECM (electronic countermeasure) planes with large "radomes" on top. The RA-5C was a Mach 2+ aircraft, capable of electromagnetic, optical, and electronic reconnaissance. It could operate at altitudes from sea level to above 50,000 feet. And finally there were smaller "COD" prop planes for personnel and mail transport.

If a plane approached that was in trouble there would be sirens on the flight deck and we would watch and hope the plane made it. Occasionally they would come down hard. We were involved in the rescue of one pilot who had to eject, and although the carrier's helo got to him first, we recovered the parachute, which was returned to him as a souvenir. If they had unexpended bombs left on their return they jettisoned them before landing. We particularly admired the pilots who flew these missions when they had to make night landings in low visibility or choppy seas.

One bit of distraction promoted by our captain for this long stint at sea was a beard-growing contest. I had never grown a beard and for the first few days I did not participate, but at the urging of men in my division I joined in. By that time some already had noticeable growths. A few years later when I was in graduate school I grew a mustache but knew enough not to try a beard. I don't remember how the winner was chosen or what the prize was, but there were clearly some that stood out from the rest in fullness and style.

I wrote my fiancée on May 31, 1968:

> Guess what—I am growing a beard! I only have three days' growth so far so it is just in the stubble stages. I haven't really decided how I am going to trim it. I might cut off the beard part and have just a mustache. I may also go the full route with an Abe Lincoln special. It all depends on how it forms up.

After nine days I reported that the beard had formed up reasonably well and I looked like the '50s television character Gabby Hayes. Gabby became my nickname until we had to shave the beards off.

SAR

I recorded our one-day detachment from plane guard to search and rescue (SAR) on June 7, 1968:

> Our schedule has been pretty varied the last couple of days. Yesterday we were sent to the "northern outpost of the U.S. Navy in S.E. Asia," designated SAR. We are about 30 miles off the coast of NVN just south of Haiphong.
>
> Our mission is to rescue any downed pilots who have to ditch after coming back from air strikes against the north. However, during the peace talks there have not been any strikes north, so things are pretty calm.

PIRAZ

PIRAZ (Positive Identification and Radar Advisory Zone) best illustrated the disconnected reality of war at a distance. Our mission was to provide protection for a nuclear-powered cruiser, USS *Long Beach* (CGN 9). Captain Greeley had served on her as a junior officer. She was tethered electronically to a buoy whose location was set precisely by a geosynchronous satellite. The cruiser would circle the buoy very slowly and we would slowly circle outside of her and the buoy. Nobody ever seemed to appear on the deck of the cruiser. Missiles were activated automatically to intercept radar targets crossing the DMZ from north to south. We heard the noise but all we saw was a smoke trail when we went out on deck for a look.

I described this mission in a letter of July 21, 1968:

> We are operating with the nuclear powered ship Long Beach about 25 miles off the coast of Vietnam. Her task is monitoring all of the ingoing and returning air strikes and vectoring home any that are having trouble. She is also used as a defense against migs and recently shot at a couple with her long range missiles. We are getting close to some action at last.

After several days of this we were glad to be released for more interesting duty. With so many ships and planes from several countries operating in the limited confines of the Tonkin Gulf there were bound to be some mistakes. Which brings me to the HMAS *Hobart*.

The HMAS *Hobart*

The HMAS *Hobart* was an Australian destroyer operating in our area and also home ported in Subic Bay. My first knowledge of the *Hobart* was from an incident that occurred late on the night of June 17, 1968. This incident does not appear in the *Furse* Command Histories because our ship had no direct involvement, but I have pretty clear memories of what I heard on that night.

I was standing a relatively quiet watch on the bridge when I heard over the net we monitored with the carrier a report of a ship that had come under fire about 20 miles from us. The ship was identified as the HMAS *Hobart*, an Australian destroyer. The Task Force commander kept asking what was going on and no one seemed to have an answer—was the ship being attacked by enemy boats or aircraft? Or could it be friendly fire? There were reportedly some U.S. planes in the area. As we listened and awaited possible orders to assist, a report came over the net that a sailor had picked up a piece of debris off the *Hobart*'s main deck from an apparent missile that had hit them. Stenciled on it were the words Raytheon Manufacturing Company, Waltham, Massachusetts; the missile had been fired from one of our planes which, it turns out, had also fired on two of our PCFs (patrol craft, fast) that night, sinking one. Two on the *Hobart* were killed and several wounded.[8.3] I saw the damage inflicted on the *Hobart* a few weeks later when we were in Subic. It was a stark reminder that the dangers we faced were not always from our enemies.

Two days after the *Hobart* was hit I wrote:

> There have been several interesting occurrences in the past few days. First we are only about 60 miles from the DMZ. Recently there has been increased fighting down there. Occasionally we get in to about 30 miles.
>
> In the past few days American ships have been attacked by shore batteries and also, of all things, armed enemy helicopters! I was on watch during one of the firefights and could see the flares and shell bursts. We also could hear communications over our nets. So far, we have not been involved.

Could I have been referring to the *Hobart?* It certainly sounds like it. None of us really knew what happened until later; talk of attack by enemy helicopters was one theory at the time for what turned out to be friendly fire by our own aircraft. There is also a reference in the Commander Destroyer Squadron Two "WestPac Trip Report" 1968, page 2, which seems to refer to this incident:

> (2) In general, there is very little operational command, as such, exercised by the gunline commander. When two or more ships are present at the DMZ, the

gunline commander schedules and coordinates their unreps. During the "mysterious air action" of 15-16 June, 1968, the gunline commander did take charge of all ships in the vicinity and proceeded seaward in an AAW posture.

The gun-line commander ordered the rest of his ships to get out of the area so that they too would not become targets of air attack, even if by friendly forces.

The *Hobart* was in port at Subic Bay for several weeks getting repaired. We were curious to see the damage inflicted by the missile hits but wanted to be respectful of the casualties she had suffered. So it was not without trepidation that I approached her one night to ask if she could spare some paint for our motor whaleboat, which was badly in need of painting. The boatswain's mate told me we were out of the special epoxy paint needed to paint its fiberglass hull. He had tried unsuccessfully to locate some on other American ships in port. We only had one day in port to get the boat painted before we got underway for another three to four weeks at sea. I was greeted pleasantly by the OOD on the *Hobart*. He connected me with my counterpart who generously obliged me with the promise of some paint if I would send the boatswain's mate around. I could not really see her damage because an enclosure had been built around it.

The men rigged lights and by midnight had the boat painted. The next morning as we got underway the captain glanced aft from the starboard bridge wing and saw the newly painted boat. I was sent for. It was Australian gray-green, not our gray. In the evening light the *Hobart* had looked gray to me. Everyone had a good laugh at my expense, and like the missing anchor we had to sail with it for a few weeks before we could correct it back in Subic. At least it looked shiny and new.

One other incident occurred in port during this visit: one of my men returned to the ship at about 1:30 a.m., went up to the bow, and jumped overboard. We tried to get our boat in the water but had trouble starting the engine. Fortunately a Coast Guard boat picked him up. He was drunk. In one week in port I had three men with broken hands and one with a broken nose from fights, not to mention those with VD. I was happy to get away from Subic and back to sea.

Operation Sea Dragon and Gunfire Support

> Plane Guarding with AMERICA continued until 26 August when COMDESDIV 22 returned aboard by Highline from USS BOSTON (CAG 1). FURSE went directly to Naval Gunfire Support Operations off Phan Thiet, South Vietnam. The ship provided naval gunfire support for the Third Battalion (Airborne) 506th infantry and South Vietnamese units in-country. Fourteen (14) Call-for-fire and five (5) harassment and interdiction missions were fired. The ship participated in twenty-two (22) missions in Sea Dragon Operations. (FURSE *Command History of 1968*)

The first time I saw the coast of Vietnam from a distance it looked like a long, low, unbroken strip of dirty green set off by a thin strip of beach. As we got closer it looked like a resort beach, with pristine white sand interspersed with grass-topped dunes. I couldn't help thinking about the passage from Joseph Conrad's *Heart of Darkness* where he describes his first sight of the coast along the Congo River:

> I watched the coast. Watching a coast as it slips by the ship is like thinking about an enigma. There it

is before you—smiling, frowning, inviting, grand, mean, insipid, or savage, and always mute with an air of whispering, "come and find out." This one was almost featureless, as if still in the making, with an aspect of monotonous grimness. The edge of a colossal jungle, so dark green as to be almost black, fringed with white surf, ran straight, like a ruled line, far, far away along a blue sea whose glitter was blurred by a creeping mist. The sun was fierce, the land seemed to glisten and drip. [8.4]

There was something both beautiful and sinister in this coast. As T. S. Eliot remarked about Conrad, "we are continually reminded of the power and terror of Nature, and the isolation and feebleness of Man."[8.5] The stillness of the dunes silhouetted against the grey-green tree line belied the presence of a lethal enemy lurking within.

We had been given the duty of patrolling the coast above the DMZ to interdict WBLCs,[8.6] pronounced "wiblicks," which stood for waterborne logistics crafts, as part of Operation Sea Dragon, which spanned from October 1966 to October 1968.[8.7] If they were heading south it was assumed that they would be enemy boats carrying supplies to their troops. Civilian fishermen had supposedly been advised of this—our standing orders were to shoot at them until they turned back or were sunk. We encountered a sizeable WBLC early in our patrol. It appeared to be a barge or large raft a few miles away heading south.

The Commander Destroyer Squadron Two (ComDesRon Two) "WestPac Trip Report" (page 30) recommended as follows for firing at WBLCs:

WBLC's detected off shore were normally taken under direct fire. Fall of shot was observed on both

fire control and surface search radars and spots
applied accordingly. It was found that using one gun,
five salvos, for waterborne targets was cost effective
and accomplished *quick destruction of the targets with
minimum ammunition.* [italics mine]

We fired a warning shot and it kept going. Then more warning
shots, still to no effect. Finally the captain ordered us to lock on and
fire airbursts using shells with proximity fuses set to go off above
the target and spray shrapnel on the personnel below. We fired about
20 of these, again to no effect. Then we fired high explosive (HE)
shells that would detonate when they hit the target and sink it. Again,
we appeared to get some direct hits but still it kept going on a steady
course and speed. We figured it was made of bamboo too soft and
pliable to set off the HE rounds and too buoyant to be sunk when
holes were pierced in it by our shells.

Finally the captain ordered us to cease fire and to break off. He
speculated that we had already cost the taxpayers well over $10,000
in ammunition. So much for "quick destruction of the targets with
minimum ammunition" as recommended by ComDesRon Two.

We saw our first casualties within weeks of our arrival on
the gun line off North Vietnam. We were summoned to general
quarters on a clear day when three radar contacts were reported
heading straight at us at high speed. We waited anxiously, and
as soon as they were within range we locked on for a possible
order to fire. I was in CIC watching them come ever closer on
radar and wondering why we hadn't fired our chaff rounds as we
had practiced so diligently. By now they should have shot their
missiles if they had them.

The signalmen were sending flashing light authentication
codes. Every few days new codes were issued so that friendlies
could identify themselves to each other. These boats were not
responding. Soon they would be under our 5" gun firing arcs and

we would be dependent only on our .50 calibers. The captain in consultation with the XO and Ops officers chose not to fire as they got within close visual range, probably recognizing them as special operations boats. The boats were painted dark grey with no insignia or markings. The captain allowed them to come alongside. I thought at the time that these were swift boats[8.8] but later found out that they were a special class of boats called PTFs or "Nasty Boats" (PTFs: Patrol Torpedo Fast, descendants of World War II torpedo boats), heavily armed 80-foot-long wooden-hulled boats with twin 3,100 horsepower water-cooled engines that could reach speeds close to 50 knots at a burst.[8.9] "Nasty" was a fitting name for these fearsome-looking craft.

We secured from (went back to normal watch standing) general quarters, but prior to doing so were advised not to take pictures of or otherwise report this occurrence. I went out briefly and saw one of the boats idling alongside, with areas of blood on the deck and two swaggering South Vietnamese soldiers standing on the bow. The growl of the idling twin engines enhanced the powerful impression these boats created.

I ran back to my room to get my camera and snapped a few shots from inside the passageway door so I wouldn't be seen. The photos show holes where the grenades hit, the many shrapnel marks and a large area of blood on the deck where the wounded man had lain. Soon the engineering officer, who had served on similar boats on a prior tour, went aboard to assist. We had only one doctor and insufficient medical facilities to treat the wounds of those needing help. The engineering officer accompanied them to a cruiser that had been summoned to help. A sputtering jet of misty water emanated from their sterns and became a solid jet when they sped away.

The engineering officer reported to us later that the boats had stopped to search a fishing boat, and as they were about to board the crew of the boat threw grenades at them. This incident gave me a graphic reminder of what I might have been doing had I accepted the orders to swift boats as had my friend Steve Hayes. Steve sent me a letter about one of his patrols in April 1969 describing a close call with a claymore mine.[8.10]

We operated periodically with local boats with American advisers; they would pull alongside for supplies or to share intelligence. We gazed with interest at the motley crew of Vietnamese and American advisers as if they were from another world—closer to danger and freer from regulations. They saw us I am sure as equally foreign. These occasional brief encounters with the men fighting in-country gave me a subsequent thirst to learn what was happening so close and yet so far from our relatively safe position offshore.

There was much anticipation about going on the gun line, but first a little excitement from the carrier as described in my letter of August 1968:

> Last night was quite a night! At about 7:30 PM the carrier's flight deck all of a sudden erupted in what appeared to be flames and soon she was engulfed in smoke. Rich Seddon had the watch and called down to the wardroom saying "the carrier just wiped herself out." We had visions of another Forrestal. Actually what happened was that two flares carried by a plane taking off fell onto the deck and ignited. The fire crews put them out in about 5 min. and things were back to normal until about two hours later when the destroyer O'Brien reported two men were lost overboard. One had been recovered, but the other was still in the water and reportedly couldn't swim. That started a massive search by ships and aircraft in the area which ended about 4:30 AM. I had to get

up at 6:30 to take the watch. By the way, the man still hasn't been found. Today, the one that was saved said it had been a suicide attempt.

The reference to the USS *Forrestal* (*CVA 59*) in this letter referred to a devastating fire this carrier sustained in 1967 in which 134 sailors were killed and 161 injured when a Zuni rocket was discharged on the flight deck.

Cruising so close to the coastline of white beaches brought into focus the tragedy of this beautiful country, which was undergoing such a wrenching and destructive war. Years later I would go back and walk on some of those very same beaches with American veterans involved in developing resorts there. Vietnam had long been a tourist destination for the French when they occupied it as French Indochina before being ousted at the battle of Dien Bien Phu in 1954.[8.11] In fact, that long nine-year war of attrition with the French was a rehearsal for the war with the Americans in the 1960s and 1970s, with the Americans repeating many of the same mistakes.

When we got in close to the coast it looked more attractive than at a distance, as I described in this letter of August 28, 1968:

> Here we are on the gunline. It is a beautiful stretch of coast in South Vietnam with white beaches and low dunes and hundreds of small junks and sampans clustered around their fishing stakes.
>
> Right now the forward gun mount is thundering away at a suspected VC encampment. I just came back from the bridge where I found out that one of the structures was heavily damaged by our fire. Our first target destroyed! We have fired about 300 rounds so far.

We shoot from anchorage about 2.5 miles off the coast and can reach targets fairly well inland from this position. Today we even weighed anchor and moved into less than a mile—26 feet of water under our keel—a little shallow for us.

Tomorrow we weigh anchor at 3 AM, refuel at 5:15, re-arm from another ship at 8 AM, return to the line for another full day of shooting. We are in two sections (port and starboard) but have to do a lot of work when we are not on watch. Actually, we get about 5-6 hours of sleep a night (or day) which is sufficient. This is called Condition II and can generally be sustained for about 10 days before people start getting sluggish and lose their efficiency.

Nighttime was even eerier. We could see the red glow and hear the muffled sounds of distant explosions and see the staccato arcs of red tracer bullets that were too far away to hear. We were mesmerized onlookers at this spectacle of fireworks, which had little sense of reality to us.

Sometimes our mission was simply random bombardment of sectors occupied by the North Vietnamese to disrupt them—harassment and interdiction. We would anchor at a safe distance offshore and keep the ship positioned to bring to bear the mount that was doing the firing on the target area. We might or might not be in communication with a spotter on the shore. Again I was reminded of Conrad's *Heart of Darkness* as our little ship lobbed shots into the interior.[8.12] We did not question our mission, but shooting randomly into the immensity of the landscape had a sense of futility that shooting at a defined target did not.

The many fishing boats that plied the coast continued to pass close by, seemingly oblivious to our guns. This was South Vietnam where these boats weren't seen as threats to the extent they were on northern Sea Dragon operations in the vicinity of the DMZ. This was noted in the Commander Destroyer Squadron Two "WestPac Trip Report" 1968 (page 17):

> Also in the Phan Thiet area there are a large number of fishing junks, sampans and fishing net marker poles. Many of the boats and all of the fishing poles are not lighted which makes night movement of ships extremely difficult (there are frequently from 100 to 200 boats engaged in fishing in a given area). The fishermen seem unaware of the danger of crossing the Gun Target Line and do so constantly.

In order to avoid a recognizable pattern of firing, the captain devised a strategy for dividing the area into sectors corresponding to the number generated by rolling dice. As I recall there were about ten sectors, so the total of the two dice determined the sector. All night we would roll the dice, which would tell us the next sector, and we would give a coordinate within that sector to Plot, the plotting room on the first platform deck directly below the bridge containing the Mk 1A computer, Mk 6 stable element, star shell computer and spot transmitter, and the fire control switchboard. Plot would then position the guns for the next shot. We fired about once every few minutes. One time the anchor drifted and we fired into a friendly area accidentally but we never found out what, if any, collateral damage we might have caused.

After a while the sounds of guns firing day and night got to be just background noise. As we hit our racks exhausted at the end of a watch we tried to gauge how sleepy we were by how many rounds we heard before we went to sleep—like counting sheep. After (rearmost) officers' quarters was pretty close to gun mount 52 and forward officers' quarters almost underneath gun mount 51, so the noise of the guns was close to our bunks. No one could really remember how many rounds they heard, like trying to remember where you stopped counting when put to sleep by an anesthetic. We could never remember counting more than about five or six rounds.

Our logs from the period August 27, 1968, to September 5, 1968, a period of ten days, give an indication of the round-the-clock operations, when day and night merged into a timeless continuum, particularly for those of us stationed primarily in CIC with no visual connection to the outside. The statistics for those ten days and nights tell the story:

- Fired 1586 rounds, usually 100 to 300 on a given watch (one to five rounds per minute).
- Changed anchorages 14 times in the vicinity of Phan Thiet and Phan Rang on the coast of South Vietnam for harassment & interdiction and calls for fire.
- Refueled at sea five times (every other day).
- Rearmed four times, three at sea, once in Cam Ranh Bay.

With the unrelenting pace of gunfire operations we had almost forgotten about everything else including our missing anchor, which made us look like a face with a big tooth missing. One afternoon as we were preparing to come alongside a tender for resupply it sent us a message saying that our anchor was on board—did we want it? Of course it was impossible to transfer a 4,000-pound anchor at sea so we would have to wait another week to pick it up at Subic, but we were relieved to know we would soon be made whole again.

One day we were close observers of the dive-bombing of a target at the tree line on the beach about two miles from where we were conducting gunfire support operations. It looked just like a war movie, with a fighter plane swooping down, unleashing its bomb, and pulling up sharply as the bomb exploded below. This was repeated several times before the plane had unloaded all of its ordnance and flew away.

We could see a burst of smoke and flash of light from the explosion but not the target nor the damage done by the bombs. I almost had the feeling I had been a spectator at an event at an air show.

I had bought a super-8 movie camera and whenever I could I took films of whatever seemed of interest when I was off watch. I was pretty circumspect about this but no one seemed to care. Later I manually spliced all of the small reels together. Eventually I had them transferred to videotape and then to DVD. Many of the photos in this book, including those of this mission, were taken using that camera. Since they are enlarged from individual frames they are a little fuzzy.

On August 30 and 31, 1968, I wrote of our first contribution to the infamous body count that was so much a part of the nightly news during the Vietnam War.

August 30

> Just a quick note. We are still here on the gun line at anchor about a mile off the coast due east of Saigon and a little below the coastal town of Phan Thiet. We are still putting out a few rounds into the nearby countryside—mostly VC controlled.
>
> Sleep is the big activity when not on watch. I find I am getting plenty of rest—about 5-6 hrs/day even during the firing. One soon gets used to the noise.

August 31

> We just received word from the spotter that after a body count yesterday they found that we had killed 19 VC and wounded 8. The target had been described as a possible VC company encampment; intelligence reports must have been good.

It feels funny to know that there are so many VC so close. In a way it is strange to feel happy over having killed somebody, but this ship has had so little direct contact with the war that everyone feels better now that we have finally done something.

The body count became an end in itself as a metric of the success of operations in Vietnam. A ratio of 12 VC killed to each American was the magic number to win the war according to Defense Department planners. According to reports, we won the metrics, though the veracity of the body count numbers was often questioned, but we eventually lost the war.

Another issue was the effectiveness of new, relatively untested armaments such as the 5"/54 caliber guns introduced to the fleet as replacements for the older 5"/38 caliber guns we had on our ship. They were more automatic and fired at a much higher rate of speed, yet they were prone to jamming. And there were a series of premature detonations, particularly in rainy conditions (premature bursts reached 60 to 70 percent using HE/PD projectiles in heavy rain squalls according to the Commander Destroyer Squadron Two report, page 12), at least one of which resulted in gun mount casualties. On gun-line firing missions the lead ship was usually the 5"/54 ship with the 5"/38 ship firing suppressing fire against shore batteries, but the greater reliability of the 5"/38 guns sometimes resulted in reversing this order. We were content with our older, more reliable guns.

On one of our last days on this stint on the gun line, September 5, 1968, we were pretty exhausted but had too much to do to worry about it.

I am writing you finally after a rather hectic couple of days in which we steamed into Cam Ranh Bay at midnight and anchored. Then we waited until 5 AM for an ammunition barge with 400 rounds 5"/38. We had that loaded aboard by 6:30 AM and steamed 150 miles back to Phan Thiet.

Then we got an emergency call from some army troops caught in an ambush, but arrived too late. All that was left was "a trail of blood" according to the spotter, referring to the VC that had eventually fled. We settled down at anchor again only to be called an hour later to steam 125 miles north to Phan Rang where a VC battalion had been pinned down in some coastal mountains. We arrived a little before midnight and put 80 rounds into four targets in a matter of minutes. Then from midnight to 6 AM we methodically poured 200 rounds into the area. I had that watch and was on my feet for six straight hours firing one round every two minutes. Then I got 2 hrs. sleep before we pulled alongside an AO to refuel on our way back to Phan Thiet. I took the watch on the bridge after that to bring the ship alongside an AE for 1 ½ hrs. to take on 400 rounds of ammo.

I managed to get a little sleep on this watch since we are not firing tonight. It's 4 AM- 2 hrs. to go until I am relieved. At 10 AM today we will start shooting again in support of a large sweep of the area. There has been sporadic gunfire on the beach tonight. All you can see is an arc of red tracer bullets in the distance and can't even hear the noise.

In retrospect I realize that proximity to the guns while firing was probably the source of the tinnitus, or ringing in the ear, many of us developed later. We did have old-fashioned soft rubber earplugs but they often blew out or dropped out leaving our ears unprotected until we could find another pair. They did not shut out much of the noise in any case. And there were periodic "preemies," where the projectile detonated prematurely shortly after it left the gun barrel. My movies did not capture the full effect of the guns including the noise, shock wave, and acrid odor escaping from the muzzles of burnt powder.

UNREP and VERTREP

We resupplied or refueled every few days in an operation known by a typical Navy acronym: UNREP—underway replenishment— or VERTREP—vertical (helicopter) replenishment. When my wife first saw the movies I took of an underway replenishment she asked the obvious layperson's question: Why don't the two ships do this while they are stopped rather than moving? This may seem to be simpler but would actually be more difficult. Stationary ships would be wallowing in the waves whereas they are relatively stable while moving and have an easier time maintaining a constant separation between each other. Also, if attacked they could break away and already have their speed up. Finally, ships proceeding toward a destination can continue making progress while taking on fuel or ammunition.

All qualified officers of the deck (OOD's) were given the chance to bring the ship alongside. This was a maneuver that took practice and a feel for the different forces acting on the ship as it moved into station about 80 to120 feet from the supply ship. The supply ship or carrier was usually steaming at about 12 to 15 knots, so we would approach at about 17 to 20 knots. As our bow pulled adjacent to the stern of the supply ship there was a tendency for its wake to pull our bow toward it so we had to steer a few degrees out. Then as more of our ship moved alongside we had to steer back in and settle on a parallel course. We also had to cut our speed to match hers as we got alongside. As soon as we were in position with our transfer stations lined up the lines would go across for the hookups.

I described one such approach in a letter of July 28, 1968:

> I brought old Freddy alongside an AF [refrigerator
> ship] today and had one of my best approaches yet. I
> came in sharply at 25 knots (she was doing 12) cut to
> 20 and then to 10 and back up to 12 as we stopped
> right alongside at about 120 feet. I moved into 100
> feet and locked in. The Captain didn't say a thing
> [during the approach] and gave me a well done [when
> on station].

Coming alongside a carrier was more intimidating, at least
until I had done it a few times, because of the bigger wake and the
overhanging decks. But once on station it was fascinating to inspect
the carrier at close range. It seemed there was always an admiral
looking down at us from one of the various bridge levels. And we
could see all of the supplies on pallets waiting for other ships to come
alongside. In particular we could see the huge projectiles destined for
what could only be the battleship *New Jersey* (*BB 62*). We were so far
below the flight deck that we could not see what was happening up
there, but we certainly knew the experience of those serving on the
bird farm was far different from ours on a "can" (destroyers have
been colloquially called "tin cans"'or just "cans").

I described a multiship UNREP/VERTREP in a letter of June
12, 1968:

> …Then we pulled alongside the oiler for our drink;
> the carrier was on her [the oiler's] port side, we were
> on the stbd., all three ships within 80 feet of each
> other steaming along at 12 kts. A helicopter was
> transferring personnel from the oiler to the carrier
> while planes were landing on the carrier. All the time,
> a band was playing for the inspiration of the whole

show aboard the carrier. This operation is even more of a spectacle at night when all is illuminated by red lights.

While alongside we sent across a line with colored canvas flags that marked distances so the OOD could constantly monitor whether we were drifting apart or together and make adjustments. Larger ships like carriers sometimes had two destroyers being supplied simultaneously on the same side, which made staying on station critical. Oilers would routinely refuel ships simultaneously on both sides as noted in my account above. We always had to be ready to break away if there was a problem.

I only remember one occurrence of an emergency breakaway, other than when we collided with the *Lowry*. The seas were rough and we just could not maintain station once we were alongside and hooked up to the oiler. I was stationed at the forward refueling station and could see the lines getting stretched. The word came to break away as the only way to get the fueling hose loose in time was to take a knife and cut the bindings that secured it to the fueling port. The boatswain's mate in charge used his knife to cut the bindings and then released the pelican hook that held the cable that supported the hose. As the cable and hose fell away it left a trail of black oil on our deck. This was a dangerous situation that could potentially cause injury if the rig hit one of the men as it broke loose.

Nighttime UNREP was a little more challenging as I recalled in this letter of August 7, 1968:

> I brought the ship alongside for the first time at night last night. It was a little trickier. We were alongside about 50 minutes—1 hr. I was a little tense because we were not directly opposed but slightly ahead due to station alignment inequities. It seems I have gotten to perform this exercise more than any of

the others. It is satisfying to perform well under the circumstances. Of course the Captain is right there behind you if anything goes wrong.

Resupply was also provided by helicopters (VERTREP). The first time we were scheduled to receive a drop on the fantail I organized the detail of about 30 men to get the supplies off of the deck and to the storerooms as efficiently as possible. The plan was to form a line to go out one door of the deckhouse, pick up a box, and take it in a door on the other side—a one way flow. I drew up this plan neatly on a sheet with carbon paper and mimeographed a bunch of copies for distribution to the work detail.

At the appointed time we watched as a very large twin-rotor Chinook helicopter hovered overhead with a cargo net full of supplies and mail. As it slowly descended to about 10 to 15 feet over the deck the net was lowered and released to allow the boxes to fall out and be picked up. On signal the men came out in an orderly fashion to pick up their boxes. We had to get everything picked up from the net as quickly as possible so the net could be retrieved by the chopper. Every minute it hovered near the ship there was some danger of a rotor hitting part of our superstructure.

It was immediately obvious that my system was much too slow, so I motioned everyone to come out at once, grab something, and take it away. The rotor noise was so great and the wash from the rotors so powerful that verbal communication was almost impossible. Also, as the ship pitched the fantail would rise up, squeezing the amount of space between the deck and underside of the helo. When this coincided with a dip from the chopper, men bolted out from under in fear of being crushed underneath. Despite the controlled chaos this worked. The next time we did a VERTEP I drew another diagram for distribution with lots of little dots converging on the drop point.

I labeled it the "ant method" of pickup although even ants were more orderly than we were.

By the end of June 1968 we had received supplies by helicopter 70 times and I had supervised half of these. Though it was a bit of a nuisance, those of us on helo detail were the first to know if we received mail.

9

SHIP'S COMPANY

Wetting Down, Officers and Crew

When I had been in the Navy (USNR) for a year and a half I was promoted from ensign to lieutenant junior grade (LT(jg). The next time we were in port, from June 29 to July 18, 1968, for turbine blade repairs, I was due for a "wetting down" party at the officers' club. This is a traditionally raucous celebration in the U.S. and British navies and coast guard when an officer gets promoted. The "wet" part referred originally to the newly promoted officer being thrown into the sea but evolved to mean a drinking party. By tradition the promoted officer buys drinks for everyone. We came back to port after plane guard duty with the USS *America* and headed straight for the O club at liberty call. The *America* had also come into port so there was a large contingent of her officers there as well.

The officers' club was a place of refuge and relief not just because alcohol was served but also as a reminder after living in a steel shell of what it was like to be in a building with regular furniture. It was a surrogate home for a few hours. It also was a chance to get to know officers in other divisions or at a more senior level with whom you interacted less frequently or with more formality on board. We were usually pretty mellow in the O Club, but when we did express ourselves in a less restrained way these incidents became fodder for shipboard retelling, often embellished for effect. Such was my wetting down party.

At the nominal price of 35 cents a drink I was generous in buying for both *Furse* and USS *America* wardrooms who were there that night. I was joined by a fellow officer who also made Lt(jg); we each brought about $22.00 and spent all of it. I had eight gin and tonics according to a letter I wrote the next day. Looking back I question whether my memory was playing tricks on me in recalling that number.

My last clear memory was the CO of the *America* along with our CO coming over to our table to congratulate me. We offered them a drink and I apparently said to the CO of the *America*, in reference to our duty as their plane guard ship, "You put 'em in, we'll pull 'em out," or something to that effect. I eventually caught a ride back to the ship in the shore patrol wagon to suffer a worse-than-usual hangover the next day, as reported to Pam:

> This morning I awoke feeling less than outstanding, but to show resolve ate breakfast and made my normal tour of working spaces at 7 AM. Then I returned to the rack for recuperation. Lucky it was Sunday—a non-working day.

The wardroom was made up of both "regular Navy" and reserve officers who entered for a limited term. Though I had a Naval Reserve commission I did not feel in any way discriminated against as a non-career officer. We got promoted in the same time frames as career officers, at least at my level.

One could not, however, advance through the higher ranks without becoming regular Navy. The unusually large number of non-career officers in the Navy as a result of the war and the draft resulted in reserve officers comprising more than 30 percent of the officers on our ship. Many reserve officers decided to seek or were offered commissions in the regular Navy when their terms were close to expiring.

Living in close quarters and interacting so intensively every day was a communal experience where we got to know each other pretty well. This was not only true of our relationships with other officers but also with the enlisted men. On the ship we had officers from across the United States, and the social, educational, and geographical differentiators that defined us before we joined the Navy were less important than friendships borne of shared experiences. Here, unlike in college where the differences could be preserved or even reinforced by fraternities or clubs, everybody was randomly intermingled; we were all literally thrown together in the same boat.

In some ways we got to know the men in our own divisions almost as well as our fellow officers. We were really not that far apart in age, and often the sailors had chosen to join as enlisted men rather than officers in order to serve shorter tours. I enjoyed talking and joking with my men on watch or in the course of our daily work. It sounds elitist in retrospect, but we did have to be careful not to fraternize with the men too closely in order to maintain our authority. We had to use our judgment when someone overstepped the bounds as had happened with the rum-spiked coffee in Halifax, or sometimes unexpectedly on deck.

One hot day I was walking on the main deck toward a working party washing down the fantail with fire hoses. When I suddenly appeared the sailor from my division who was manning the hose turned it on me on impulse and gave me a good soaking. I was momentarily taken aback and wasn't sure whether to be angry or just take it as a harmless expression of playfulness. I ran toward the man with the hose, a fun-loving sailor in my division, and grabbed the hose, which I turned on him and the rest of the men. Everyone seemed to enjoy getting soaked on a hot day. I was quick to return to my room to get dry clothes and restore my dignity. Give-and-take with members of the crew varied with the personality of each officer. Some were absolutely chummy with their men, others more standoffish. I was somewhere in the middle.

One difference between the management of a ship and managing a business is that on a ship the boss (officer or petty officer) rarely has any say in the selection of the officers and men assigned to him. He cannot just fire someone if that person does not live up to his standards—he has to make the most of the hand he is dealt. He has to learn to capitalize on a person's strengths and work around his weaknesses. A further complication in shipboard management is that the turnover is pretty constant in both the officer and enlisted ranks. Each ship is to some extent unique, so institutional knowledge has to be continually retaught to new arrivals. Every action is therefore treated as a training opportunity. This is particularly true if a person is reporting from shore duty or another kind of ship.

Social Evolution

Two areas of sensitivity then and now are attitudes about gays and women in the Navy, which I view through the lens of my time on *Furse*. We had a gay officer on *Furse*, though at the time most of us never truly knew nor did we ask. This officer was popular, very competent, and a real asset to the ship. He roomed with another officer who was pretty open-minded and did not seem offended when we would all come back to the ship after some heavy drinking and his roommate would make humorous but mildly suggestive comments. This was the "don't ask, don't tell' policy in a nutshell, and it worked for us. I speculate that there were other gay men on board that I did not know about. This is an area that I personally think is a nonissue.

The presence of women on ships has undoubtedly altered the dynamic of shipboard life since my days on the *Furse*. The language, for one thing, was generally very colorful, with expressions that I, at least, would find totally inappropriate around women. We had all fallen into that mode and had to recalibrate when we entered the civilian world at the end of our tours. I would be curious to know if things have cleaned up or are just as salty on ships today. From what I have overheard walking on college campuses today, these sensitivities no longer exist between the sexes.

This transition has apparently happened and is working, though there have been bumps in the road such as the Tailhook scandal of 1991,[9.1] where former Navy pilots got together for an alcohol-heavy reunion and groped their female counterparts, and the recent off-color videos sponsored by the XO of the carrier *Enterprise*.[9.2] In the latter case many of the women on board came to the defense of the XO, which I find perplexing though others find it relatively harmless. I recently took a Fleet Week tour of the USS *Roosevelt* (DDG-80) and saw almost as many women officers and enlisted personnel leaving the ship on liberty as men. It all seemed very natural and shows that when there is a concerted effort by leadership to implement a policy it can be, and apparently has been, accomplished successfully, even on a small combatant.

The gap between enlisted men and officers is institutionalized by different uniforms, different living quarters, separate dining facilities, and the convention of officers referring to enlisted men by their last names whereas officers are called Mr. and their surname. Efforts were made to ensure that the officers stayed in tune with the living conditions of the men. Each week an officer ate dinner on the mess decks, the name for enlisted dining. I always enjoyed these occasions to sit and talk with my men in a more relaxed setting and also getting away from the stiffness of wardroom dining. And the food was generally pretty good.

As Welfare & Recreation Officer I conducted bingo games on the mess decks on Saturday nights. Though I was often tired and not enthusiastic about doing this, once we got started the banter with the men gave me an opportunity to connect with the crew in a more informal way.

Every few weeks I would inspect the crew's quarters to ensure that decent living conditions were being maintained and no unauthorized items were being stashed, particularly alcohol. This was in advance of an inspection of the living spaces by the captain or XO. The crew's compartments usually housed about 50 men, each in "racks," canvas stretched across a metal frame with a minimal mattress, stacked three high. Clearance from the lower rack to the one above was about 18 inches. A person's face was almost touching the underside of the rack above him. At the bottom of a tier were lockable metal compartments where each man kept his clothes and personal effects. Officers' quarters were luxurious by comparison. It was easy to see how minor personal animosities could escalate into fights in these tight quarters. The petty officers bunked with the men and kept the peace.

At times there were more men than bunks so the bunks were shared in a practice known as "hot-bunking." When one person was on watch another could sleep in his bunk, still warm from its previous occupant so that overall utilization was more than 100 percent. This situation was supposed to be only short term since it was both unhealthy and bad for morale.

I was always a little uncomfortable going down into the living quarters of the crew. It seemed I was invading their one small bit of personal space. Whereas the officers had small desk areas and space for a few personal items, the sailors had to tape family photos or more suggestive photos to the bulkhead beside their racks. The mess decks served as their wardroom when off duty.

As a concession to morale I agreed one time to let the men in my division paint their living compartment any color they wanted rather than the pale green designated by the Navy for these spaces. The color had apparently been chosen because of its soothing psychological effect. They chose pink. After living with this for a few months they eventually went back to pale green.

As the draft dragged on and the war got less popular the educational level of newly arriving crew members seemed to decrease. Many were from economically disadvantaged families or areas of the country. New arrivals sometimes had little idea where we were geographically when we were at sea or visited foreign ports. I think they sincerely benefitted from this broadening experience. In this regard the military was a positive force for bringing citizens from different socioeconomic backgrounds in touch with one another, giving many an expanded understanding of the world as a whole, and giving many access to a higher and more regular level of health care than they received at home. Likewise, it gave officers from a relatively sheltered background such as mine a more direct exposure to a cross section of American life.

Protester

The war protest movement was developing momentum on the home front and even among some discontented ground troops, but it seemed distant from us at sea. That is, until one day when a seaman in my division held his own personal protest by sitting on a bollard (a short, rounded metal post) on the fantail and refusing to budge. He would not even come in and speak to anyone so I went to him. He said that he and a couple of others in the division were opposed to the war and did not want to be part of the gun crews any longer. He was one of the brighter and more enthusiastic members of the division and as I recall had recently made third class. But I suspected he had heard about conscientious objectors and thought this might get him reassigned to shore duty or out altogether. His two accomplices had matured from out-of-shape boys when they joined the *Furse* into hardened young men with a certain degree of insolence. They had not put themselves on the line as the protester had, though they all wore some item with a peace symbol on it to flaunt their individuality.

I knew they had no particular liking for me because they had threatened me one night in port when they returned drunk and I was standing watch on the quarterdeck. This had happened to other officers at times when men in their divisions had some gripe against them, and one officer actually slept with a .45 by his bed for a week. This was always a ticklish situation because you didn't want to provoke a drunken sailor but you also had to be firm. I was on duty when someone took a punch at the other officer on watch with me. The officer fended it off and sent the sailor to his bunk without reporting it, knowing that the man would be in a lot of trouble if he chose to play by the book.

I told the seaman that he had sworn an oath to defend the country when he joined the Navy and his refusal to do his duty could result in disciplinary action. I also reminded him that trained members of the gun crews were hard to replace. He remained firm, but I did not want to play into his hand and create a confrontation though I was tempted, and I didn't want to lose a key member from the gun crew. So I changed his General Quarters (GQ) station to the magazine below the mount so he would not be in the same space as the actual firing of the guns. I reassigned the others to the handling room, also below the mount, and never heard any more about it. I was not about to escalate this into an incident and was inclined to give them a chance to come to their senses, at least this time. They all performed fine for the rest of the deployment, though I kept a close watch on them as did the petty officers.

Doctor (?) on Board

Normally medical care was administered by a first class medical corpsman whose routine duties called for treating minor ailments, the flu, shipboard accidents, and the inevitable cases of venereal disease. Occasionally a more serious situation would develop that required a doctor. This could be a problem when we were at sea.

In our transit across the Pacific between Hawaii and Midway, one of the crew members reported to sick bay with sharp pains in his lower back and abdomen, which the corpsman diagnosed as kidney stones. The corpsman had no treatment except to give him painkillers and plenty of fluids to facilitate passing the stones. The communications officer made contact with a support ship with a doctor on board that was a two-day sail from us. The seas were rough at the time, which made matters worse. We felt great sympathy as we passed by sick bay and knew how he was suffering. There was absolutely nothing anyone could do, and we all suffered mentally with him. As we got within range of the other ship, the man passed the stones. He was transferred by helicopter for observation and eventually returned to the ship.

When we entered the combat zone, we were required to have a doctor in addition to our medical corpsman. The first one we got was brought to us by helo from the carrier. When he was firmly on deck and was led up to the bridge to report for duty he already looked a little green. This quickly escalated into full-scale seasickness, and he was assigned to sick bay for treatment. He gamely tried to tough it out but never could shake it. After several days he had to be taken back to the carrier. That the doctor of all people would be the sick one made us feel hardier than those stationed on the relatively stable carrier.

The second doctor assigned to us was the antithesis of the image of a caring physician. He was a crude-talking bull of a man whose primary interest was playing poker in the nightly game in the boatswain's locker. He had no other real duties that I could see, so he spent his time looking for amusement on board. One night I was getting ready to go to sleep and was lying in the top bunk. He came in and thought it would be funny to push the bunk up into the wall with me in it.

I was caught by surprise and was suddenly squeezed up against the bulkhead and the mattress and could hardly breathe. I could dimly hear laughing while I tried to push back to get enough airspace in front of my face to breathe. My roommates saw the danger and tried to get me down but had to fight off the doctor to do so. When I finally emerged gasping for air he was in hysterics. I let him know what an asshole he had been, especially for a doctor. He was unfazed. Fortunately he didn't stay on the ship more than a few weeks. I suspect he got bored and found a way to be transferred to more entertaining duty.

"Hey, Skinny!"

We had two R & Rs on the deployment, the first in early August 1968 to Hong Kong after we had been in the Tonkin Gulf about two and a half months and the second to Tokyo (actually Yokosuka, which is 40 miles south of Tokyo) toward the end of our tour in mid-September. We were all looking forward to this. I had been to Hong Kong in 1964 when I was 20 years old with my sister on our way back to the United States after a summer in Tokyo visiting our parents.

We arrived in the harbor amid colorfully adorned junks and small craft. I loved the exotic feel of the harbor and city clustered right up to its edges. Brightly decorated boats trailing ads for electronics from their masts caught our eye, a stark contrast to our haze-gray hulls.

I also knew that the tradition upon arrival of a U.S. Navy ship was to be approached by boats offering to paint our sides in exchange for the garbage from our galley or nylon line. Our garbage was valued for the food content still left in it, and the line could be made into ornamental objects. We knew this was coming and the boatswain's mates had put aside some scrap line to be ready. But the XO had said this security risk would not be tolerated. Absolutely no one would be allowed aboard or near the sides of the ship. This meant that my men would have to spend part of their R & R cleaning, scraping, and painting the sides. I gave the bad news to Boats (nickname for a boatswain's mate, usually the lead boatswain's mate).

Sure enough we were quickly approached upon anchoring and the duty officer on the quarterdeck shooed them away. They were all hardened women who knew the drill and persisted. I told them the same thing. They told us that all of the other ships that came into port had allowed them to paint. All they wanted was some line. They said they could paint the whole ship in a day if we would supply the materials. I rechecked with the XO who held his position. The boatswain's mate was involved in these discussions as well.

We spent the afternoon cleaning the deck areas and readying for liberty the next day. The boatswain's mate had assigned the crew that would begin painting in shifts in the morning. We assembled at quarters early in the morning in our whites. Just as we were about to break up we heard a loud woman's voice shout, "Hey, skinny!" She was alongside in her boat and had singled me out. All of the other officers started razzing me—"Hey, skinny, she wants you!" I was pretty thin then and was known as Skinny for the remainder of our stay in port.

One of the seamen who was about to start painting came over and said he had promised the woman that I would reconsider. I petitioned the XO one more time. In the end it was arranged that a couple of our men would be on deck watching them and that absolutely nothing of value to us would be traded to them. I left the rest to the boatswain's mate and most of the men were released for liberty. These women got to work and by the end of the day had done a job that would have taken us twice as long. Boats gave them some line and food and what else I never knew.

Hong Kong was known as place where electronics, tailored clothes, and other goods could be bought cheaply. By bringing them back on the ship, import duties and shipping costs could be avoided.

By the time we left, our hangar was filled with two motorcycles, oriental rugs, stereos, and various smaller purchases. I bought a tape deck and an amplifier that I stored in the room I shared with three others, which itself was becoming packed with gear.

I went ashore in civilian clothes with the weapons and supply officers. We climbed to the top of Victoria Peak where we looked down at the cluster of U.S. Navy ships at anchor in the harbor against the backdrop of Kowloon, followed by dinner at one of the large floating restaurants. We were happy to be off the ship and out of uniform for a few hours. We knew it would just be a memory soon enough.

When we left Hong Kong the ship looked new and the crew was refreshed. Within days the usual spate of sexually transmitted diseases started to emerge and the corpsman was ready with antibiotics.

I returned to Hong Kong in 1995 with my wife, anticipating the visually rich environment I remembered from my earlier trips. Much to my disappointment the harbor seemed almost devoid of small boats and junks and the water seemed brown and lifeless. The Star Ferry, which was the primary means of crossing between the island (Victoria) and the mainland (Kowloon), still operated and the floating city still remained, albeit in a reduced and more orderly state than I remembered. New big-box stores had moved in and supplanted a lot of the smaller, more vibrant shops.

Typhoons in this part of the world are like hurricanes in the Caribbean and Gulf of Mexico but have their own dynamic. A typhoon is the name given in the western Pacific for a storm that is essentially a hurricane or cyclone.[9.3] As the *Furse* returned to the Tonkin Gulf we steamed through the aftermath of typhoon Shirley and tropical storm Rose.

There are accounts of many ships in World War II being lost or badly damaged while trying to keep formation in typhoons.[9.4] There is a recommended track to follow to minimize exposure and damage in this kind of vast tropical disturbance that is determined by the course of the storm and where the ship is relative to that course.

Depending on whether you are navigating in the "safe semicircle" or in the "dangerous semicircle," the wind should be kept off of the starboard quarter or bow.[9.5] The swells were huge but I don't remember feeling in danger, just pretty uncomfortable much of the way.

We returned to the relative calm of the Tonkin Gulf where we resumed our plane guard duty. Shortly afterward I learned I was to be assigned as defense counsel in a special court-martial for a sailor who had been absent without leave for 24 days. I had taken a correspondence course in the Uniform Code of Military Justice (UCMJ) but had no practical experience. I consulted with the XO who advised me to request a qualified counsel for the defendant. This was granted and relieved me of a duty that would have required a lot of study and preparation. On a selfish level I was also concerned that the trial would be during our next R & R in Yokosuka and I would miss liberty.

Civilians often view the military justice system as closed and calculated to preempt due process in order to obtain quick judgments against guilty-until-proven-innocent defendants. I had no training in law but did appreciate that the UCMJ was codified in a way that was pretty clear and the process could move quickly for relatively minor offenses in a shipboard setting. In my brief exposure to the system I saw both discipline for the unrepentant and compassion for the guilty, including those who were AWOL for just a few hours or even a few days, often to take care of a family emergency.

USS *Long Beach* (CGN 9) on PIRAZ

"Nasty Boat" (PTF) alongside after grenade attack; note grenade holes, shrapnel marks, and blood on foredeck

10

A SHIP HAS NO BRAKES

Watch Officer

The rigors of being at sea continuously, including underway replenishment every few days and steaming in multiship formations, forced each of the watch officers to develop his proficiencies at an accelerated rate. Just ten days after arriving in the Tonkin Gulf on May 30, 1968, I became qualified as an OOD Independent (OODI) in a simply worded memo from the Captain: "As a result of ability demonstrated on board this ship, you are hereby considered qualified and designated as an Officer of the Deck, Independent."

This was the equivalent of a nautical driver's license. In a letter about two months later on July 21, 1968, I talked about what I had gained as an OOD:

> I think my experiences as an officer of the deck in a
> war zone have taught me how to take responsibility
> and bear its consequences like few other situations
> could. It may sound trite, but when everyone else
> on the ship is asleep except the watch section,

and you are responsible for their actions, and the safety and proper performance of the whole ship depends on you for four hours, you definitely feel the responsibility. I think these years as a junior officer in the Navy will stand out as some of the most challenging I will ever face. I only wish I got paid better for it!

It would take me another year to qualify as an OOD, Fleet, (OODF), the designation for conning the ship in the presence of other ships, including maneuvering in multiship formations with minimal supervision from the captain or other superior officer.

There was no ceremony. I had simply gained the confidence of the captain and XO as one who could be trusted to run the ship with skill and good judgment. Good judgment meant calling the captain or XO when a situation was developing that was beyond the abilities of the OOD or otherwise affected ship operations in a significant way. This included signals received from the task force commander to execute a formation change or from the carrier that she was about to change course for flight ops. Admiral Stavridis describes in his book *Destroyer Captain* the constant calls he got as CO of the USS *Barry* (DDG-52):

> I cannot escape them. It seems they ring about every ten or fifteen minutes, giving me some bit of information deemed vital to my performance as commanding officer underway—the ship's course or speed, the barometer's rise or fall, the sprained ankle of a crewman or the healed virus of a ship rider, tasking from the admiral, a crisis on the mess decks— the flow of information seems, and is, endless.
>
> I will not escape the shrill ring of phones until long after I leave this place, I think. It is tiring. It is,

I am sure, the highest price of command. There is simply never a moment to relax, a moment when the ring of a phone does not signal some new rumor of war, or slight catastrophe, or lurking fear finally realized.[10.1]

I believe that captain of a naval vessel is one of the most demanding jobs in the world. A ship at sea is always moving, often in the close company of other ships. The captain is responsible for the safety of the ship, its crew, and meeting operational commitments 24/7, with only sporadic sleep for weeks or months at a time. He must train his officers and crew—most if not all of whom he had no role in choosing—to exercise good judgment in his absence. He must constantly walk the narrow line between being a mentor and a disciplinarian while keeping morale strong. A lapse in any of these areas can cost lives not to mention his career. A good CO makes his own good luck through skill and good leadership.

These are similar to the demands a captain of industry, a CEO whose ship can, metaphorically, go down if he or she fails to exercise leadership, good judgment, and decisiveness. It is with good reason that a sea captain is the paradigm of a leader in many professions.

At night the officer on watch about to be relieved would send a messenger down to the berthing compartments and staterooms 30 to 45 minutes ahead of the next watch to make sure all reliefs were awake. No reliance on alarm clocks. The messenger was not allowed to touch a person to wake him even if the man was sound asleep. I can still hear a particular seaman's loud voice booming in my ear: "Mr. A., you've got the watch!" He would stand there until I got up. Others in the room just slept through it.

When an officer came up to the bridge for his watch he was expected to report to CIC about 15 minutes ahead of time to familiarize himself with the ship's situation. This included noting the locations of other ships as well as any radar contacts that looked like they might pass close to us. If the bearing of the contact remained the same and the range (distance) was decreasing, it was on a collision course. This familiarization period also allowed the officer to adjust to the red lights at night and get fully awake.

Nevertheless, I often went to the bridge still groggy from being awakened from a deep sleep and still only partially acclimated to the dimness. Until my eyes adjusted I would have to ask who someone was even though he was standing only a few feet from me. In addition, one had to distinguish the important from the irrelevant chatter on the various radio nets that were piped into the bridge. Sporadic and often static-filled messages were in code—broadcasting "in the clear" was only for emergencies. The consequences of missing or misinterpreting an important instruction were significant, so our ears became fine-tuned to pick up critical words and call signs. Our call sign ("staircase," as I recall) was generally the same, but sometimes would be changed for a specific operation. This was multitasking to the ultimate before that term was popularized.

Signals between ships were sent by flashing light (visual Morse code), semaphore (flags held by hand and positioned in patterns for each individual letter), signal flags hoisted on the mast, or by radio or teletype. Audible signals would be executed by the words *stand by* (pause), *execute*. Visual signals were verified and executed by hoisting and then lowering a set of coded signal flags. We came to know the basic meanings of the most common flag combinations but had the flag book close at hand as well. The meanings of some common signal flag letters were:

Bravo	Ship is handling explosives or fuel oil
Five	Ship is broken down; cannot maneuver on its own
Oscar	Man overboard
Papa	Personnel recall. All hands return to ship
Quebec	Boat recall. All boats return to ship

Flags and pennants were used in combination to indicate specific maneuvers, such as the corpen pennant and the sierra (S) flag, which together meant to execute a search turn.

It was the job of the signalmen to verify new flag messages as soon as they went up. The OOD also tried to decode the simpler ones. We used to spend slow time on watches quizzing each other on the signal flags and Morse code. Picking up these new languages was good training for learning and assimilating the arcane jargon of architecture and construction later on.

Boatswain's Pipe

Intraship communication was by sound-powered phones. These were powered simply by someone picking up the handset, pressing the key (a button that would activate to phone), and talking into it. When information is to be transmitted from the bridge, the boatswain's mate of the watch (BMOW) keys the handset and says the message, which is broadcast via speakers throughout the ship. To alert people that a message is coming, the BMOW will first pipe a particular series of notes into the speaker. Each sound corresponds to a particular message, so that if you miss the words you will recognize the sound and know what was transmitted. These calls are described in *Watch Officer's Guide*:

> Many ships of medium size have boatswain's mates (or men skilled with the boatswain's pipe) on watch a greater part of the time. These men preface their passing of the word with the more common boatswain's calls. Among these are: "all hands," "pipe down," "mess gear," and "attention" (or "passing the word" or "word to be passed"—identical calls under different names). Many ships preface the word to be passed with "now hear this," or "now hear there."

185

These three words prepare the listeners for an announcement. *A sudden announcement with no preface is too abrupt for many people. They would comprehend only the latter part of the message. If the boatswain's call is used, there is no reason to use a preface such as, "now hear this"* [italics mine].[10.2]

The boatswain's pipe (or boatswain's call) is a 5 to 6-inch long slightly curved flat metal device with the general profile of a smoking pipe. Its use can be traced back to the Crusades in the Middle Ages. It has been used by the British Navy since the late fifteenth century to pass orders. The boatswain's mate blows into one end and the sound comes out of the bowl of the pipe. The bowl is a small sphere of about a half inch in diameter that is open at the top. By melting wax into the bowl and denting it in a certain way it can be tuned. The bowl is held in the palm of one hand while the stem is held between the thumb and forefinger of the same hand. By moving fingers cupped over the bowl, notes are produced.

It takes practice, and some boatswain's mates get it more quickly than others and become proficient enough to sustain a nice trill during the piping of the note. And some never really get the feel of it. It was traditional to give a new third class boatswain's mate his own silver-plated boatswain's pipe, which became a prized possession. He would engrave the flat edge below the stem with his name or initials and attach a lanyard so he could wear it around his neck on watch. I obtained a pipe and attempted to tune it myself but ended up giving it to one the boatswain's mates to tune for me. I could barely achieve a trill.

To this day I love to hear the plaintive call of the boatswain's pipe in old movies of World War II sea battles; nothing conjures up the unique atmosphere of the ship as well as these special sounds trailing off into the air. It is telling that in *The Bluejacket's Manual of 1940* (tenth edition), the de facto seaman's handbook, a whole chapter replete with photos and diagrams is devoted to the use of the boatswain's call. The 2009 twenty-fourth edition gives it only one short paragraph. With the march of technology these sounds will probably be prerecorded and activated by pressing a button, just as electronic bugles now play taps at military funerals.

"Now Relieve the Watch"

No matter how complicated the situation the oncoming watch officer is inheriting, he is expected to relieve his predecessor within a few minutes of coming onto the bridge with this simple exchange, executed with salutes:

"I am ready to relieve you, sir."
"I am ready to be relieved."
"I relieve you, sir."

These words are simple but carry great weight, which justifies their formality. The relieving officer is not obligated to relieve the watch until he is satisfied that he understands everything and that the ship is not out of position. There is an old Navy saying, "Relieve in haste, repent at leisure."

One afternoon as we steamed alone off the coast without much going on, my relief appeared from CIC and before I could brief him on the situation he informed me that we were closer than the mandated distance from shore. We were technically still within range of enemy shore batteries. He was right, but to me we were close enough to our designated area and it was extremely unlikely that we were actually in any danger. I thought he was joking but he held his ground. I was annoyed and didn't immediately do anything. However, I realized I wouldn't get relieved so I brought the ship out to the required distance, extending my watch by 10 or 15 minutes.

In the scheme of things this was a relatively trivial incident and only stayed in my memory because it was so unexpected. I was caught in a bit of a quandary since he was right, but I wanted to let him know I was not happy about it. It turned out that this little occurrence became the stuff of dreams later.

If an army marches on its stomach, as Napoleon supposedly said, the Navy steams on coffee. It is said that if a ship stays moored to a pier for too long it will become mired in its own coffee grounds. Coffee is the fuel that sustains the men on watch. On our ship there was a small built-in table on the rear bulkhead of the bridge where the coffeepot was set and the cups were stored. It had a small lip around the edges to keep the cups from sliding off, but inevitably they did and the only ones left were the plastic ones that didn't break. Sometimes at night we would get down to just one shared cup, which we had to use if we wanted our fix of caffeine. No one ever seemed to suffer any ill consequences—we used to say that the coffee was so bad that it killed any germs.

There was no head (toilet) on the bridge so some ships installed their own open-air urinal aft of one of the bridge wings. If you visit the *Joseph P. Kennedy* (DD-850) at Battleship Cove in Fall River, Massachusetts, you will see an open urinal built into the back of the port bridge wing. We, however, just had to hold it until the watch was over. Or, if desperate, appeal to the captain to use the head in his cabin right behind the bridge.

Every watch was different, and I always tried to maintain an overall awareness of what was coming so I was mentally prepared for my next watch. After several months at sea and countless watches I had become pretty confident in my abilities to cope with almost anything. One sunny day I confidently took the watch just before we were scheduled to come alongside another destroyer. It would be my job to get us there. We were steaming independently and I tracked the other destroyer's course and speed and calculated a course to intercept. The captain was not on the bridge but the XO was on the signal bridge one level above. The problem with my predicted path was that there was a line of several destroyers between us and the target ship. I confidently decided that I could steam between two of the ships that were spaced pretty close together—only a few multiples of their 390-foot lengths, which did not leave much room to pass through.

The whole situation had a sense of unreality about it. I was buoyed by the beautiful weather and went into a zone almost like I was playing a video game with real ships instead of icons on a game board. It was a personal challenge to slip my ship between them—how neat would that be! I even envisioned kudos from the captain or XO for pulling off such a skillful maneuver.

As I approached a point of no return, reality snapped me to my senses. If I miscalculated or the ships did not stay precisely on their current course and speed I might be in big trouble—and a ship has no brakes to bring it to a screeching stop! Just as I started to veer off and lower speed to pass astern, the XO appeared on the bridge and looked at me intently. He had been watching this potentially dangerous situation unfold and came down to take the conn if I didn't pull away. He did not say anything but stayed on the bridge until I got around them and was making my approach to bring the ship alongside.

I was but one of many junior officers who had responsibility for these ships with hundreds of men aboard and it was a wonder that serious accidents rarely seemed to happen. Only I and the XO knew how close I had come to crossing into the danger zone, and it sobered me for the rest of my brief naval career.

We got occasional tastes of what was happening in-country from aircraft and helicopters that passed close to us. Once an Army Cobra helicopter came out from the coast and wanted some target practice with its M197 3-barrel Gatling gun that fired 20mm rounds at a rate of 700 rounds per minute—that's ten rounds a second! This fearsome weapon was mounted in its nose and when it fired all you heard was a loud whirring sound. We threw wooden boxes overboard. When they had drifted to a safe distance the Cobra would make a pass and in seconds the boxes would be completely pulverized.[10.3]

Navy pilots from the carriers would also occasionally buzz us. One early morning watch as I was standing on the port bridge wing at about 0500 the rear lookout reported planes approaching dead astern. The report reached the bridge at the same time that two F4 Phantoms roared by just above sea level and not more than a hundred feet on either side of us. The noise was deafening and the whole ship shook. The captain came running out onto the bridge from his sea cabin to see the planes in a steep climb in front of us doing spins as they rose, pilots laughing all the way I am sure.

11

BATTLEWAGON AND
BATTLE STATIONS

Japan

By mid-September 1968, only about a month after our trip to Hong Kong, we were headed for our next R & R in Japan. This interval seemed a lot longer. Countless hours of plane guard duty, thousands more rounds of shore fire bombardment, and many underway replenishments had inured us to this seemingly endless routine of round-the-clock watches and sleep deprivation.

When the time came to go to Japan we were almost too tired to get excited. We headed north with a first stop for replenishment on the west coast of Taiwan in the port of Kaohsiung. There were two cities by that name on this coast, and there was some midcourse discussion between the XO, who was the ship's navigator, and the Ops officer to confirm that we were heading for the right one. They decided we were heading for the wrong one and we altered course accordingly. As we steamed in the next morning there were hundreds of small craft clogging the channel. It seemed inevitable that we would hit one of them. It was a conning officer's nightmare even with a pilot aboard. We were told that if we did hit one the boat owner could apply for reparations that would enable him to buy a new boat. Whether this was hearsay or fact, we managed to avoid them and they us.

We eventually arrived at Yokosuka (pronounced Yokooska), our port for the next few days. The U.S. Navy was an accepted but not always welcome presence in Japan due to periodic incidents by U.S. sailors involving Japanese citizens, mostly women. We were advised to be on our good behavior.

I went the 40 miles north to Tokyo by train with the weapons officer. We saw the Ginza and hit a few bars along the way. In one bar two obnoxious girls literally tried to drag us upstairs, and when we resisted they raked our faces with their long nails before we could get out of there. Aside from this it was a pretty low-key trip; we were just glad to be off the ship and enjoy the sights of Tokyo. I had lived in Tokyo for a summer with my parents so I was the de facto tour guide.

Tokyo is one of those cities that seems to transform itself almost every generation while retaining a strong sense of its heritage and cultural identity. As one who studied architecture I always felt an affinity with the calm beauty of its parks and the shrines. Japanese architecture has been refined for many hundreds of years into beautifully crafted gates (torii) and temple enclosures.

I steered my fellow officers to the Meiji Shrine (destroyed in World War II and rebuilt) near the emperor's palace in central Tokyo; we rested a bit on a bench and watched the kids run around in tight little robed outfits complete with obis (wide sashes pulled tight around their torsos) in the case of the little girls. They skittered around among their parents and the park workers who swept the grounds in wide arcs with brooms made of tree branches.

To be able to sit in the midst of trees and grass was a rare treat for us. I devoted a disproportionate time to recording these scenes with my new super-8 camera as I sat peacefully observing the calm surroundings animated by the kids. Our time was short so we did not try to do too much—just get a flavor for the city. Unlike Hong Kong, Tokyo had not lost any of the vibrancy I remembered from my previous trips. I wished we have been able to stay longer and vowed to return for an extended trip when out of the Navy. Regretfully, I have never been back. We would return to Yokosuka about a month later to refuel on our trip home, but for an even more abbreviated stay.

We went right back to the gunline and the relentless pace of days and nights merging in a continuum of general quarters, replenishments, and sporadic sleep. We resumed Sea Dragon operations off of North Vietnam on September 23 and then relieved the USS *Boston* (CAG-1) as flagship of Southern Sea Dragon on September 28; we also operated with the USS *MacKenzie* (DD-836). Then it was back up north to relieve the USS *New Jersey* on October 5, 1968.

Battleship *New Jersey*

> On 5 October COMDESDIV 22 relieved Commanding officer, USS NEW JERSEY (BB62), as Commander of Northern Sea Dragon Operations, and FURSE joined that task unit. USS BERKELEY continued operating with FURSE attacking water-borne logistics craft, and lucrative land targets including bridges, choke points, supply points and gun emplacements in North Vietnam with spotting assistance from carrier and shore based aircraft.
> *(FURSE Command History of 1968)*

In the course of the six months we were in the Tonkin Gulf I had the opportunity to bring the ship alongside other destroyers, oilers, ammunition ships, refrigerator ships, and aircraft carriers. And now the battleship *New Jersey!* Battleships, or battlewagons as they were once called, were the grandest dreadnoughts of the premissile Navy with their array of large-caliber guns ranging up to 16 inch, the largest in the fleet.

The Iowa class battleship *New Jersey* arrived in the Tonkin Gulf in September 1968 with 16-inch guns that could reach 85 percent of targets in North Vietnam, according to Lawrence M. Greenberg, contributing editor of *Vietnam Magazine,* in his account of naval operations in Vietnam. The *New Jersey* last fired in anger 15 years before in the Korean War. Her 1,900-pound shells could wreak havoc on targets far in excess of the 5-inch and 8-inch shells on destroyers and cruisers then operating on the gunline.[11.1]

Her arrival in the gulf created a buzz among the rest of the fleet. When I first saw her she had just arrived and many ships diverted to pass close by for a firsthand look. Her profile was distinctive with its long, sleek lines terminating in a powerful, bulbous bow—a beautiful and awesome real-life example of the era of the battlewagon. The crew of the *New Jersey* had been carefully selected from many volunteers who longed to have the chance to serve on a legend. I have since visited her in Camden, New Jersey, where, even in her somewhat deteriorated condition, she is still an object of grandeur.

A little after 6 a.m. as the sun came up, we made our approach to her starboard side to relieve her. The sea was calm and the air still cool as we slid into position. It was eerily serene to see the shape and details of this magnificent vessel emerge from the early morning mist into the glow of the rising sun. We were alongside for 25 minutes. I was busy making sure we stayed in position and that the midships highline transfer went smoothly. I knew that this was going to be a real photo opportunity so I had persuaded one of the other officers to record it with my movie camera so I could study the details at my leisure later.

Below is my log entry for the 04–08 watch on Saturday, October 5, 1968:

04–08 Underway as before. 0600 set the special sea and highline detail. 0620 maneuvering to take station 500 yards astern of USS New Jersey (BB 62). 0630 on station astern of New Jersey, base course 000, base speed 12 knots. 0634 commenced approach, OOD at the conn. 0635 alongside starboard side of USS New Jersey. 0637 first line over. 0656 transfer of turnover material completed. 0700 all lines clear. Maneuvering to clear starboard side of USS New Jersey. 0700 clear of New Jersey, C/S 25 knots. 0705 C/C 000, C/S 15 knots. 0725 C/C 290.

H. H. Abernathy, Lt(jg) USNR

I recounted the experience of coming alongside and of our last few days on Sea Dragon in a letter to my parents three days later:

I had the distinction of being the officer of the deck when we highlined with the battleship New Jersey about three days ago. I conned the ship in alongside and got a compliment from the Captain of the New Jersey on the approach (we have a phone line rigged between ships). We see the New Jersey firing her 16" guns from a distance of about 12 miles—the noise and sight are distinctive.

Last night on watch I saw a SAM missile hit one of our planes. It was dark and all I could see was the explosion. Not more than a few minutes later another aircraft reported his partner was down and safe in the water. A helo was dispatched from one of the SAR (search & rescue—a job we had for a while) ships. The pilot was safe aboard shortly thereafter.

We steam up and down the coast just out of gun range hunting for WBLC's (water borne logistic craft) and LUCTARS (lucrative targets) such as supply dumps, truck convoys, etc. Highway 1A runs close to the coast and is easily vulnerable to interdiction.

We have three more days on Sea Dragon until we head for home. We really feel like we are earning our combat pay here.

Everything about the ship was unique—the size of the guns and gun mounts, the anchor chain lying on the broad foredeck with anchors snugged up below the massive hawse pipes, the teak decks, the sweeping bridge. We all had the sense that we were seeing a sight that would soon be lost to naval history. When we broke off and pulled away I got a shot bow-on that revealed a wide, low profile of great power in comparison to the slim profile of the next destroyer to come alongside. The designers of those ships knew how to integrate form and function to create a truly impressive object of power and beauty.

Less Is More

A bit of a digression here for some personal observations as an architect about the evolution of ship design, from ships like *Furse* and the *New Jersey* to modern ships. Recently I saw a ship from my office window in New York making its way silently up the Hudson River for Fleet Week, an annual event where naval ships moor in New York Harbor and can be visited by the public. This ship was a modern destroyer. All of the surfaces were smooth and beveled. There was one small gun mount forward of the canted superstructure, which was topped by a narrow band of dark windows marking the bridge. A cluster of radar domes sat atop the pyramidal mast. It was the nautical equivalent of the stealth fighter aircraft.

In the words of modernist architectural pioneer Mies van der Rohe, "Less is more." Just as minimalist glass skyscrapers replaced heavily ornamented masonry structures replete with cornices, balustrades, and pillars, sleeker hull designs made with composites have replaced the articulated ship designs of World War II. Today's designs have removed almost all surface protrusions and have certainly made ships easier to maintain. Form has been reduced to its functional essence.

The evolution of warship design from WWII-vintage destroyers like the *Furse* to sculpted ships has paralleled the evolution of automobiles. For instance, my 1953 MGTD, built in the same era as the *Furse*, has its headlights mounted on separate brackets, an articulated grill, a gas tank attached with metal straps behind the rear seat, flowing fenders, and running boards. Modern-day equivalents have all of these elements blended smoothly into an aerodynamically designed body. The *Furse* had all of her topside gear exposed and articulated—gun mounts, torpedo tubes, ASROC launcher, life raft cages, capstan, whaleboat, damage control gear—whereas few if any of these are visible on the exterior of the modern destroyer.

The evolution from guns to missiles and from exposed elements to smooth radar-deflecting surfaces is a manifestation of modern technology. Destroyers, like submarines, have become indoor environments in which warfare is fought with electronics controlling missile launches. Ships have been turned outside in. The open deck seems to be a vestigial environment in these ships. I remember in the evening how our chief boatswain's mate would sit on a bollard below the torpedo deck and smoke a cigarette while gazing out to sea, and how the cooks would retrieve flying fish on deck in the mornings that they would cook for breakfast. Maybe this is nostalgia, but a deck on a ship is like the porch of your house—a place to get some psychological relief from living in a warren of passageways and windowless, equipment-packed compartments.

This new generation of ships is epitomized by the new Zumwalt-class destroyers:

> DDG 1000 will have a "tumblehome" hull form,
> i.e. a design in which hull slopes inward from above

the waterline. This will significantly reduce the radar cross section since such a slope returns a much less defined radar image than a more hard-angled hull form.

Requirements for the integrated deckhouse EDM is that it is fully EMC [electromagnetic-compatibility] shielded with reduced infrared and radar signatures. Measures to fulfill these conditions include an all-composite superstructure, low signature electronically steered arrays, an integrated multi-function mast and low radar and infrared signatures. Other measures to reduce the vessel's infrared signature include the development of an exhaust suppressor.[11.2]

This new destroyer will be almost twice as long as the *Furse* and is certainly a significant improvement in just about every way. And it was designed with Human Systems Integration (see page 29, *Proceedings,* USNI, "From Minimal to Optimal," July 2011) to optimize the size of the crew—this new ship will have a complement of only 148 officers and men, half the number of the *Furse.* Less crew equals more savings in manpower. The one aspect that has thankfully stayed the same is that when seen from a distance the classic destroyer profile is still recognizable.

The long, low profile of the *New Jersey* with guns bristling from mounts packed neatly into and around the superstructure will be remembered with pride by those who served on and with her. Even at a distance this profile was unmistakable.

Before we departed we got a chance to see the *New Jersey*'s 16-inch guns fire. She could cruise in close to the shore without fear of shore batteries since her hull was too thick to be in danger of penetration by guns in use by the North Vietnamese. She would simply fire away on a steady course and speed. As we steamed ahead of her I could look back and see the puffs of smoke emerge from her guns after a round was fired. When I later visited the *New Jersey* on exhibit in New Jersey I learned that after the shell left the barrel a charge of nitrogen was sent through the barrel to eject any leftover combustibles. As I became more practiced I could see the brief blip of the projectile arcing up out of the smoke. I could also see the ship rock very slightly sideward after a shot was fired from those enormous guns, a testament to their power.

The *New Jersey* was rearmed at sea as well as in port. Sometimes when we were alongside a supply ship we could see pallets with huge projectiles and the powder charges stacked on the deck awaiting transfer to her. She also took on ammo by helicopter, the first instance of rearming a heavy battleship by this method.[11.3]

We were now on Northern Sea Dragon duty well north of the DMZ and very near the 19th parallel, which marked the northern limit of bombing and shore fire negotiated at that point in the peace talks. We were definitely in more hostile territory than we had been in the south. I liked the heightened sense of anticipation of being at the leading edge of our military presence in Vietnam. We could tune in the radio to listen to Hanoi Hannah, the North Vietnamese equivalent to Tokyo Rose of World War II. We found these broadcasts amusing but had to admit that she had a pretty seductive voice and near-perfect English. We occasionally found bits and pieces of electronic gear floating in the water, which we dutifully retrieved for any possible intelligence value.

Taking a Hit

During a search for water-borne targets on 7 October, FURSE was taken under fire by enemy shore batteries. Approximately 24 rounds were fired at FURSE with one direct hit on the flight deck. Although damage was superficial, one member of a damage control party, EMFN Robert E. Ferguson,

was injured in the arm and evacuated by helicopter.
(FURSE Command History of 1968)

We knew that there was always the possibility of encountering hostile fire from the shore on our firing missions, but we never thought too seriously about it. Every time we went to GQ we had to put on our flak jackets, vests with heavy plastic plates sewn inside, and our helmets, which were cumbersome in the close confines of CIC. Some took them off in the stultifying atmosphere. Even the fairly unlikely chance of being hit was enough to convince me to keep them on. But we were pretty far north of the DMZ where there was little U.S. opposition to the placement of NVA guns along the shoreline. South, in the vicinity of Phan Thiet, where the U.S. presence was more concentrated there was little threat to us along the coast.

Our log entries from October 7, 1968, the day we were hit, commencing with the 00–04 am until the 12–16 watch, give an idea of the frenetic activity of gunfire operations prior to taking hostile fire. We went to General Quarters for firing missions on each of these watches and received a helo on the 12–16 watch while steaming with the USS *Berkeley* (DDG-15) within a few miles of the coast near the city of Vinh. This meant that we were essentially always on duty with little or no opportunity for sleep.

The 16–20 watch started out routinely but would quickly evolve into a few minutes of intense activity that would bring the reality of our own vulnerability sharply into focus and put our many hours of training to the test. The normal procedure was to race in perpendicular to the coast, turn sharply to parallel it, unleash our fire on the targets, and race back out to a safe distance. On this day we were in a column formation at about 4,000 yards astern of the *Berkeley*. In this formation the lead ship fires at the targets while the ship astern fires "shotgun" at possible shore battery installations. Normally the ship with the 5"/54 caliber guns, in this case the

Berkeley, was responsible for firing at the primary targets due to the greater rate of fire and range of these newer guns.

At 1614 we increased speed to 25 knots as we approached the shore in a line abreast with the *Berkeley* and executed a 90-degree turn to port, which put us in a column formation parallel to the shore. We steadied on course 140 degrees at 15 knots to stabilize the fire control computer, then started firing at our assigned targets inland and laying down suppressing fire on the beach. This was the danger period before we could zigzag to make it more difficult for enemy coastal batteries to hit us. At 1632 we commenced receiving the first hostile fire of our deployment, which belied my previous letter that it was all one-sided.

The North Vietnamese had set up bamboo stakes at regular intervals as visual references to track the course and speed of our ships. I was in CIC as gunnery liaison officer, with communication to the gunnery officer in the fire control director atop the ship and with personnel in Plot and on the bridge. I heard some popping sounds and the word came from the bridge that rounds from a shore battery were exploding around us, falling almost vertically. Since we were inside this didn't register immediately with us, and some of the men were so tired that they hardly looked up when told we were under fire.

For those on the bridge and in the director who could see the shells it was much more real. The gunnery officer's voice was noticeably excited as he was heard to say to the FT in the Director "Shit, they're shooting at us!" as they proceeded to direct counterbattery fire. There was no clear target, consistent with the ComDesRon Two "WestPac Trip Report" observation that these shore batteries used low visibility, flashless powder to disguise their location. I also sent a firing coordinate to Plot of a location on the nearest beach. The hazy conditions and lack of direct visibility of the target camouflaged within a tree line made a damage assessment impossible.

As we were firing there was a report of a hit near Mount 52 (the gun mount just aft of the flight deck and forward of the fantail). Then the popping stopped. We seemed to continue on course and speed a few moments before we turned away to steam out of range of the shore guns and eventually secured from General Quarters.

We had fired 37 rounds of counter battery in two minutes, nearly 20 rounds a minute, which was our maximum rate of sustained fire, evidence of the effect of adrenaline when under fire and of the skill of the gun crew. We had experienced our first contact with hostile fire, and except for those in the immediate vicinity of the hit, we were too tired to have much of a reaction.

The actual log entry for the 16–20 watch on October 7, 1968, as written by F. R. Seddon, Lt(jg), USNR, reads:

16–20 Underway as before. 1612 C/C 140^0, 1614 C/C 230^0, C/S 25 Knots. 1621 C/C 140^0, C/S 15 knots. 1632 commenced receiving hostile fire. C/S 27 knots. C/C 070 °. 1636 C/C 030°. Commenced firing on coastal defense site. 1638 ceased firing. 1639 C/C 090°. 1642 C/S 15 knots. 1643 maneuvering to take station bearing 315°, 4000 yards from the Berkeley. Base course 120°, base speed 12 knots. 1704 set material condition Yoke. 1708 secured from General Quarters. Ammunition expended 37 rounds full service smokeless powder charges. Damage: hole in flight deck 2 ft. in diameter caused by a shell, which also shattered glass panels at front of ship's store, numerous holes and dents in after passageway, overhead deck, and bulkheads due to shrapnel. Numerous holes in hangar door due to shrapnel. AN/ULQ -6B port antenna rendered inoperable due to shrapnel damage. Casualties: Ferguson, Robert E. B60 40 96, FN, USN, sustained shrapnel wounds on upper right arm and right wrist. Treatment administered by COMDESDIV 22 staff medical officer. Disposition: to be evacuated by helo to the USS Bennington (CVS 20) for further treatment.

FN Ferguson, the sailor from the damage control party stationed below the hatch who got hit, was taken to the wardroom to receive medical treatment before transport to the aircraft carrier. The wardroom table doubled as a surgery table when necessary. We were one of 29 ships that sustained hits from shore fire, and probably one of the last.[11.4]

Our experience was consistent with that of other ships on similar firing runs as noted in The Commander Destroyer Squadron Two "WestPac Trip Report" 1968 (pages 26, 27):

Operations in North Vietnam revealed several shortcomings in our current peace-time gunnery practice. "Text-book" counter-battery training is misleading in that shore batteries encountered today include dual-purpose AA weapons located at strategic positions to counter both air and surface targets. These guns are highly mobile, have short, quick muzzle flashes and give off very little smoke (usually dark) when fired. They must be caught in the act to spot, and studied to locate. Large white puffs of smoke are not characteristic. *Initial warning has almost always been splashes or bursts alongside the ship.* (italics mine)

After we secured from GQ, we went back to the hangar deck and saw the hole where the round had penetrated, right above where the damage control party was standing. The hangar deck and door were peppered with small holes, and I managed to pick up a piece of the shrapnel as a souvenir. Those with new items from Hong Kong were anxious to check the condition of purchases they had stored in the hangar. The captain reportedly had a rug that sustained only light damage from the shrapnel that had penetrated the light-gauge aluminum hangar door. It was obvious from the number and size of the holes in the door that a lot of shrapnel had sprayed across the deck, fortunately an unmanned topside area during GQ.

I wrote letters home every few days and mentioned this incident to allay any fears in case it had made the news in the United States. My account to my parents on the afternoon we received fire was pretty brief:

> First and foremost, we received our first hostile fire this afternoon about 3 hours ago. We were bracketed by perhaps 15 rounds of probably 85 mm projectiles. They splashed all around us but only one hit. It blew a big hole in our flight deck and sprayed shrapnel all around the area. Luckily, only one person was hurt— he received shrapnel in his left arm and wrist. He was evacuated to one of the aircraft carriers.
>
> We returned fire as we turned away at maximum speed until out of range.

The incident appeared in a *New York Times* report on daily action in Vietnam and was picked up by local papers. A few weeks later I received a letter from my parents enclosing an article from our local paper mentioning my name as one of the officers on board. Our next-door neighbor had seen a news item about it and called my name into the local paper. Here is an excerpt from that article:

> SAIGON (UPI) . . . Off the northern coast, Navy spokesmen said, three American sailors were

wounded when Communist shore batteries opened up on a pair of Navy destroyers 13 miles southeast of the coastal city of Vinh and scored a direct hit on the destroyer USS *Furse*.

Damage to the *Furse* was reported as minor, mostly from shrapnel sprayed across the decks in shelling that occurred Monday.

(At least one Delawarean is aboard the *Furse*. He is Lt. (j.g.) H.H. Abernathy Jr., 24 the son of Mr. and Mrs. H.H. Abernathy Sr. of 802 Princeton Road, Westover Hills.)

Spokesmen said 24 rounds of shells from Communist shore batteries exploded around the destroyers but a haze over the beach prevented crewmen of the *Furse* from spotting the shore batteries.

My parents first heard we had been hit from the newspaper and immediately contacted Bill Roth, the senator from Delaware at that time. His office quickly responded that I had not been hurt. No e-mails or cell phones then!

This was the first incident of *Furse* being involved in direct combat. The captain had a plaque made with a piece of shrapnel mounted on it and an inscription memorializing this event:

A Souvenir from the
North Vietnam Government
Delivered on Board
USS Furse (DD 882)
7 October, 1968
In Consternation over Services
Rendered While a Unit of
Sea Dragon Forces

When I returned to Vietnam in the late 1990s I visited a war museum near the coastal city of Vinh. By then more than half of the people living in Vietnam had been born after the war and these war museums were relics to them, mostly gathering dust. But I was curious about how the war had been portrayed from the North Vietnamese point of view. The central display was a large pile of metal made up of parts from downed US aircraft. This struck me as a crude but a visually powerful display. Around the walls were maps and commentary on military actions as well as photos of North Vietnamese army officers and troops. One map portrayed the coast and showed an image of a US destroyer steaming offshore with what looked like statistics of ships hit by shore guns. We were about the only visitors to the museum for the 20 minutes we were there and the few staff looked at us curiously, probably sensing that we were American veterans. At a similar museum in Hanoi there were a few older Vietnamese men sitting on the steps, probably former NVA soldiers, who also eyed us. Though the park of this museum was well attended, there were no visitors to the museum other than us.

I was impressed by how far this beautiful country had progressed and by the openness of the people, particularly the children. Americans were welcomed back, and many veterans, including the ones who had invited me, were actively involved in commerce with their former enemies. Vietnam had been involved in wars with its neighbors and occupying powers for centuries and our war was just their latest. Whether the appearance of having healed from the carnage of the war was real I couldn't tell.

One image in particular struck me. On a visit to the countryside we chanced upon a forlorn old building sitting in a field. We were told this simple masonry building with rectangular openings in the walls for windows, a bare dirt floor, and a worn blackboard on one wall was a one-room schoolhouse. About 20 primitive wooden chairs were lined up facing the blackboard. On the blackboard were still visible what must have been the last lessons of the previous session—algebraic formulas in neat script. This was reportedly an elementary school, and if so the level of math being taught in this remote farming community was well beyond what was being taught to similar ages in the United States.

Literacy in Vietnam was well above 90 percent. There was also evidence everywhere of the ingenuity of people to achieve surprising results with limited resources. Street vendors, often young kids, sold surprisingly realistic model planes cut and shaped from empty Coca-Cola cans. Roads in the cities were constructed in muddy areas by pounding thousands of bamboo stalks into the ground at close intervals to provide a solid mat foundation on which the paving was poured. Bamboo was lashed together into scaffolds to help construct buildings of ten stories or more in height. No wonder damage we had done with our guns got repaired so quickly and efficiently.

There was also a great sense of health consciousness at all ages. While in Hanoi I would go out for early morning runs as soon as the sun rose, only to find the parks already swarming with people engaged in tai chi or other exercises. Of course it was very hot and humid and the early morning was prime time for this before the heat of the day became intense. There were many groups of older people exercising in seemingly choreographed movement sequences—slow sweeps of arms and legs more like judo in slow motion. These routines looked like they had been developed over years and had a mystical as well as physical dimension to them. They also spoke of the inner strength and patience of the Vietnamese people who had outlasted their enemies for centuries.

Call the ball

Chasing the bird farm, author on bridge wing

Damage to HMAS *Hobart* from friendly fire,
June 17, 1968 (image Wikipedia)

Author being lowered in the motor whaleboat

Deceptively peaceful coast off Phan Thiet

Visit from in-country allies and adviser

Junks fished while we prepared to fire

Junks continued fishing while we fired

Cleanup before next firing mission

Looking up at the *America* as she looks down at us

Author on ASROC deck with replenishment detail

Mary and her crew paint the sides while the chief watches

Dinner in Hong Kong with supply and weapons officers.
(author in center)

The captain is on the bridge

The USS *New Jersey*, a beautiful sight at dawn in the Tonkin Gulf,
October 5, 1968

Author bringing *Furse* alongside the *USS New Jersey* (BB 62),
with CO and XO on the bridge

Two Navy classics, bow-on

Author with his 1953 MGTD

Proposed *Zumwalt* (DDG 1000) class destroyer

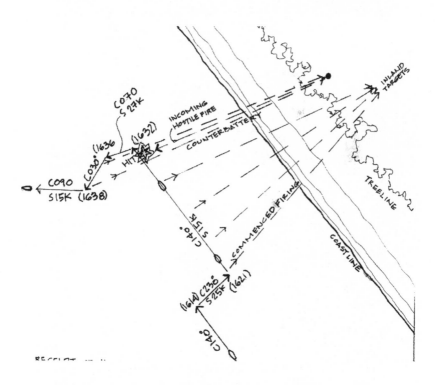

Ship's path when hostile fire received October 7, 1968

Furse fires back

Furse takes a hit on the hanger deck

Hanger deck damage from below

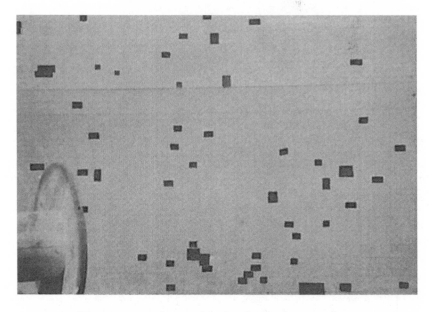

Tape covers shrapnel holes in the hangar door

Entering San Francisco, a grey but happy day

A long, hot day in the locks

Eight months and 70,000 nautical miles later...

Home at last

Captain Greeley

Author (center) receiving CINCPACFLT Letter of Commendation

Pam in our elegant Norfolk apartment

July 1969- one more month!

Fall 1969 at Rice

Entering port

First Division--irreverent, irrepressible, indispensable!

12

BACK TO THE FUTURE

On 9 October, the Commanding Officer of the Australian Guided Missile Ship HMAS PERTH relieved COMDESDIV 22 as Northern Sea Dragon Commander. 10 October was a good day for all hands as FURSE departed the Tonkin Gulf operations area on the first leg of the transit back to Norfolk, Virginia. *(FURSE Command History of 1968)*

Like the 1985 movie,[12.1] we had been in a state of suspended animation from our regular lives. The difference is that we couldn't just rev up the engine and blast through the time warp—it would take us more than a month at 15 knots to return to Norfolk.

Departure and Return to the United States

My thoughts in our last month were on my wedding in mid-December, just two weeks after we were to arrive back in Norfolk. Every few days I awaited the mail drop for the latest letter from my fiancée telling of how the plans were going. Fortunately Pam and her mother were (and still are) extremely well organized and were taking care of all arrangements. I expressed an opinion about silver and china patterns when asked but ultimately was happy to leave these decisions to her. Through the years she and I have remained remarkably in agreement over design matters; whenever we have renovated houses I have relied on her suggestions as much as my own design sense.

When the day arrived for us to leave Vietnam we were steaming as usual along the coast when, without any hoopla, an announcement came over the 1MC that we were changing course for home. It was as if we were just going on another mission. There was no celebratory reaction among the crew except for a palpable relaxation in tension and conversations that turned to home. I wrote to Pam on October 10, 1968:

> This morning we turned our bow eastward. The psychological impact was tremendous—everyone felt the strain finally begin to ease. It was a beautiful morning. We have been operating with the Australian destroyer HMAS PERTH; her CO was task unit commander. He called us this morning via radio and said tersely: "You are released to proceed home to a well-deserved leave."
>
> As a reward for our service, the Captain has given each of the three officers of the deck that stood all of the bridge watches during Sea Dragon a week without watches. I got mine between Yokosuka and Midway. We each had averaged 4 or less hrs. of sleep/day for 12 days.
>
> I am a little curious about whether our hostile fire incident was reported in the local news. If so, how?

Our last stint on northern Sea Dragon had in many ways been the most intense, with all other thoughts shoved to the background to keep our minds focused on staying alert on little sleep while fulfilling urgent and often unpredictable missions. And then all of a sudden not only did things return to normal operationally but we were headed home. We had to reestablish the ties to our previous lives. But we could not recalibrate instantaneously even as we left behind the intensity of the previous weeks and months. My reaction to this was to enjoy the moment before facing up to responsibilities I had put on hold, mostly related to my fast-approaching marriage.

I exchanged many letters over the following weeks with Pam and my family. Each helo that dropped mail to us was a symbol of our tenuous connection to the real world. Reality would appear at the sight and sound of its rotors and recede again as it disappeared. But the measured pace of the trip in the vast open ocean gave me time to sort out my emotions and emerge from my narrow focus solely on my shipboard duties.

The return trip was basically a repeat of the trip out—long periods of steaming at 15 knots to conserve fuel. We island-hopped and eventually arrived in Hawaii again. I took another spin on the beach before we resumed our journey. I also spent a day trying to learn to surf but all I had to show for it were scarred legs and hands from falling onto the coral reefs a few feet below the surface. Training was still held but at a relaxed pace. No more firing chaff rounds.

Our route was slightly altered along the West Coast going south to the Panama Canal. Our first port in the mainland United States was San Francisco, followed by Acapulco, Mexico. We couldn't complain. It had all been a pretty routine crossing of the Pacific, but a few more bumps in the road awaited us.

Murder on Board

> San Francisco was the next stop on the way home,
> with 5 days in port from 5 to 10 November. *(FURSE
> Command History of 1968)*

I was looking forward to San Francisco because Pam was flying out to meet me. At 0605 on November 5, 1968, on my watch we sighted the San Francisco lightship and stationed the special sea detail for entering port. First Division huddled in their blues on the foc's'le in an expectant mood. A small boat approached with a pilot and at 0753 we passed under the Golden Gate Bridge as the fog and cold dissipated and the sun was rising. Passing beneath the Golden Gate is the West Coast equivalent to entering New York Harbor under the Verrazano Bridge with the Statue of Liberty in the distance. It was a gray but happy day. At 0813 we passed Alcatraz and at 0823 passed under the San Francisco–Oakland Bay Bridge. At 0858 we were moored port side to berth 9 Pier 2, U.S. Naval Air Station, Alameda, California. We had arrived in the continental United States.

I left the ship just before dinner and headed into San Francisco to meet Pam at her hotel. When I returned to the ship the next morning the pier was cordoned off by shore patrol officers. As I approached to show my ID I asked what was going on and was informed that there had been a murder on the ship and everyone who was on board at the time was being detained pending an investigation. I had been very lucky to be off of the ship when it had happened.

I went immediately to the wardroom to find someone who could fill in the details. The supply officer told me that he had been sitting in the wardroom in the early hours of the morning when he heard noises in the adjacent cook's compartment. The door burst open and one of the stewards carrying a bloody butcher knife rushed by and headed out the aft wardroom door chased by one of the cooks. It was alleged he had stabbed a very well-liked first class cook who had returned from liberty drunk and could not defend himself.

The steward was chased off the ship and down the pier by a group of angry sailors intent on meting out their own retribution on behalf of their popular shipmate, but fortunately for the steward he was apprehended by the shore patrol first. Both perpetrator and victim were taken to the naval hospital and at 0402 the ship received word that the cook had died of stab wounds to the chest. At 0541 Naval Investigative Service agents came aboard.

The cooks and stewards coexisted amicably. The stewards served the officers exclusively, so they interacted with the cooks primarily in meal preparation. The stewards were by and large accepted and well liked, or so it appeared to me. They had general quarters stations and assisted with working parties like the rest of the men. The altercation between this particular steward and cook could have been for any number of reasons—there are no records that I could find on the investigation or disposition of this tragic occurrence.

This was a shock to all of us and cast a pall over our reentry to the United States. The next morning I left as early as I could to see my fiancée and avoid entanglement in what promised to be a significant hiccup in our return journey. I stayed off the ship with her as much as possible until she had to return to the East Coast. We took a trip down the Big Sur coast by car and then back to San Francisco. It was great to watch the waves pounding on the shore and the seals cavorting on the rocks along this scenic drive south of San Francisco. At one point seagulls swarmed about us in a scene right out of Hitchcock's movie *The Birds*. I would be retracing this route in a matter of days by water.

The ship was delayed for a few days for witnesses to be interviewed and for the onboard part of the investigation to take place. It was all pretty clear-cut from what I had heard, though I never found out what sentence had been set. According to the others there had been an argument between the steward and the cook earlier in the day and the steward was lying in wait. This was a scene right out of the popular program now airing on television called *NCIS* (Naval Criminal Investigative Service), but in this case there was really no mystery and lots of evidence.

We steamed out of Oakland on a foggy morning with lookouts on the bow. The abutments of the San Francisco–Oakland Bay Bridge loomed up out of the murk about 50 yards away before we passed close by them, a little disconcerting for those of us on the bow. Visibility had partially improved by the time we passed Alcatraz and exited under the Golden Gate Bridge, again marveling at the structure as we passed below. We had a close call when we were in open sea still thick with fog. A sailboat that must not have shown on the radar in the choppy waters suddenly appeared just off our bow. This time both we and the sailboat altered course to avoid getting dangerously close, though she had the right-of-way.

San Diego

When we arrived at our pier at the San Diego Naval Base my friend Steve Hayes was there to meet us. I saw him on the pier as we approached but was busy supervising getting our mooring lines and the brow across to the pier before he could come on board. Steve had recently started Swift Boat school at Coronado across the bay.

We had a mutual friend from Wilmington who was living in San Diego at the time and we joined him for dinner. Steve told us about his training and the Swift Boats, which he really seemed to enjoy after a year slogging away on an LST, one of the slowest, hardest-riding ship types in the fleet due to its flat bottom. He regretted that he would miss my wedding. He had known both me and Pam since we were kids and had been a surrogate brother to me growing up.

Acapulco and Return to Norfolk

> Manzanillo, Mexico was used as a fuel stop on 15 November; FURSE arrived in Acapulco, Mexico, for R&R on the 16th. COMDESDIV 22 hosted a luncheon for local Mexican military commanders and the Mayor of Acapulco on board FURSE during the visit. Guests included Admiral RIGOBERTO OTAL, commander Eight naval Zone, and Senora Otal; Brigadier general SALAZAR, Mexican Army, representing the commander, Twenty-Seventh Military Zone, and Senora SALAZAR; Lieutenant General CASTRO, Mexican Air force, and Senora CASTRO; and Senor HEREDIA, Mayor of Acapulco. *(FURSE Command History of 1968)*

We remembered our previous near debacle fueling in Manzanillo and were happy this one was smoother. Then on to the destination we all were awaiting, Acapulco.

Acapulco Harbor is a beautiful round bay embedded in the southwestern coast of Mexico just north of its boundary with El Salvador. It is justifiably known as one of the most attractive tourist destinations in Mexico, and we arrived in mid-November when tourist season was strong. We anchored in the middle of the bay. Shortly after we anchored the ops officer asked if anyone knew French—our captain had received an invitation from a French ship in the harbor to a reception on board and someone needed to answer the invitation and deliver it. I knew enough to help draft a reply and wrote it as neatly as I could on the ship's stationery before entrusting it to a very squared-away junior officer from the Naval Academy to deliver by boat. When he returned he was sopping wet. He had stepped off of the boat to board the French ship and slipped and fell into the water. He had managed to hold the invitation above his head and was able to climb out and deliver it still dry.

We had invited the local Mexican military commander to come to an evening reception on board our ship the following day. The deck crew was sent over the sides on stages (planks suspended by lines) to clean and repaint. Someone noticed that there seemed to be some oil in the water coming from our ship. Somehow one of the bilge pumps had been activated and was pumping oily water over the side, creating a thick slick of oil that ringed the ship, extending outward about 200 yards. Immediately our whaleboat was rushed into action to put booms around the expanding slick while dispersant powder was sprinkled on it. We just hoped we could keep it from reaching the beaches and from being noticeable to those coming out that evening for the reception.

I was designated to accompany the XO in the boat sent to transport the commandant from the pier to our ship at anchorage. We waited as long as we could to depart to give the sun time to fade and our crew maximum time to clean the oil before picking him up. The boat coxswain returned on a less than direct course to avoid the worst of the spill as the XO kept him in conversation so he would not notice still visible clumps of oil. It all seemed to work and he was eventually returned ashore without an inkling of the problem. Crews worked late into the night with dispersant and had it pretty well cleaned up the next day.

While in Acapulco we were granted complimentary use of the facilities at an upscale resort called Las Brisas at the south end of the harbor. A few of us rented a "sailfish," a small sailboat with a centerboard, which we sailed out to the ship in the afternoon in light breezes. We arrived as others were swimming off of the side of the ship. Several intrepid sailors jumped or dove off of the bridge wing almost 20 feet above the water. They thoroughly enjoyed the rare treat of using the ship as their diving platform. Returning our rented sailboat took some time since the breezes had slackened and our sailing skills were mediocre. We spent the evening in town and left the next day sunburned from too much exposure.

The trip down the coast and back through the Panama Canal was routine. Going through the locks was less exciting on the return trip—basically sitting out in the hot sun for hours monitoring the lines as we slowly ascended from the Pacific and descended to the Atlantic in the locks. Finally we were back in our home ocean.

I don't remember much about the trip through the Gulf of Mexico and along the East Coast of the United States. We passed Cape Hatteras, a point jutting into the ocean off the coast of North Carolina where storms and heavy seas are the norm. On an earlier cruise from our annual Springboard exercises in the Caribbean we had run into a severe storm there that had caused the ship to heel over almost to its maximum righting moment (the position from which it will not return to a vertical position). Steve Hayes and I had spent several weeks each summer on Nags Head, North Carolina, just north of Hatteras and had roamed the beaches where the remains of wooden hulls from earlier ships wrecked along that infamous coast had washed ashore. I hoped we didn't join them. It was the only time in the Navy I remember being truly scared. The captain, as usual, seemed unconcerned, or hid it well from the rest of us.

Our return to Norfolk on November 26, 1968, the day before Thanksgiving, marked the end of an eight-month deployment that seemed more like a year. We steamed back into our familiar harbor and to our pier where a small band was playing and family members were waiting. I knew no one was going to be there to meet me since I would be returning home within a few days. I was glad that I would have those few days to adjust to being in port and getting my shipboard duties in order before making my way north.

The letter Captain Greeley wrote on the title page of the *Furse WestPac Cruise Book* sums up his and our sense of what we accomplished during this deployment:

From the Captain:

The cruise we made together through the troubled waters of the Tonkin Gulf will long stand in my memory as the most satisfying deployment of my Naval career. This is so primarily because of the vital nature of FURSE's mission in waters off Vietnam as an instrument in the Allied fight against the Communists.

Beyond that, I take particular pride in your performance throughout the demanding cruise. You were called upon to work long hours with only a minimum amount of sleep. You were expected to do many things, from refueling underway on dark nights to responding on short notice to calls for fire from Allied units on the beach. You carried out our varied assignments expeditiously and in a highly professional manner, earning for FURSE numerous plaudits for her excellent performance.

As you know, the deployment was a difficult and demanding one. But few things worth doing are easy, and you have returned from this cruise much better men for the experience. That you handled every task assigned you professionally has earned you my lasting respect, and it is for this reason that I dedicate this book to you, the men of FURSE.

Well done and my best wishes
M. T. Greeley
Commander, United States Navy
Commanding Officer

I had stored my car at home before I left so I took a bus, a somewhat lonely but peaceful trip through Maryland and Delaware.

I was the only person on the bus in uniform—not sure why I did not travel in my civilian clothes. I think because my identity was now as a naval officer and I wanted to present myself both to the public and my family in this image. My parents and fiancée picked me up from the bus station. They were curious about the various ribbons since all they had seen when I left was the small red National Defense ribbon everyone gets when they join. I knew I was returning to a world where there was some hostility to the Vietnam War and those who fought in it, but I was comfortable in the uniform and proud to wear it.

The next two weeks were a blur of wedding activities culminating in our marriage on December 14, 1968. Most of my ushers were fellow officers on the ship. No crossed swords over the departing bride and groom—we decided to keep it nonmilitary, and in any case there wasn't time to work this into the ceremony. It had started to snow when we left the reception and were driven to a hotel at the Philadelphia airport for an early morning flight to San Juan, Puerto Rico, for a connecting flight to the island of Virgin Gorda in the Caribbean. As we flew in the small plane from San Juan to the island I looked down at one point and saw a ship that looked like a destroyer. I knew that that would be me again before too long on another Springboard. I was surprised that even on my honeymoon I identified with a ship similar to mine. I still clung to it as my home.

When we returned we rented an apartment in a complex that was 90 percent Navy personnel, a few miles from the base. For the first time I would be living off of the ship and driving daily to the base like it was just a job. The ship would no longer be my home. My stateroom would now just be a place I slept when I was on board. It would belong more to the other officers who lived on the ship full time. I was like a student who moved off campus coming back to stay with his former roommates in the dorm occasionally.

We furnished the apartment with an eclectic mix of furniture from parents and college. I put up some shelves and artwork I had done in school. We used a folding card table as our dining table. One weekend we took a trip to Washington, D.C., and went to some trendy shops in Georgetown. We loved the idea of picking out our own things as a married couple and bought, among other things, an inexpensive inflatable chair.

In a letter to my parents describing our new apartment I wrote:

> We have fixed it up to some extent now. Pam has made curtains for the bedroom and living room. Her maiden effort, but a considerable one without a sewing machine, especially considering the size of our windows. We still don't have a dining room table, but have been content to eat off our coffee table.

As a newly married couple we participated shortly thereafter in Mess Night on the ship, a formal dinner on board with dress uniforms and long dresses for the wives. Pam had now become a Navy wife.

One of the traditions of the Navy is for a newly married couple to call on the captain and vice versa. In each case the protocol is to leave a calling card unobtrusively in a silver dish in the hallway. We arranged a date to call on the captain at his house in a suburb of Norfolk and eventually settled on a date for him and his wife to call on us at our apartment. The captain and his wife arrived right on time and we showed them into the apartment. We had our little dish in the living room where he left his card.

After showing them around our three rooms we all sat down in the living room where we served hors d'oeuvres and drinks. The captain's wife sat on our Danish-modern sofa, we sat on our folding dining chairs, and the captain opted for the inflatable chair. As the conversation went on we noticed him sinking further and further into it—it was slowly losing air and he was trying to remain nonchalant. Finally one of us said, "Sorry about that chair, why don't you move to the sofa?" He was a good sport and we had a good laugh about it later.

Captain Greeley was diligent in ensuring that his officers and men were credited for their contributions while in the Tonkin Gulf. There was an awards ceremony at which the XO presented medals and commendations. I was pleased to receive a Commander Pacific Fleet (CINCPACFLT) Letter of Commendation, signed by Admiral Hyland.

There is a degree of cynicism related to the issuance of medals by the military. Some feel that there is a political dimension to the choice of who gets recognized. Looking at those to whom these honors were granted on the *Furse* there are none that I would question. Both officers and enlisted personnel were represented at almost every level. But not one boatswain's mate was on the list to take his place alongside the machinist mate, the signalmen, the radiomen, the electronics technician, the supply clerk, the gunner's mate, the hospitalman, and the quartermaster. The men from First Division were unsung in comparison to others but certainly had been indispensable in both deck and gunnery operations during the deployment. Everyone received the Vietnam campaign ribbons as well as the combat action ribbon. It is also interesting that of the 33 awards, only four were for those in the Naval Reserve (USNR) versus regular Navy (USN), and all of those were for junior officers. All but one of the enlisted awards were for third class petty officer and above, which would generally only include regular Navy.

Civilians often think that military personnel are showing off with their chests full of medals. I had a teacher in high school who was a decorated veteran who displayed his ribbons in cases at his home. In the age of the antihero I thought this was a bit self-aggrandizing when I saw them at a class party at his house one day. But after serving I came to understand the pride of those who had achieved these distinctions.

Corporate equivalents are less colorful but no less recognizable in the cut of one's clothes, the car one drives, the club one belongs to, and the neighborhood one lives in. Professional degrees mounted on the office wall are de rigueur for doctors and lawyers. In sports, letters are given for making a team or stickers on helmets for special plays made in football. We seem to have a need to display our distinctions. So the military is not alone, and one could argue that military ribbons are more objective since they are about documented campaigns or actions and do not carry a social or class dimension.

13

INTO THE SUNRISE

Leaving Norfolk

On 24 February FURSE sailed for SPRINGBOARD with Captain K. J. Cole, COMDESDIV TWO TWO embarked. Extensive ASW operations were conducted with Task Group 83.7 and officers and men prepared for the strenuous operations scheduled for the Puerto Rico Operations area.

During SPRINGBOARD FURSE successfully completed all required gunnery validation exercises, with an average score of 140 percent. Two ASROC exercise shots and two torpedo tube exercise shots were conducted, all being evaluated hits.

Ports visited during SPRINGBOARD included San Juan, Puerto Rico from 11 to 14 March, St. Thomas Virgin Islands, 18 to 20 March, and St. Croix, Virgin Islands, 24 to 26 March. *(FURSE Command History of 1969)*

We had been mostly in port for three months prior to heading to another Springboard in late February 1969 and then east, this time into the rising sun, a voyage with a totally different vibe than our westward adventure toward the setting sun. Though taking me away from home once again it was also taking me toward the advent of my new civilian life. But first I was sent to gunnery school in anticipation of relieving the soon-to-depart gunnery officer, whom I had first met when we briefly roomed together at Dam Neck at the start of our tours on *Furse*.

I went back to Dam Neck to gunnery school with little enthusiasm since I already knew a lot about gunnery, but I also knew I needed a refresher to pick up knowledge about administrative and maintenance duties. In addition to taking apart and reassembling a .50 caliber machine gun and firing it on the range my strongest memory is of a rat scurrying under the table where we ate lunch and up the leg of one of our instructors who shook it off and chased it with a pipe as we all howled. I did learn about calibrations that had to be done on our 5"/38 caliber guns including one called arbitrary correction to hit (ACTH) that I would be required to compute later.

I remember thinking I had more experience than the others and should finish first in the class of 11, but I was beaten by one other guy and finished second by a whisker. He also knew we were close, and after the final grades I avoided him so he would not have a chance to gloat. Whereas I had good memories of DASH school at this same facility at the beginning of my days on the *Furse*, this minicompetition was about all that made this school interesting in the last half year of my naval career.

Arbitrary Correction to Miss

I was called upon to perform the arbitrary correction to hit calculation during a gunnery exercise at sea not long after gunnery school. I conferred with the first class gunner's mate to make sure we did it correctly. It involved firing at a surface target and recording the deviation of the actual landing point from the calculated landing point. This deviation was recorded for a lot of shots to determine the fudge factor (arbitrary correction) necessary to be applied to the guns so that the projectile would hit the target. This is a little like sighting a rifle and applying windage.

I stayed up practically all night with a multipage form running the many calculations required. The next morning I gave the calculated correction to the first class gunner's mate so he could enter it prior to the day's gunnery exercises. At the end of another day of shooting we had substantially improved our accuracy. I called the gunner's mate to my stateroom to congratulate him, and by implication myself, for such a good job with the abstruse and lengthy calculations. He informed me that he had ignored what I had given him and put in a correction based on his own long experience with our guns. He popped my bubble, but who cared as long as we were hitting the targets. His experience beat my blind reliance on rote calculations. I later learned from Captain Greeley's daughter that he bragged about how good his "shooters" were.

I eventually relieved the outgoing gunnery officer. Relieving a fellow officer is an exercise in noting all existing deficiencies in materiel, equipment, and personnel. The officer being relieved is obligated to correct as many deficiencies as possible prior to the date of relief; those deficiencies that remain are included in the relieving letter. It's a little like a punch list in building construction. For example, items d and e in the relieving letter with the former second division officer (gunnery assistant) stated:

> d. Training Status-Director and mount crews will be rusty initially due to loss of experienced personnel, particularly the pointer, trainer, and Director Officer in the director.

e. Equipage Status-Borescope and bore erosion gauge are rusting from lack of preservation. Many landing force items are rotting from submergence in salt water during the ordnance storeroom flood last Springboard.

The fact was that a lot of gear and equipment was in less than satisfactory shape at any given time, and these turnovers were opportunities for correcting the most serious deficiencies, or at the very least of bringing them out in the open. The landing force items referred to were not taken too seriously since it was almost certain that we would never mount a landing force, for which we had virtually no training.

We departed for my final Springboard on February 24, 1969, and our temporary home port, San Juan, Puerto Rico. I knew the drill but it was still physically taxing. The trip down was rough, with many sick sailors. Going back to sea was an adjustment even in good weather. I wrote on February 28, 1969:

> This morning was tiring. I conned the ship alongside an oiler for almost 3 hrs. while refueling. I was on the bridge from 7 AM to 1:30 PM and have watch again tonight from 8–12 PM.
>
> Time is becoming meaningless. One day runs into the next with little distinction. Standing watches around the clock is the reason.

I also had to learn some new skills at my new GQ station in the fire control director.

It was nice to be in the open air at the very top of the ship rather than in the dimly lit, stuffy confines of CIC. I was almost totally dependent on the target acquisition skills of the second class FT responsible for locking on the targets. All I really had to do was to give the command to commence firing to the gun captain once I got it from the bridge and we were locked on. Though there were a few new people in the director, the second class FT who had the most experience was still with us and made me look good.

On the return trip to Norfolk on April 3, 1969, we helped sink a World War II destroyer for surface gunnery practice. These aging hulks were prepared as targets by closing all of their watertight compartments to make them harder to sink. A line of eight destroyers made the approach and successively unleashed their 5-inch batteries as their guns bore on the target. It was awesome and somewhat unsettling to see pieces of superstructure fly off the hulk as she was hit. Eventually she sank and we tracked her descent with sonar. This gave us a feel for what it was like in WWII surface battles, albeit with a stable target. We got the most hits of any destroyer by patiently using the bracket-and-halving method before firing for effect.

Springboard was, as usual, a trial of endurance and sleep deprivation. When we returned to Norfolk my wife had fixed an elaborate meal for our first evening together in eight weeks. I walked into the door of the apartment and headed straight for the bed where I fell fast asleep and could not be awakened until the next morning. What a relief to be home! My wife served what she could salvage the next night, not too happy I missed the full production the night before.

Early Out

At this point I had about seven months left in the Navy. The military had initiated an early-out program for those who planned to go back to school. A person could be granted a three-month early out if he was accepted into a school and provided proof of acceptance. I knew by now that I wanted to go back to school and get either an architecture or business degree, which would mean two or three more years. But I also knew I would have to work fast to get accepted into a school and get the paperwork submitted to be able to enter the following September.

I went to a local Norfolk business school to retake the GMAT boards I had taken before I entered the Navy. As soon as I got accepted I filled out the forms and got the captain's endorsement. When the early-out authorization to enter this school eventually came through, I realized I really wanted to follow my true interest, architecture. So I contacted both an architecture professor and a professor of English I knew well at my undergraduate school, Rice University. Both of them graciously said they would allow me to return without reapplying. I would have to repeat a year as a condition of my acceptance since I had been away from architecture now for five years. I withdrew my application from the local business school and got the paperwork amended to designate Rice as the school I would attend.

Meanwhile, Pam was making the best of Norfolk. The weapons officer and his wife lived across the street so we did a lot of socializing with them. She also learned to drive my stick shift car, with some memorable attempts at parallel parking, and she got a job at a local university. One of her qualities that I really admired (and still do) was her ability to adapt to circumstances in the most positive and supportive way. She was also a good sport when I had duty at night; she would come aboard to watch the movie with me even though the slightest rocking of the ship made her queasy.

One weekend in May 1969 we had a family cruise. Members of *Furse* families could come aboard for a day of steaming off the coast of Virginia Beach to see what our life at sea was like. My father could not come but my wife's father did. He would later become an Assistant Secretary of Defense in the Nixon/Ford administration and reconnect with our captain in the Pentagon. Pam's father was curious by nature and later flew in some of the advanced Air Force fighters when he was in the Pentagon.

We had great weather and went through some drills such as man overboard, in which an orange dummy that floats named Oscar (Oscar is the signal flag raised to indicate man overboard) is thrown over the side without warning and the OOD, who in this case happened to be me, goes to flank speed and does a 360-degree turn (a Williamson turn) toward the side from which the man went overboard which eventually comes back to the spot where he went in. The captain took the conn as we approached the dummy in order to make the final pickup. I was hoping I could do this but he had excellent ship-handling skills and wanted to make sure it all went smoothly for the spectators.

Sometimes it was easy to get lost in determining what effect the engine orders were actually having on the motion of the ship, particularly at low speed when tide, wind, and current also were factors. If things were really confused we would stop the engines and put the rudder amidships so the vessel could settle and we could see which way it drifted relative to small objects such as cigarettes that were dropped into the water. Then the engine orders could be given with more confidence. This technique was useful in man overboard drills to nudge the ship right up to the man without overshooting. I would often think of this later as a lesson for making sense of a confusing situation where the best action was to slow down, take a deep breath, and let things settle before proceeding.

Giving orders to change speed on a ship is not like using an accelerator on a car. There is a lag between the order given by the OOD and the actual execution in the engine room. The verbal order is first given to the helmsman using both a general speed range and a specific speed. For instance, "all ahead standard, make turns for seventeen knots" tells the helmsman that the order is for both engines (all), is for forward motion (ahead), is in the standard range (about 15 to 22 knots as I recall), and specifically for 17 knots. The helmsman communicates it by an electromechanical device, the engine order telegraph (EOT), to a person in the engine room who hears a bell and sees the dial of a slave device move to the same position. The engineman then moves the handles of his EOT to that position, which signals to the helmsman on the bridge that the order has been received. He next adjusts steam to the turbines to achieve this speed. This takes several seconds at least. Often speeds are changed less than a minute apart, which means a new speed is hardly achieved before the whole sequence repeats itself. In modern ships this operation is quicker with electronic and LED light signals.

The OOD has to be cognizant of the sequence of the orders. For instance, If he were going from "all ahead two thirds" to "all back two thirds" he would go through "all stop" first to create an orderly reduction in steam to the turbines. Of course in an emergency an "all back full" could be given—this was as close to slamming on the brakes as we had, but it still took some time to stop the ship's forward motion. I can't document this but my recollection is that at 15 knots it might take us several ship lengths, or about 1,000 feet, to stop the ship's forward motion after an "all back full" order.

At the end of the day the weather was starting to deteriorate and all were happy to get back to the pier. Our ship's family event was a nice outing for all, and the pride both the crew and their family members had for the ship and the U.S. Navy was obvious.

We had gotten orders to go on a six-plus-month Indian Ocean deployment, which meant that I would be on this cruise for only about two months before I would be released from the Navy. This struck me as wasteful since I would have to be flown back at the Navy's expense. Why couldn't I just be given shore duty in Norfolk for the remainder of my time? The captain did not see it this way and told me I would be going. One reason was my experience in enabling us to renew our gunnery qualifications at Culebra, as if thousands of rounds in Vietnam had not been enough.

Magical Mystery Tour

> On 2 July in company with USS RICH (DD 820) FURSE got underway for the Middle East. After gunfire support exercises in Culebra, fuel stops were

made at Roosevelt Roads, Puerto Rico from 5 July to
7 July and at Porto Grande, Cape Verde Island, from
14 July to 16 July.

FURSE crossed the equator at longitude 00–
00 on 21 July and all Pollywogs were duly initiated
into the Solemn Mysteries of the Ancient Order
of the Deep. Luanda, Angola, was the stopover
point from 23 July to 25 July. *(FURSE Command
History of 1969)*

As the 1967 Beatles song says, "The magical mystery tour is
waiting to take you away."

Once the ship left for the Indian Ocean cruise on July 2, 1969,
I would not be coming back to Norfolk. We packed our furniture
and Pam went back to Delaware to live with her parents for the two-
and-a-half months I would be away. I was beginning to withdraw
mentally from the Navy and to think ahead to life afterward. I tried
to resist developing the proverbial short-timer's attitude on this
final cruise. In particular I was anxious to score well again in our
requalifications at Culebra. I had become the gunnery officer and
a new ensign was now first lieutenant. Nothing had changed in the
format of the annual gunfire support qualifications (in spite of the
Commander Destroyer Squadron Two recommendations to make
them more realistic for conditions in Vietnam) and we were able to
achieve an almost perfect score.

My sentiments for the upcoming trip were expressed in a letter
of July 7, 1969:

We are in Roosevelt Roads after a hectic Saturday
of shooting and loading ammo. Today is Sunday,
and believe it or not, a working day for the crew. My
heart is not in it, though I am still going through the
motions.

Tomorrow at 8 AM we will leave for Porto Grande, Cape Verde Islands. The sooner, the better, as far as I am concerned.

I have not yet received mail here. This may be one of the last ports in which we will get mail on time. I feel like the ship is about to depart on a journey to the end of the earth. I can't wait until I am off—it's hard to believe that it will be less than a month.

I should mention one small occurrence before we left—the retirement from the Navy of my chief boatswain's mate, Chief Clemons. He was so experienced and so good with his men that he rarely needed to shout. It was hard to see him go. He was one of the older chiefs, which gave him an added air of authority. Though he was not loud he could be biting when disciplining someone. He knew every expression to bring a man down to size, and I only regret I did not write them down at the time.

In his final evaluation I gave him perfect scores in every category to honor his long and distinguished service. As was the custom when a chief retires we stationed an honor guard at the quarterdeck for his departure from the ship. He appeared in his dress uniform and we piped him ashore. As he came to me to say good-bye before saluting the flag and exiting down the brow, he gave me a salty salute and handed me his boatswain's knife, the most personal of a boatswain's mate's tools of the trade. I was deeply touched and still have it with its well-worn leather case and honed blade that attest to years of use.

The perfect score I gave the chief was well deserved, but there was a good deal of grade inflation in annual personnel evaluations. Anything less than an almost perfect score could slow down one's advancement at the higher levels. Comments were generally positive, but an experienced reader could discern whether they were sincere or simply damning with faint praise. This was particularly true at the level of lieutenant commander and above. At higher levels good words on the evaluation were not enough; an advocate at the captain or flag (admiral) level was invaluable if not required for further advancement.

Since we needed to conserve fuel we steamed at about 15 knots as we had across the Pacific. This was in many ways an idyllic crossing of the Atlantic. The temperatures were mild and the seas generally calm. We were treated to a succession of events both natural and unnatural that kept us entertained during this transit along the route of the sailing ships going back to Columbus's time that followed the east-west trade winds at these latitudes. It was an enjoyable and relatively low-key denouement to my three years in the Navy. I felt that I had been on the ship long enough and was mentally beginning to disengage. This cruise gave me the time to do so in a measured way.

One day we were visited by a good omen of maritime myth, an albatross. The bird appeared one day flying above us and eventually perched atop our rotating radar antenna on the forward mast. This posed a quandary for the ops officer: do we try to shoo it off to avoid interference or let it be? He was not about to defy the maritime spirits recalled in these stanzas from Coleridge's "Rime of the Ancient Mariner":[13.1]

At length did cross an Albatross,
Thorough the fog it came;
As if it had been a Christian soul,
We hail'd it in God's name.

It ate the food it ne'er had eat,
And round and round it flew.
The ice did split with a thunder-fit;
The helmsman steered us through!

And a good south wind sprung up behind;
The Albatross did follow,
And every day, for food or play,
Came to the mariner's hollo!

Though we were not dependent on breezes there was still a belief that good things would come to a ship that harbored an albatross. We were all surprised that it seemed to be unfazed by this constantly turning perch, but it stayed there for at least an hour before flying off. It eventually came back and perched on another, more stable part of the mast, and we felt comforted to know it had chosen us. It sometimes flew away for hours and would return again over a period of several days until it disappeared.

Dolphins also accompanied us on our steady course, flashing in and out of our bow wake and occasionally jumping clear of the water. The playfulness of these aquatic acrobats coupled with our visit by the albatross gave the journey an aura of being blessed by the sea gods.

One evening when the weather was calm someone noticed a blue glow circulating around parts of the ship on the upper decks. I had read about St. Elmo's fire and now was seeing it invade the superstructure of our ship. This electrical phenomenon, which normally accompanied the onset of thunderstorms, was named after the patron saint of sailors and was regarded with almost religious awe.[13.2] The faintly bluish globs were more defined as it got darker; they seemed to cling to the masts and lines and very slowly move over and around them like alien organisms touching and inspecting us and then slowly dissipating when their curiosity was satisfied. They lasted about a half an hour.

I was now glad that I had not been granted shore duty for these last few months so as to be able to witness these things I had only read about in classic seafaring novels. When you are far out at sea in a relatively small vessel, there is a feeling at times that you are in another world, enveloped in an expanse of ocean and sky that is fused into a continuum, and that events that would be strange elsewhere can happen here. When out of sight of land with the ocean as the only visible landscape, and especially when on the main deck only a few feet above the surface of the water, the texture of the waves—their ripples, their surges, their reflections and shadows—make it seem both mysterious and alive. The phosphorescent glow of plankton in our wake as the sun goes down was like going through a carpet of embers briefly rekindled as our bow knifed through them. These phenomena are timeless and link us to mariners of the past and draw men back to sea in spite of its rigors.

This experience is a qualitative one and greatly diminished for those on larger ships such as aircraft carriers and cruise ships where one is so far above the water. At that level the sea seems solid and detached, even hostile. The only glow one sees at night on a large cruise ship is from the myriad lights of these floating hotels. Ocean sailors, on the other hand, experience the sea most intimately as it washes over the gunwales when they heel or tack. The boat and crew become part of its contours as they rise and fall on its swells.

One early morning I reported for the 04–08 a.m. watch to relieve the engineering officer. I came out onto the bridge a little before 4 a.m. and he was in discussion with others on the bridge about a very bright object about 20 or 30 degrees above the horizon in front of us. It was too big to be a star and too small to be the moon. I immediately thought it was a planet such as Venus whose size was exaggerated by being so close to the horizon. But all of us agreed we had never seen Venus look so large. He decided to call the captain to report it since it was so out of the ordinary. The captain and the navigator also marveled at its size. As the day dawned it gradually grew fainter and disappeared with all of us none the wiser as to its cause or nature: UFO? Space object? Atmospheric aberration? I recently checked a website that allows one to see the sky at a particular location on a particular date, and sure enough there was Venus, but looking nowhere near as large as it had seemed to us that night.

We arrived in the Cape Verde Islands for a one-day stopover. These islands are volcanic in origin and have a rather stark, ashen landscape rising to a small volcanic peak. I visited the vibrant marketplace in an open barnlike building that was simple in shape and elegantly constructed. I took lots of pictures that I would later show to fellow architecture students at Rice as an example of indigenous architecture. Some sailors who had started their own rock band set up on the fantail to practice. This drew a cluster of curious onlookers fascinated by the blaring sounds in this otherwise peaceful setting. I wrote on July 16, 1969:

> We have left Porto Grande now enroute to Luanda Angola. I spent about two and one half hours seeing Porto Grande. It was hot and dusty, and the beer wasn't cold.

No question about my priorities—cold beer.

As we left Porto Grande and closed in on the coast of Africa the reality of my impending departure began to rise in my consciousness. I held it at bay, though, because in one sense I really couldn't believe it was happening and I did not want to appear any different to my shipmates. I had seen others leave the ship and remembered how ambivalent I had felt knowing they were going to another world while the rest of us had to soldier on. I took it a day at a time, unobtrusively savoring quiet moments of enjoyment in this low-stress cruise. Our collective consciousness was diverted for a day by the upcoming moon landing.

The first landing by a human on the moon was by Apollo 11 astronauts and took place as we crossed the Atlantic about mid-ocean.[13.3] It occurred late at night on July 16, 1969, and we listened to it on a static-filled radio fed to the bridge wing speaker. I was thankful we were hearing it at sea with the moon and stars brightly visible in the clear night sky, which made us feel more connected to astronauts Armstrong, Aldrin, and Collins circling and setting foot on our nearest celestial neighbor as we listened. We did feel a bit cheated that we could not see the live pictures until later since we had no TV on board.

I wrote to Pam on Sunday night, July 16:

Just finished listening to the moon landing on the radio. They have broken through man's age old dream, and I will cross the equator for the first time in just a few hours. I wanted more than anything to be able to watch on television—I've been at sea for every one of the Apollo missions. I hope you watched for both of us.

Five days later, on July 21, 1969, I wrote that the cruise was taking on a new, more mellow tenor:

For the first time in my naval career I have been having a good time. The weather has been balmy—I have had time to do some sunning, plenty of reading, and even some strumming on John Vaughan's guitar.

I still feel it hard to think of being off of the ship. I have begun to check days off my calendar, but this does not really help.

We sailed directly south along the coast of Africa and soon we were approaching the equator. About half of us aboard were about to be initiated into Neptune's realm in the Crossing the Line (equator) ceremony.

The ceremony of Crossing the Line is an initiation rite in the Royal Navy, U.S. Navy, U.S. Coast Guard, U.S. Marine Corps, and other navies that commemorates a sailor's first crossing of the Equator. Originally, the tradition was created as a test for seasoned sailors to ensure their new shipmates were capable of handling long rough times at sea. Sailors who have already crossed the Equator are nicknamed (Trusty) Shellbacks, often referred to as Sons of Neptune; those who have not are nicknamed (Slimy) Pollywogs.[13.4]

This took me a little by surprise since I knew very little about it. The ship slowed and the announcement was made that all duties were suspended for the day; all Pollywogs were to be judged to see if they were fit to become Shellbacks. King Neptune and his court were summoned to the main deck to prepare the tests of worthiness. All Pollywogs were to stay off the main deck until ordered to report for judgment.

A BT chief (boiler tender chief) who was the oldest and most experienced chief on board was King Neptune. As we waited for the festivities to begin, one of the more senior officers announced he was not going to take part—it was all too juvenile and he saw no reason to subject himself to the petty abuse he knew was coming. In the end he relented and joined in the spirit of the occasion.

When announced, we reported to the foc's'le in bathing suits or underwear to begin the gauntlet. We were ordered by Shellbacks dressed as mermaids to crawl on our knees to the first station where our hair was chopped off crudely with barber scissors. On the way we were paddled on our butts by Shellbacks. Then we entered a long rubber tube about 3 feet in diameter and 20 feet long filled with garbage collected from recent meals. When we emerged we were led, still on our knees, to another "throne," where a mermaid asked us to open our mouth and receive Neptune's libation. A green, foul-tasting liquid (I never found out what it was) was squirted into our mouths by a large syringe. Then finally to the throne where sat King Neptune; we were read the charges against us and judged by Neptune, who with a wave of his scepter forgave our crimes and pronounced us Shellbacks. The general and specific charges against me read (spelling mistakes and all):

> **Whereas**: You have conspired to enter the royal domain without visa, passport or proper authorization.

> **Whereas:** You have failed to maintain the personal hygienic perfection required to enter this domain. To Wit: you have allowed to cover your body and

enter into your mind a certain amount of slime
that is usually found on pollywogs and other lower
specimen of the realm.

Whereas: You are further charged with brown baggery,
mopery, dopeing off, chit requesting, apple polishing,
sympathy seeking, gun decking, procrastination, gold
bricking, liberty hounding, and reveille neglecting.

Whereas: You are specifically charged with Heinous
crimes of: 1. Planning to leave the ship in Lourenço
Marques. 2. Threatening to throw the royal coffin
over the side.

Wherefore: The people of the domain of Imperium
Neptuni Regis, state of the raging main, Equatoria,
pray that the defendent be brought before the royal
court forthwith and be tried before the benevolent
judges presiding.

When the court dismissed the charges and allowed us to enter
the kingdom we were hosed off with a fire hose to get the muck off
of us. I described the ceremony in a letter of July 24, 1969:

We crossed the equator in a ceremony in which great
swathes of my hair were removed without any design.
The deepest cuts leave about ¼". There is still enough
long stuff to comb over the stubble. Hopefully the
scars will be mostly healed by the time I return. At least
my shaggy tufts will keep the airline stewardesses away.

It was all in good fun though some groused that the paddling
had been a little vindictive. Officers were treated no differently than

enlisted men. Unpleasant as it was at some points, most of us were glad that we got the full treatment rather than some token facsimile of this traditional ceremony. I was impressed by the planning that had gone into it before we left port, including creating and personalizing the Crossing the Line certificates. This was certainly more memorable than the Golden Dragon certificate we had received for crossing the international date line (the 180th meridian) on the WestPac cruise, which was issued with no ceremony.

The ship was cleaned up as we proceeded on our way to Luanda, Angola. Angola is a former Portuguese colony located about midway down the western African coast below the bulge.[13.5] We had been advised that it was on the verge of civil war and highly unstable and we should remain aboard. If we did go ashore we should stick to bars close to the ship where the shore patrol was present. I was assigned as one of the liaisons with the local police who came on board to meet with us; they looked like hardened criminals themselves carrying not only guns but sheathed machetes and hats with a skull symbol on them. I found it hard to accept that they were even legitimate police. Their advice was basically the same— neither they nor anyone could protect us from indiscriminate acts of violence that could and did occur regularly. We were only there for a day and were happy to leave.

The departure from Angola was an important milestone for me in this cruise. I would be discharged from the ship at the next port, Lourenço Marques (now Maputo), Mozambique. From a practical standpoint the watch list would have to be adjusted at my departure for one less person. At this point my reluctance to set myself apart was weakening and I asked the XO if I could be taken off the watch list a day or so before we made port. I wanted to enjoy my last couple of days at sea, particularly our rounding of the tip of the African continent, the Cape of Good Hope, without standing watch.

The XO obliged me so I could be a sightseer for this portion of the trip. I tried not to be too obvious since the other officers were now standing watches slightly more frequently, but I did have a couple of days to muse on the last three years and what this ship had meant to me. I did not realize it at the time but disengaging from these experiences, both the good and the bad, would take many, many more years, and to this day more than forty years later they are still fresh in my memory.

Like Cape Horn at the tip of South America, this was a critical passage in trips between the Atlantic and Indian Oceans, though much less dramatic in steam-powered vessels.[13.6] The weather, like that of Cape Horn, can be tempestuous. We were fortunate that our passage was relatively calm, mostly large swells but no storms. With binoculars we could see Table Mountain in Cape Town, South Africa.

On August 1, 1969, we moored at a pier in the capital, Lourenço Marques at the southern end of Mozambique on the east coast of Africa. I finally began to let go and almost could not believe that the next day I would be leaving the ship. I felt a combination of euphoria and sadness to be leaving the steel shell that had been my home for so long. When you are young a year seems like a long time, and three years almost a lifetime. It's funny about a ship; it takes on its own spirit, its own soul. Its creaks and groans, its odors—all become part of its unique aura. When I visited the USS *Joseph P. Kennedy Jr. (DD 850)* in Battleship Cove, Fall River, Massachusetts, in the summer of 2011 I got occasional whiffs of the familiar odor of the interior passageways that brought memories rushing back. Leaning on the side of the bridge wing as I had so many times on watch, it all seemed to fit as I was transported back to that comfortable and familiar place. A little of the *Kennedy*'s aura still survived when reawakened by a kindred spirit.

Since it was my last night on the ship I went ashore with the weapons officer to ease the transition with some drink. We ended up going from bar to bar, talking about what we were going to do when we got out. The last thing I remember was putting one of the small shot glasses down too hard on the table to make a point and it shattered. Then another and another. I was pretty far gone when we returned to the ship. The next morning I had to be roused out of bed for quarters. I struggled to get into my whites and up on deck to hear the plan of the day. I don't remember what was said to me except that I took some ribbing for the shape I was in.

A few hurried farewells and I was released to see the captain prior to my departure. I met him in the wardroom where he said he would recommend me for a commission in the regular Navy if I would extend. He knew I was eager to get on with my life but dutifully went through the motions of making the offer. I had fleetingly thought about the Navy as a career, but I knew it would not be my future.

My orders noted that I had a leave balance of 52½ days and that I was allowed 66 pounds of baggage and 22 pounds of excess baggage traveling second class. All I was actually bringing was a navy duffel bag that weighed well under the limit. I took my foul weather jacket with my name stenciled on the back, which did not survive long after I reentered civilian life. I left as I had come on, this time in reverse—a salute to the OOD, to the flag, then onto the pier. But I was a good deal saltier after almost three years, both literally and in spirit—green verdigris encrusted the brass buttons on my hatband and belt buckle. My shoes were cracked with exposure to the salt water. The ship was no longer a mystery, rather had become too familiar—I was ready to leave it all behind. At least I thought so.

I hardly remember my actual departure from the ship except that the weapons officer was detailed to get me to the airport and make sure I got on the plane on time. I certainly could not have done it on my own. I slumped down into the seat for a relatively short flight to Johannesburg, South Africa, where I would connect to flights home. I had been told that I would not be allowed out of the airport in uniform since there was so much animosity toward the United States for the embargo that had been imposed during apartheid. I think I slept most of the way back on the flights from Johannesburg to New York.

I was still in the Navy for another week while I was processed out at the Brooklyn Navy Yard, though mentally I was out when I left the ship. I met my wife in New York and the next day went to the Brooklyn Navy Yard where I presented my orders for discharge. The staff officer impressed upon me never to lose my discharge papers, form DD 214, which was the official evidence of my service and my ticket to GI benefits. Among other things I was given a dental checkup and asked if I wanted to have a couple of incipient cavities filled courtesy of Uncle Sam before I became a civilian. I would rue this later when they both came loose and had to be replaced by my own dentist. I was paid for my unused leave and departed in a cab with about $1000 in cash in my pocket.

Polliwogs dress for audience with King Neptune

And the band plays on

Captain Greeley
welcomes new Shellback

14

THE WORLD

Vietnam vets referred to returning to the United States as going "back to the world"—an apt phrase encapsulating the transition from the otherworldliness of war to the normalcy of the real world. In my case the transition was not so dramatic, but it was a transition with subtle symptoms I did not realize until years later. The ship had wormed its way into my psyche like an invading organism that would take years to leave its host. My daughters experienced a version of this when they hiked the Appalachian Trail for a couple of months with a small group from their summer camp in Maine and then returned to the main camp for a final week with the rest of the campers. The counselors cautioned both the resident campers and the parents of the returning girls that they would need some time and personal space to reacclimate to the group dynamics of the camp after living on the trail with their small, tight-knit group in spartan conditions. And they had only been in their cocoon for two months.

Older and Wiser

On August 7, 1969, I was out of the Navy and on my own to build the rest of my life. I was reentering civilian life at a time of increasing polarization over a war that affected more and more families who had lost loved ones or knew of someone who had. The stories and pictures that had emerged of brutality by American soldiers epitomized by the My Lai massacre made returning soldiers objects of anger to those who watched the war on the nightly news. There was little if any decompression time afforded returning soldiers, many of whom suffered post-traumatic stress disorder from the mind-numbing experiences they had endured.

I did not suffer from these effects since I had been buffered from the grueling combat experiences of the ground troops. And our journey back took a month versus a plane ride straight out of the jungle and to the United States a day later. Nor did I have animosity to those who chose not to serve by going to Canada, getting educational deferments, or going into the Peace Corps. I had friends who had done each of these. I had made my choice and did not regret it, and they had made theirs. I was now supermotivated to make the most of school and eager to get started. I would be three years behind my peers due to my military service. But I would be ahead in ways I did not realize at the time.

The next step for us was to relocate once again, this time to Houston, the home of Rice University. In some ways it was like coming home to a city we both knew from our dating years in college. Rice is an oasis a couple of miles south of the downtown area, and I looked forward to the life of a student in that serene environment.

We drove from Delaware and after a short search found a garden apartment a few miles from campus that was pretty new and was populated by mostly older couples, which was fine with us—it would be quiet and allow me to study without distraction. We arrived about a week before school began, giving us time to set up the apartment, apply for the GI bill, and let my hair grow some more. As in our Norfolk apartment, the first few weeks were pretty basic living, as Pam describes in a letter to my parents (August 24, 1969):

> Things here are still pretty unsettled and chaotic—we're waiting for our furniture which evidently hasn't left Norfolk yet—the wheels of Navy red tape turn exceedingly slowly and we're itching to get settled and organized before school starts next week—we're camped out in our apartment tho like real hippies—sleeping on a mattress, eating off elegant paper plates & seated on lovely cardboard boxes at a very sturdy and effective table. Hank is about to start construction tho on a dining room table for us—actually it will be a combination dining table and drafting table—

We finally got our furniture three weeks later.

Pam also was able to get a job on campus in the office of the Dean of Humanities, which was convenient because it was right across from the School of Architecture allowing us to meet for lunch. Her administrative skills and upbeat personality made her an immediate hit with the dean and the other professors and staff in the department.

When the other students arrived they looked so young to me. I did recognize a few who had been freshmen when I left and were now a year ahead of me. It was a little awkward but I decided to just put my head down and study without worrying about fitting into this younger group. The age difference was more pronounced by the maturity I had developed in the past three years and the fact that I was the only married person in the class. This came to a head when our professor announced that we would take a class trip to Los Angeles at one of the breaks and everyone was expected to go.

I declined on the pretext of having other family commitments. The reality was that I could not see riding in a bus with all of those "kids" with whom I had almost nothing in common.

I also decided not to leave the Navy behind completely and joined the local Naval Reserve unit. A professor I knew, an exsubmariner, encouraged me to join. I could also continue to advance in rank, albeit at a much slower pace, and be paid a small allowance. I explained my new studies and decision to join the reserves to my parents on September 14, 1969:

> I spend much of my nights in the architecture lab or library so only get a chance to relax on the weekends and have to work then too. Actually, compared to standing watches at midnight the whole week is sort of a rest. Now that my uniforms have arrived, I imagine I will be calling the reserve center soon seeing if they want me. I am not too excited about it actually, but still have some feeling for the Navy and might like to keep my hand in it for a while.

So I put on my uniform one night and went over and joined. My hair was a little longer than regulation. I filled out some forms and was scheduled for a physical. When I stripped for the Navy doctor he asked me if my heavier right arm and shoulder were a result of throwing Molotov cocktails at student demonstrations. He had already typecast me as a student activist. I am not sure if he bought my explanation that I played a lot of tennis, which was why my right arm had developed more—I resented even having to give an explanation. This was my first inkling that I would not be welcome here. Most of the men were older and had not served in a time of combat and were suspicious of those who had served in Vietnam.

I decided to give it a chance and joined a class in computers. There was no option to go out occasionally on a ship, which was my idea of the Navy. The third or fourth time I went there was an inspection in our dress uniforms. A lieutenant commander who had probably been a Lt(jg) like me when he entered the reserves stood in front of me and told me one of my ribbons was upside down. It happened to be a combat action ribbon that neither he nor many, if any, of the others had. I told him he was wrong and refused to change it. This was another indication that this was a club for armchair sailors building their retirement benefits. I dropped out after a few more sessions in spite of the $20 a meeting pay I received for attending four nights a month. Another officer I met later had had better luck at this reserve unit and was able to go out on a reserve destroyer one weekend a month from Galveston, Texas.

As the war ground on protests got more violent at universities throughout the country; even Rice University in the conservative state of Texas was shut down for a day. The incident that embroiled Rice in the counterculture "wars" was whether to allow Abbie Hoffman on campus. I wrote my parents:

> Rice U. is in a turmoil over having Abbie Hoffman come to speak. The students say yes, the president no. Already the dean of students' office has been burned down. The games they play on campus these days.

I was clearly feeling above it all but had begun to develop less than favorable opinions about our political leadership and their prosecution of this war that had no clear objective, with the troops as the victims. Popular support was below 50 percent, while more and more troops were being sent over and more and more died. The troops themselves were vilified on their return, which was unprecedented in American wars.

One day Vice President Spiro Agnew came to give a speech to a local group and a demonstration was planned in front of his hotel on South Main Street. While I recognized that he was basically a voice box for the president, I resented his deprecating, alliterative pronouncements such as "pusillanimous pussyfooters" written for him by Bill Safire and Pat Buchanan. Others included "nattering nabobs of negativism" (written by Safire), and "hopeless, hysterical hypochondriacs of history." He once described a group of opponents as "an effete corps of impudent snobs who characterize themselves as intellectuals" I had to admit these were humorous in a ridiculous sort of way. What I objected to was being typecast (now called "profiled") as an unpatriotic radical just because I was a student.

Agnew would eventually meet his own political end when he pleaded no contest to tax evasion charges and resigned as vice president in 1973.

I had already felt more alienated by the local reserve officers than I had by the students who seemed more tolerant. I went to an orderly demonstration in front of Agnew's hotel with a small sign saying something pretty tame, I don't remember what. I watched the line of kids and really did not feel like one of them but wanted to register my own opposition to Agnew so I joined in for a few minutes before stepping out and going home. I did not feel radicalized but felt an urge to stand up against the negativism being fostered by a political leader I did not respect.

Though I felt like an observer to the protests and violence on both sides, it was apparent to me that the Vietnam War was a different kind of war and could not be won in the clear-cut terms of past wars. America's most respected journalist, Walter Cronkite, felt compelled to express this sentiment in a personal statement on air on February 27, 1968, excerpted below:

> For it seems now more certain than ever that the bloody experience of Vietnam is to end in a stalemate. This summer's almost certain standoff will either

end in real give-and-take negotiations or terrible escalation; and for every means we have to escalate, the enemy can match us, and that applies to invasion of the North, the use of nuclear weapons, or the mere commitment of one hundred, or two hundred, or three hundred thousand more American troops to the battle. And with each escalation, the world comes closer to the brink of cosmic disaster.[14.1]

Many younger people who were being drafted were not resisting just to avoid the danger of military service but because they truly did not believe in the mission. The draft was in many ways a good thing. It was pretty egalitarian, particularly as deferments became harder to obtain. It also brought the public into the war in a much more real way than an all-volunteer military. And in the end it was this wider public consensus, including respected voices such as Cronkite's, that pushed the political structure to bring the war to an end. The Navy was somewhat more insulated from this influx of draftees but was increasingly dependent on them to fill its manpower needs as the war continued.

Recently the wars in Iraq and Afghanistan did not directly touch the majority of Americans. The Department of Defense (DOD) has been able to maintain troop levels by cycling career military personnel through several tours and calling up reserves. A draft is neither desired nor palatable to the DOD or the public as a whole. And in spite of arguments that these wars are fundamentally different from Vietnam they also have gone on a long time in countries where the culture is quite different from ours and where the indigenous populations have resisted unwanted occupiers, whether friend or foe, for many centuries. Unlike the Vietnam War most Americans support our mission in these countries, which is based on protecting the human rights of their populations and on their strategic importance. And the daily death toll, while significant, is relatively modest in comparison to Vietnam. Where there is protest in the United States it is about the economy, whether government spending or Wall Street greed, not about these wars.

There was, at least, one big benefit to the era of social activism in the late 1960s and early 1970s: powerful music with compelling messages and sounds. The music of these years reflected the disenchanted but also hopeful soul of the youth of that era. Just watch the movie *Good Morning, Vietnam*, which illustrates the music the troops craved versus the bland songs they were being fed by Armed Forces Radio. The music of the late sixties, with its strong beat and its association with that compelling era, is still my music of choice for running, in addition to my other favorites, bluegrass and Sousa marches.

The music I listened to on the ship on my tape deck was mainly from cassettes sent by my fiancée, which tended more toward jazz: Astrud Gilberto, Herbie Mann, and Ray Charles. This was calming and reminded me of Pam. We all listened to the Beatles, Rolling Stones, Simon & Garfunkel, and Bob Dylan. It was a mixture of relatively innocent music with the more strident and psychedelic songs of the early '70s as protests became more confrontational. Just watch the surreal Stanley Kubrick film "Full Metal Jacket" for songs by Sam the Sham & the Pharaohs (Wooly Bully), The Trashmen (Surfin Bird), The Rolling Stones (Paint it Black) and others.

Part of my agreement with Rice in being re-admitted was that I would become an undergraduate again and repeat my sophomore year, the year I had dropped out of architecture previously. Though I had no interest in any subject other than architecture I still had to take a language, history of art, and other non-architectural courses. When I discussed this with the two young architecture professors at Rice they suggested I transfer to their alma mater, Princeton. I jumped at this because I could concentrate solely on architecture. I filled out the application including a request for financial aid and waited. Eventually I received a reply that asked if I would come if I did not receive aid. I said yes. I was elated when I was admitted with full financial assistance.

After just a year in Houston we packed up again and took a weeklong trip to Mexico City by train, after leaving our car at a parking facility just across the border in Mexico. On our return we were detained for several hours by the Texas border patrol who profiled me as a hippie who was probably importing drugs—my hair had grown and I had a mustache (much to the chagrin of my wife's family). They took our car apart and did find some bottles of rum I had gotten duty-free in the Navy; fortunately I had a copy of my trusty DD 214 on hand to prove I was a veteran. We were still charged an import duty and eventually let go.

We drove back east in the summer of 1970. The war was dragging on, but my attention was focused on school. I was in a graduate program with older students, a few of whom were also Navy veterans. We hardly ever spoke of our duty though it was comforting to know there were others in program with similar experience. The students in grad school also had a similar sense of commitment and work ethic. The architecture lab was permeated by the smell of marijuana, which was prevalent on campuses everywhere at the time. Though I did not partake I certainly got some secondhand smoke, which may have assisted my creativity!

I thought I would try the reserves again and found a local unit that was more tolerant of students. But it lacked energy, and my chances of being able to go to sea occasionally did not look promising. I did advance in rank to lieutenant, though I never sewed on the new stripes and eventually dropped out of the unit due to my workload.

As the war entered its final phase in 1972 I was increasingly at odds with the tactic of heavy bombing of Hanoi, including civilian areas. I understood that we needed to back up our demands with military pressure against legitimate targets. Even though we claimed the targets were military we acknowledged what the newspapers had discovered on their own—that 1600 civilians had been killed in Hanoi and Haiphong.[142] This kind of "collateral damage" did not occur in targeted bombing.

It did not seem honorable to me that we would resort to bombing civilians to force the North Vietnamese to surrender. Of course they had been brutal in their treatment of our prisoners as we would later find out with the release of those incarcerated in the Hanoi Hilton. And wars have often been brought to a close only by bringing the devastation to the enemy's homeland. But this still did not sit right with me. I protested in my own way by sending back my Pacific Fleet Letter of Commendation to the senator from my home state of Delaware, Bill Roth. As it happened, my friend Steve Hayes was now out of the Navy and serving as an aide to Roth; he received it and sent it back acknowledging my protest.

Those of us who had served got on with our lives with the memories gradually pushed to the background. I looked at this time in the Navy as another chapter that was necessary at the time but was now behind me. Three years, over 150,000 miles at sea, and living in confined quarters with 300 men cannot be dismissed so easily.

Dreams

For the first five years that we were out of the Navy about five or six of us kept in sporadic touch, especially if something happened, usually not something good. A happy-go-lucky young officer, who was like a frat brother, died from cancer with almost no warning. His upbeat personality and enthusiasm coupled with the suddenness of his death increased the sense of loss. My wife and I went to his service and I found myself in tears afterward with so many emotions suddenly unleashed—mostly just the suddenness of it and the loss to his family. But also probably the destruction of the closeness we had developed based on the bond of our intense shared experience.

Gradually we ceased to communicate and lost touch with one another. The supply officer and I saw each other a couple of times in New York but were pursuing separate paths and ceased to remain in contact. I found out a few years later that he had died. I did keep in touch with the weapons officer for a few years, but since we did not live close to each other this communication gradually died out as well. The bond between us was gradually supplanted by new bonds in our personal and professional lives . And as with the men in my company at OCS, the chances that we would meet again in the future were small. With one exception.

Fairly recently I found the ship's website and looked at the listing of shipmates who had signed the roster. Very few of those on the list were from my vintage. Plus I had a new life and did not want to dwell on old memories. But when I got the urge to record my experiences on the ship I took a look at the website to see what historical information there might be.

I noticed immediately that in the ship's history there was no mention of the WestPac cruise except for a shell casing provided by the one officer I did know commemorating the time we were hit. The website contact was helpful in providing me with his telephone number. In a brief exchange of calls and e-mails he said something that struck me: "I just got over the nightmares I had from being in the Navy a few years ago." I took this to be a commentary on his memories of the confining lifestyle or other discomforts of a small ship.

But his comment jogged in me a sudden recall of the periodic dreams I had had about the ship that only really subsided after about 30 years. These dreams were usually of being back on a ship in some situation of stress for which I was not equipped. For instance, going on watch when the ship was in a narrow channel at night at high speed and having to avoid obstacles in the water. Or having reserve duty on a ship for two weeks and not remembering basic information about a destroyer. Or forgetting how to wear my uniform properly. There was always a sense of anxiety strong enough to cause me to wake up from a fitful sleep.

When I followed up with my former shipmate and asked him what his dreams were he said he had two. The first was that he reported aboard the carrier *Coral Sea* in his mature years as the oldest Lt(jg) in the Navy and was put in charge of the engineering plant, which was impossibly complicated and way beyond his knowledge.

The second was that he forgot to relieve me on watch because he had rigged a specially constructed mattress to keep himself from falling out in rough weather. He followed by saying he hoped it never actually happened. He had, in fact, been the officer who had failed to relieve me for being too close to shore while on the gunline; that distant occurrence may have triggered this dream. What struck me was how similar our dreams were of returning to the ship in our later years and being out of place. I have subsequently heard from another former destroyer officer of the same vintage of his recurring dreams.

I took these dreams to be much like the dreams many of us have had about our school days, such as going to class having not done our homework. Or, in my case, skipping a whole semester of math classes and suddenly having to take the final exam.

My own interpretation, not being a psychologist, is that our dreams were manifestations of our immersion in a whole different world compressed inside a floating steel shell where a completely new framework for living and working had to be learned, until that framework became our new reality. This new world had to be embraced and internalized in order to survive—just like at OCS where eventually I learned to march to a new rhythm, both literally and figuratively. Then, after three years, we were thrown right back into "the world" to resume our previous lives in the old framework. Every veteran probably experiences this to a greater or lesser degree, but living within the confines of a small ship probably intensifies the dichotomy. And it takes a long time to work its way out of one's system.

EPILOGUE

I wrote the basic story recounted in this book in a little over one month. I realized that I needed to get events in the right order and corroborate my memories with historical facts. I discovered that I could obtain the ship's Command Histories and selected copies of the daily logs from the National Archives and Records Administration. These records enabled me to construct an accurate timeline and to flesh out my own memory of key events, which put the story on a sound historical basis. I also found a box full of letters from those three years that brought to light in a very personal way how I reacted to events. The letters were in effect my diary of those years. I spent the next five months cataloguing, reading, and weaving the logs and letters into the narrative. I have excerpted these letters as written without conforming them to the editorial conventions of the general text. Finally, I found the movies I had taken and prevailed upon my daughter Kate, a film editor, to help me transfer them to digital media so that individual frames could be extracted as illustrations.

In actuality, when I wrote this story I was thinking very little, if at all, about the intended audience. It was a way to make sense out of this dynamic and formative period of my life with the benefit of forty plus years of perspective. One of the most interesting discoveries was to check my own memories against the actual logs. I found that they were pretty close. It was gratifying to see my own log entries, in my own handwriting and with my own signature, which made it all the more personal for me. It was enlightening as well to read the immediate context of many of the events, including the hours immediately before and after our receipt of hostile fire.

I also found out that the logs, the most detailed surviving written records, simply did not mention significant events of a nonoperational nature. I felt a responsibility to fill in missing detail as I experienced it, though from the limited perspective of one person. Because ships in the Tonkin Gulf were not involved in the intensity of combat that was in the forefront of the nightly news, there were relatively few accounts written of the blue water Navy in Vietnam. Some ex-shipmates have contacted me about our possible exposure to Agent Orange since we were very close to the coast and went into Cam Ranh Bay, considered in-country. I have told them I did not think we were exposed, but the *Lowry* whose operations closely matched ours, has received a similar designation as members of the so-called brown water Navy entitling her crew to compensation.

I have met other former junior officers who were veterans from the Vietnam era. When we discover our common history we end up ignoring others around us to compare our respective duties and experiences. We always come to the conclusion that this was an intensely memorable and significant period in our lives. We all seem to agree that the Navy was the best school for living that we have had. It challenged us, often under adverse and uncomfortable conditions, and gave us a great deal of responsibility and leadership training at an early age.

I used to think I wasted three years learning a lot of stuff I would never use again, which in a way is true. But I learned how to learn fast and how to keep going when I really didn't want to, both of which have gotten me through some difficult periods. I also learned to live simply and to function on little sleep when necessary. And unpredictable challenges seem to occur at the least opportune times, just as they did on watches. In rereading the description of my division—First Division—from our WestPac cruise book, I realize that I learned the basic elements of working with and leading a group of disparate people in the Navy:

> Cool, calm, and collected, Lt (jg) Abernathy "minded" the First Division helm ably assisted by "Pappy" Tetting (the old man of the sea) and "Plowboy" Sanderson, who won the coveted FURSE Lavoris bottle award for having the most powerful set of lungs on board. First Division played a significant role in nearly every evolution during the cruise, taking its cues from choruses of "Topside!" "Station the Planeguard Detail," and "$#!!&*!!!"

"Pappy" Tetting and "Plowboy" Sanderson were the lead boatswain's mates in my division and characters right out of the musical production *South Pacific.* I could only stand back and marvel at the range and creativity of their verbal cajoling when marshaling the men to action. Managing them was mostly a matter of making sure they knew what evolutions were coming and providing them an audience in front of the men to reinforce their authority. Like all good petty officers they had learned the fine line between toughness and empathy and when to apply each. I learned more by observation than by intervention, though I also learned when the latter was necessary.

I have always been more of a carrot than a stick person, trying to facilitate the natural abilities of those working for me by coaching rather than criticism. I often wonder what would have happened had I made the Navy a career—I was probably too much of a "minder" than a forceful leader. Captain Greeley was my ideal of the right combination of traits— a good coach with a passion for his profession, a confident and unquestionably competent officer who led by example.

Those of us who served are, I believe, stronger citizens as a result. I feel I have earned the right to offer constructive criticism on public policies. I may take issue with a military policy but never with those who serve, having felt that sting in a small way myself on return from our deployment to Vietnam. The all-volunteer military certainly has many merits, but the citizen soldier/sailor model invests the citizenry in a direct and personal way in the military mission.

Not long ago when going through our storage locker I came upon the uniforms I had saved. They were wrinkled and musty after having been jammed into a seabag that I had appropriated from the ship when I left. My wife asked me if it wasn't finally time to throw them out. I agreed to give up some of the pants that would never fit my expanded waist and some of the white shirts that had yellowed with age. But when I came to my double-breasted blue jacket with my Lt(jg) stripes I took it out and sent it to the cleaners. It now hangs in our storage locker in a plastic bag where I can keep it safe.

Likewise, I have kept the small leatherette case I got in OCS to keep ribbons, belt buckles, brass uniform insignia bars, buttons, shoulder boards, dog tags, and other mementos of my Navy days. A piece of shrapnel from the round that hit us, the broken link from the anchor chain that snapped in our collision with the Lowry, and a black-and-white photo someone took of me as an ensign standing at attention on the quarterdeck are in it. This box is stored behind my T-shirts and socks in a cabinet in our bedroom. I only take it out and open it very occasionally, but I know that these objects, like my jacket, represent a core part of my life that I will always keep close at hand.

ACKNOWLEDGMENTS

My wife, Pam, who read and edited many drafts, coached me to transform a series of events into a story. To the extent that I succeeded is primarily due to her. Not to mention saving every letter I wrote her!

My daughter Kate, a film editor by profession, read the early drafts and was indispensable in extracting key photos from my 43-year-old super-8 movies. My daughter Emily assisted in editing the Index.

Christine Valentine's insight and professionalism in the final editing of the manuscript raised it to a significantly higher level of consistency and clarity.

My sister Janet offered encouragement and proofreading assistance as well as forgave me for missing her wedding while I was at sea!

My parents raised me to be able to withstand the rigors of the Navy and saved my letters and those they wrote to me which were invaluable in reconstructing events.

Elizabeth Stier and her sister, Erin Nieder, daughters of Michael Greeley, provided encouragement and comment on their father's service. Erin's excellent editing of the manuscript resulted in significant improvements, and helped me with the details of the coke bottle game!

Roger Guichard, my brother-in-law, carefully edited the manuscript and also urged me to provide historical context that improved overall understanding of *Furse*'s service in the Vietnam era. He also suggested a stronger emphasis on the theme of the citizen sailor, having been one himself.

John Farrell, former Lieutenant and communications officer on the USS *Davis* (DD-937), who served in both the Atlantic and Pacific at the same time as I, read and edited the manuscript and gave me his perspective as a former citizen sailor. His encouragement helped me maintain momentum through the final stages of completing the book.

Steve Hayes read my first draft and gave me encouragement as well as perceptive comments, while writing his own book, *Light on Dark Water.*

Robert (Bob) Cressman, Director of the History & Archives Division, Naval History & Heritage Command, let me into the Archives minutes before they officially closed to go through and make copies of the Command Histories of USS *Furse*. He later also sent the Commander Destroyer Squadron Two "Westpac Trip Report, 1968," which provided valuable insight into squadron-level planning and lessons learned.

Nathaniel S. Patch, Archives Specialist, Archives II Reference Section (NWCT2R), Textual Archives Services Division, found and sent me copies of the daily logs of the *Furse*. I am in his debt in particular for expediting copies of the critical dates, which enabled me to proceed with the account on a solid historical footing.

Jack Masey gave me early advise on how to put a book together from his own experience of writing two books on his experiences producing innovative exhibitions with the United States Information Agency (USIA).

Tom Reid, whom I met just after OCS and ultimately relieved as gunnery officer on the *Furse*, contributed his experiences in the chapter on dreams as well as encouraged me in the early stages of writing this account.

Cynthia Keiser and Dorothea Danzico read the manuscript and offered valuable editing advice and critical comment.

Finally, though I made an effort to check facts and provide references, I take full responsibility for any inaccuracies.

AFTERWORD

Fifty Year Anniversary of the Vietnam War

In September 2017 Ken Burns (with Lynn Novick and Geoffrey Ward) aired a landmark PBS series, *The Vietnam War*. The local PBS affiliate in New York, WLIW, aired a companion series on New York-area Vietnam veterans. See: https://www.wliw.org/legacies-of-war/

I was invited to be interviewed for recollections of my service, and in the process met some of the other veterans as well as protest organizers. Though there have been many books on this war and era, this series interviewed North Vietnamese veterans about their war experiences and the huge losses they suffered while continuing to pursue the war effort. There was very little about the Navy's role, though the importance of the interdiction of supplies by sea was noted.

Spate of Destroyer Accidents

In 2017 there were six serious accidents involving the Navy in the Seventh Fleet. Five involved ships and one a plane. See: https://www.cnn.com/21/08/2017/politics/navy-ships-accidents/index.html

The causes have been identified as overstressed crews, turning off collision avoidance radar to avoid detection, and increased ship congestion in the area. I submit that the re- positioning of CIC on today's ships from a location immediately adjacent the bridge to a lower floor inhibits the opportunity for the CIC officer to walk out onto the bridge and converse with OOD while looking at the actual situation, not just at specks on a radar screen.

GLOSSARY

1 MC	The ship's general announcing system, over which word can be passed to every space in the ship; this is an electrically amplified one-way system. J-systems,on the other hand, are sound-powered and do not require electrical power.
AAW	Antiair Warfare
ACTH	Arbitrary Correction to Hit
allowance	minimum staff to operate a ship. See also *complement*.
ASROC	Antisubmarine Rocket ("If you can't sock 'em, ASROC 'em.")
ASW	Antisubmarine warfare
AWOL	Absent Without Leave
birdfarm	nickname for aircraft carrier
BMOW	Boatswain's Mate of the Watch
"Boats"	boatswain's mate, usually the lead boatswain's mate
boatswain's mate	enlisted rate for deck seamanship specialists
bollard	short metal deck post for securing a line
BOQ	Bachelor Officer Quarters
brow	gangplank that connects the quarterdeck with the pier
bulkhead	wall
bullnose	chock with a hole in the middle

BUPERS	Bureau of Naval Personnel
C/C	change course
C/S	change speed
can, tin can	nickname for a destroyer
captain	The commander of a ship is also called captain though he/she might be a commander by rank.
captain's mast	a nonjudicial summary judgment procedure under the UCMJ
CDO	Command Duty Officer; the CO's representative in port when the CO is not aboard
CIC	Combat Information Center, or just combat
CO	Commanding Officer
combat	shortened form of Combat Information Center
ComDesRon	Commander Destroyer Squadron
complement	normal manning level in officers and men. This was noted as 275 (15 officers and 260 men) in *Jane's Fighting Ships* of 1967–1968.
conn	control of the ship; "take the conn"
CPO	Chief Petty Officer
DASH	Drone Antisubmarine Helicopter
DCA	Damage Control Assistant
DE	Destroyer Escort
DESDIV 22	Destroyer Division 22
DesRon	Destroyer Squadron
DMZ	Demilitarized Zone
DOD	Department of Defense
ECM	Electronic Countermeasures
EOT	Engine Order Telegraph
faked down, flaked down	line laid out in a coil or in loops on the deck
first lieutenant	officer In charge of deck operations, part of the weapons department on a destroyer
fo'c'sle	forecastle, or forward-most part of the main deck

FT	Fire Control Technician
gangplank	See *brow*.
gig	at OCS, a point awarded for bad (red) or good (blue) performance
Gitmo	Guantanamo Naval Station in Cuba; sometimes abbreviated GTMO
GQ	General Quarters; combat or emergency stations
grinder	at OCS, parking lot
hawser	lines larger than 5 inches in diameter, used for mooring or towing
head	toilet
HMAS	Her Majesty's Australian Ship
Hollywood shower	any shower lasting longer than about 2 minutes
IFF	Identification Friend or Foe
Irish pennant	loose thread or string
JOOD	Junior Officer of the Deck
knot	one nautical mile per hour; 15 knots is about 18 mph
LCDR	Lieutenant Commander
LED	Light-Emitting Diode, a type of light
liberty	time off the ship. See *on the beach*.
list	lean to one side
LST	Landing Ship Dock; a transport ship
Lt(jg)	Lieutenant Junior Grade
LUCTAR	Lucrative Target
MOD	at OCS, Mate of the Deck
MPA	Main Propulsion Assistant
nasty boat	See *PTF*.
nautical mile	6,076 feet or about 2,000 yards. A useful property is that one nautical mile is equal to approximately one minute of arc measured along any meridian.
NESEP	Naval Enlisted Scientific and Education Program
NVA	North Vietnamese Army

OCS	Officer Candidate School, Newport, Rhode Island
on the beach	on liberty; off of the ship
OOD	Officer of the Deck
OODF	OOD, Fleet
OODI	OOD, Independent
pay out	let out line
PBR	River Patrol Boat (Patrol Boat, rRver). A small, fast (25–29 knots) boat with a crew of usually four enlisted persons and a junior officer.
PCF	Patrol Craft Fast, also known as Swift Boat
pelican hook	quick-release hook with a profile like a pelican's beak
piece	weapon; at OCS, M1 rifle
PIRAZ	Positive Identification and Radar Advisory Zone
plot	short for the plotting room, a secure interior compartment of the ship containing the gyroscope
PMS	Preventive Maintenance System
premie	premature shell detonation
PTF	Patrol Torpedo Fast; in Vietnam known as Nasty Boats
rack	bed
rate	a person's rate, or rating, is his/her specialization, such as signalman, boatswain's mate
rat guards	conical-shaped metal pieces placed over a line with the open end toward the pier when moored to prevent rats from coming aboard
river patrol boat	See *PBR*.
ROTC	Reserve Officer Training Corps
SAM	Surface to Air Missile
SAR	Search and Rescue
Seabeas	Naval Construction Battalion (CB) Personnel

SEALORDS	Southeast Asia Lake, Ocean, River, and Delta Strategy was a campaign to cut enemy supply lines from Cambodia.
Swift Boat	See *PCF*.
UCMJ	Uniform Code of Military Justice
UNREP	Underway Replenishment
USN	United States Navy, or "regular Navy"
USNR	United States Naval Reserve
USS *Furse* (DD-882)	United States Ship *Furse*, destroyer, number 882; shortened to *Furse* or the *Furse* according to preference
U/W	underway
VERTREP	Vertical (helicopter) Replenishment
watch	Watches are on a 24-hour clock and are generally as follows:

        0000–0400   mid watch

        0400–0800

        0800–1200

        1200–1600

        1600–1800   first dog watch

        1800–2000   second dog watch

        2000–2400   evening or first watch

WBLC	Waterborne Logistics Craft
WestPac	Western Pacific
XO	Executive Officer
Yippee	See *YP*.
YP	Yard Patrol craft at OCS, aka Yippee

TIMELINE

1966

June, 1966	Graduated from Rice
23 Jul	Reported to OCS
25 Nov	Graduated from OCS
5 Dec	Report to *Furse*

1967

winter	Overhaul, Boston Naval Shipyard
17-20 Apr	Gunfire Support School
10 May	Return to Norfolk
29 Jan-18 Mar	DASH School Dam Neck, Virginia
29 May	Leave for Key West
13 Jun	Grounding on shoal off of Key West
5 Jul	Arrive Gitmo
20 Aug	Return to Norfolk
2 Oct	ASW Operations off of Virginia Capes
26 Oct	John McCain shot down over Hanoi
6 Nov	Depart for joint US-Canada ASW exercise, CANUS SILEX, North Atlantic
17-19 Nov	Halifax, Nova Scotia
22 Nov	Return to Norfolk for tender upkeep and holidays

1968

16 Jan	Depart for Spring Board
Jan-Feb	Tet Offensive and Battle of Hue in Vietnam
9 Feb	Return to Norfolk
19, 20 Feb	NASA space capsule recovery, Virginia Capes
5 Mar	Hull Repairs, Norfolk Naval Shipyard
20-22 Mar	Naval Gunfire Support School, Little Creek
9 Apr	Underway, SE Asia
14 Apr	Panama Canal
22-25 Apr	San Diego
May-Aug	Mini Tet offensive in Vietnam
1-5 May	Pearl Harbor
7 May	Midway
15 May	Guam
18 May	Collision with *Lowry* (DD-770)
20 May	Arrive Subic Bay, Philippines
25 May	HA appointed Lieutenant (junior grade)
28 May	Depart Subic Bay for Tonkin Gulf Operations-- Planeguard USS *America* (CVA-66)
30 May	HA qualified as Officer of the Deck, Independent
6 Jun	Search & Rescue operations with USS *Prebble* (DLG-15)
17 Jun	HMAS *Hobart* Incident
22, 23 Jun	Screen ship for Soviet trawler *Bargraf*
29 Jun to 18 July	Subic Bay, turbine blade repairs. HA wetting down.
19 Jul	PIRAZ Station as escort to USS *Long Beach* (CGN-9)
28 Jul	escort Long Beach on TALOS missile station
5-7 Aug	escort USS *England* (DLG-20) on Northern SAR
8-10 Aug	transit to Hong Kong
16-17 Aug	leave Hong Kong via Kao-Hsiung
26 Aug	Planeguard USS *America* (CVA-66)
6-Sep	Proceed to gunfire support off Phan Thiet in support of Resume planeguard
11-16 Sep	transit to Yokosuka

23 Sep	underway for Sea Dragon off of North Vietnam
28 Sep	Relieve USS *Boston* (CAG-1) as flagship of Southern Sea Dragon Operations
until 2 Oct	Operated with USS *MacKenzie* (DD-836)
5 Oct	Relieve USS *New Jersey* (BB62) as Commander of Northern Sea Dragon Operations
7 Oct	Taken under fire by shore batteries-direct hit on flight deck
9 Oct	Ship participated in (22) Sea Dragon operations Relieved by HMAS *Perth* as Northern Sea Dragon Operations Commander
10 Oct	Departed Tonkin Gulf for return trip to Norfolk
12 Oct	Fuel stop Kao-Hsiung, Taiwan
15 Oct	Arrive Yokosuka, Japan
18 Oct	Underway with USS *Lind* (DD-703), USS *Lowry* (DD-770), and USS *Harwood* (DD 861)
23 Oct	Fuel stop Midway
26 Oct	Arrive Pearl Harbor
30 Oct	Underway
5-10 Nov	San Francisco
13 Nov (?)	San Diego
15 Nov	Manzanillo
16-19 Nov	Acapulco
23 Nov	transit Panama Canal after overnight stop in Rodman
27 Nov	Return to Norfolk
14 Dec	Hank and Pam wedding

1969

1 Jan-21 Feb	tender availability
24 Feb	underway for Springboard & ASW operations
11-14 Mar	San Juan

18-20 Mar	St. Thomas
24-26 Mar	St. Croix
	Return transit to Norfolk
3 Apr	Surface gunnery-sunk WWII destroyer escort hulk with 8 destroyers
4 Apr	Returned to Norfolk
22 Apr	HA designated as Officer of the Deck, Fleet
24-30 May	Local Ops, Vacapes
June	Preparation for Middle East deployment
2 Jul	Underway for Middle East
5 Jul	Gunfire support exercises, Culebra
14-16 Jul	Fuel stop Porto Grande, Cape Verde Islands
20-Jul	First Moon Landing
23-25 Jul	Luanda, Angola
	transit around Cape of Good Hope
1-3 Aug	Lourenco Marques, Mozambique (H. Abernathy departed the ship)
7 Aug	Released from the Navy
Sep	Return to Rice University

1970-1973

Sep 1970	commenced Princeton University School of Architecture
May 1973	Graduated from Princeton

SOURCES AND BIBLIOGRAPHY

Archival material

Readers interested in United States naval archives are referred to National Archives and Records Administration, Michael C. Lang, and Nathaniel S. Patch, Archives Specialist, Archives II Reference Section (NWCT2R), Textual Archives Services Division, NWCT2R 111-1652-MCL, College Park, Maryland. The *Deck Logs of USS* Furse *(DD-882)*, various December 31, 1966, to August 3, 1969, can be found here, in Box 1161.

Another important archival source is Naval History & Heritage Command, History and Archives Division, Washington, D.C. Robert Cressman, Director.

I also consulted the November 1966 records of the United States Naval Officer Candidate School, Newport, Rhode Island, specifically Seachest 701.

I consulted my own archives of the time I spent on the *Furse*, including orders, Plans of the Day, and other documents between December 1966 and August 1969, such as *USS* Furse *(DD-882)*, a record of our 1968 WestPac Cruise 1968 produced on board the Furse by ship's personnel.

Commander Destroyer Squadron Two, "WESTPAC Trip Report," 1968. Report of Destroyer Squadron TWO Deployment to WESTPAC 26 March 1968 to 30 November 1968.

Commander Destroyer Squadron Two, Commanding Officer, USS FURSE (DD-882), Command Histories, 1967, 1968, 1969.

Books

Conrad, Joseph, *Heart of Darkness and Secret Sharer.* New York: Bantam Classics, 2004. First published in 1902.

Cutler, Thomas J., *The Bluejacket's Manual,* United States Navy, 24th ed. Annapolis, MD: Naval Institute Press, 2009.

Dana, Richard Henry, Jr., *Two Years Before the Mast.* New York: Signet Classics, 2009. First published in 1840.

Drury, Bob, and Clavin, Tom. *Halsey's Typhoon: The True Story of a Fighting Admiral, an Epic Storm, and an Untold Rescue.* New York: Atlantic Monthly Press, 2007.

Jane's Fighting Ships 1967–1968, Blackman, Raymond V.B., ed. New York: McGraw-Hill Book Company, 1968.

Knight, Austin M., *Knight's Modern Seamanship, 14th ed.,* revised by Captain John V. Noel, Jr., USN.

New York: Van Nostrand Reinhold, 1966.

Leahy, William D., *The Bluejacket's Manual,* United States Navy, 10th ed. Annapolis, MD: United States Naval Institute, 1940.

Marolda, Edward J., *The U.S. Navy in the Vietnam War.* Washington, D.C.: Brassey's, Inc., 2002.

Stavridis, Admiral James, USN, *Destroyer Captain: Lessons of a First Command.* Annapolis, MD: Naval Institute Press, 2008.

Sumrall, Robert F., *Sumner-Gearing-Class Destroyers: Their Design, Weapons, and Equipment.* Annapolis, MD: Naval Institute Press, 1995.

Watch Officer's Guide, 9th edition, revised by Captain John V. Noel, Jr., USN. Annapolis, MD: United States Naval Institute, 1961.

Sloan, Jack D., Chairman

U.S.S. *Swanson* (DD-443) Historical Committee, 1991

U.S.S. *Swanson* (DD-443)

World War II

Destroyer at War!

Copyright 1991, Printed by Georgia School for the Deaf, Cave Spring, Georgia

Websites and links, in order of appearance in text:

USS *Furse* History:
Department of the Navy—Navy Historical Center
805 Kidder Breese SE—Washington Navy Yard
Washington, D.C. 20374-5060
http://www.history.navy.mil/danfs/f5/furse.htm

DASH helicopters and Gearing Class Destroyers:
Gyrodyne Historical Foundation
http://www.gyrodynehelicopters.com

Lead Line (Sounding Line) Description:
The Navy & Marine Living History Association
http://www.navyandmarine.org

"Go West, young man" quote:
LLRX.com Law and technology resources for legal professionals
http://www.llrx.com/features/quotedetective.htm

"A collision at sea will ruin a man's whole day" quote:
http://quoteinvestigator.com/2010/11/21/collision-at-sea/

USS *Lowry* (DD-770) website:
For history including collision with *Furse*
http://hawgheadtoo.tripod.com

HMAS *Hobart*
Gunplot a privately owned website about the Royal Australian Navy:
http://www.gunplot.net/vietnam/hobartvietnam.html

Swift Boat Information:
http://www.swiftboats.net

Nasty boat information:
http://www.ptfnasty.com/ptfHistory.html

French history in Vietnam including Dien Bien Phu:
http://www.olive-drab.com/od_history_vietnam_french.php

"Ship Commander Under Fire For Lewd Videos He Filmed":
www.gantdaily.com

Description of the AH1 Huey Cobra helicopter:
http://www.minihelicopter.net/AH1HueyCobra/index.htm

Battleship *New Jersey*
http://www.ussnewjersey.org/1968_narrative.htm

DDG-1000 Zumwalt Class destroyer
http://www.naval-technology.com/projects/dd21/

Crossing the Line ceremony:
http://www.goatlocker.org/resources/nav/crossline.pdf

Letters of Henry Abernathy Jr., Pamela (Mendolia) Abernathy, Mr. & Mrs. Henry H. Abernathy, Ann Abernathy, Martha Abernathy, Janet Abernathy, and Stephen Hayes from January 1966 to October, 1969. In possession of author.

NOTES

Preface

P.1. USS *Furse* (DD-882/DDR-882) was scrapped in 1991 after serving in the Spanish Navy under the name *Gravina*. The *Furse* was a Gearing-class destroyer of the United States Navy and was named for Lieutenant John H. Furse, USN (1886–1907). *Furse* was laid down by the Consolidated Steel Corporation at Orange, Texas, on September 23, 1944, launched on March 9, 1945, by Eugenia A. Furse, sister of Lieutenant Furse, and commissioned on July 10, 1945. Readers wishing to learn about the ship's service history are referred to the seven-volume *Dictionary of Naval Fighting Ships* (DANFS) at http://www.history.navy/danfs/f5/Furse.htm and to http://www. hullnumber.com/DD-882. Information is also available through Wikipedia.

Introduction

I.1. See http://www.gyrodynehelicopters.com/frank_Knox_class.htm.

1. Even Somebody with No Rhythm Can Learn to March

1.1   See *The Bluejacket's Manual,* 24th Edition, United States Navy, p.108, under Nonjudicial punishment (NJP):

This is basically a hearing in which the commanding officer (CO) handles a relatively minor offense rather than sending it to court. While it is not a "trial" in the civil justice sense, it is held with formality and is not a pleasant experience for anyone involved. Instead of having a lawyer, the offender is represented at NJP by her or his division chief and division officer. Because these proceedings are nonjudicial, the offender may be punished but will not have a criminal record. In the Navy, NJP is usually referred to as "captain's mast."

On hearing the evidence, both for and against, the commanding officer determines whether the accused is guilty or not and then, if necessary, assigns and appropriate punishment. Some of the punishments that a CO may award are:

- Restriction to the ship (or shore station) of not more than 60 days
- Extra duties for not more than 45 days
- Reduction in grade (for E-6 and below)
- Correctional custody for not more than 30 days (for E-3 and below)
- Forfeiture of not more than half a month's pay per month for two months

2. Don't Just Stand There with Your Hands in Your Pockets!

2.1. For a story of this company and anecdotes about those who flew the QH-50 drone, see http://www.gyrodynehelicopters.com.

2.2. See Knight, Austin M., *Knight's Modern Seamanship*, 14th edition (Princeton, NJ: D. Van Nostrand and Company, Inc., 1966), p. 238:

The first thing the Captain or salvage officer of a grounded ship should do is to notice whether the ship is lively, i.e., is affected by the swells. If so, it may be possible to refloat her at once by sallying ship, backing full speed, and pulling by any large tugs or other vessels which may be available. Should these measures be unsuccessful, the next step is to send out an anchor astern with a wire to hold the ship in her original grounding position. Put and keep a heavy strain on the wire. Swells tend to force ships farther up the beach and to turn them broadside to the sea.

2.3. Stavridis, Admiral James, *Destroyer Captain: Lessons of a First Command* Annapolis, MD, US Naval Institute Press, 2008), p. 125.

2.4. Stavridis, *Destroyer Captain*, p. 36.

4. North Atlantic

4.1. U.S.S. *Swanson* (DD-443) Historical Committee, *Destroyer at War!* (1991), p. 4.

5. A Shark Nearby Makes a Good Swimmer Great

5.1. See http://www.navyandmarine.org/planspatterns/soundingline.htm for a description of the lead line.

5.2. See Commander Destroyer Squadron Two *"Westpac Trip Report"* (1968), p.16:

14. one of the most revealing lessons learned in NGFS was the marked difference between firing on a practice range and firing in combat. It was discovered that often spotters were young and relatively inexperienced, unsure of themselves, and excitable under the stress of combat. When these situations arose, the "school book" solution went out and the ship assumed the responsibility of leading the spotters through the missions by prompting them for information and required data. Occasionally, it appeared that some of the less experienced spotters had very little concept of the amount and types of ammunition carried by destroyers. However, when requested to temper their requirements, they did so willingly and often apologetically.

5.3. "main brace" is defined in: http://www.navy.mil/navydata/traditions/html/navyterm.html as follows:

In the age of sail, ship's rigging was a favorite target during sea battles because destroying the opponent's ability to maneuver or get away would put you at obvious advantage. Therefore, the first and most important task after a battle was to repair damaged rigging (also known as lines—but never "rope"!). Examples of lines include braces (lines that adjust the angle at which a sail is set in relation to the wind) and stays (lines supporting the masts).

The main brace was the principal line controlling the rotation of the main sail. Splicing this line was one of the most difficult chores aboard ship, and one on which the ship's safety depended. It was the custom, after the main brace was properly spliced, to serve grog to the entire crew. Thus, today, after a hard day (or, not so hard day), the phrase has become an invitation to have a drink.

7. Go WestPac, Young Man

7.1. See http://www.llrx.com/features/quotedetective.htm.

Fuller concluded in an article in the September 2004 issue of the *Indiana Magazine of History* that "John Soule had nothing whatsoever to do with the phrase" and he was also unable to discover "Go West, young man" anywhere in Greeley's writings, including those in the *New York Tribune* and other sources where various people have claimed it occurred. I did, however, uncover the following quote cited in a recent biography of Greeley: "If any young man is about to commence the world, we say to him, publicly and privately, Go to the West" (from the August 25, 1838, issue of the newspaper *New Yorker*). "Go West, young man" may well have been a paraphrase of this and other advice given by Greeley.

7.2: See: http://www.eclipse.co.uk/~sl5763/panama.htm.

The length of the Panama Canal is approximately 51 miles. A trip along the canal from its Atlantic entrance would take you through a 7-mile dredged channel in Limón Bay. The canal then proceeds for a distance of 11.5 miles to the Gatun Locks. This series of three locks raise ships 26 metres to Gatun Lake. It continues south through a channel in Gatun Lake for 32 miles to Gamboa, where the Culebra Cut begins. This channel through the cut is 8 miles long and 150 metres wide. At the end of this cut are the locks at Pedro Miguel. The Pedro Miguel locks lower ships 9.4 metres to a lake which then takes you to the Miraflores Locks which lower ships 16 metres to sea level at the canals Pacific terminus in the bay of Panama.

7.3. See http://hawgheadtoo.tripod.com/LHIST-5.html:

LOWRY sailed from Norfolk on the morning of 9 April in company with *U.S.S. FURSE (DD-882)* and *U.S.S. WALLACE L. LIND (DD-703)* with Captain K.J. Cole, U.S.N., Commander Destroyer Division TWENTY TWO embarked in *FURSE* as Commander Task Unit 27.5.2. In the afternoon of 11 April, the *U.S.S. HARWOOD (DD-861)* joined the Task Unit after departing her homeport of Mayport, Florida. The transit of the Panama Canal was completed in a twelve hour period on Easter Sunday, 14 April 1968 with a brief stop for fuel at the U.S. Naval Station, Rodman, Canal Zone.

7.4: See Commander Destroyer Squadron Two, *"Westpac Trip Report, 1968,"* p. 61, for this description of a refueling at Manzanillo:

The ship was held off the pier by means of this line and the starboard anchor as there is a severe lateral surge in the harbor at all times. There is only one fuel hose on the pier. The after fueling station was placed adjacent to this hose. Fuel was then transferred forward as it was being pumped aboard. Six hours were required for the entire evolution. The pumping rate is slow and fuel quality, although good, is highly viscous... Apparently it is well to enter port early.

7.5. See http://battledescription.com/sinking-of-the-eilat:

On October 21, 1967, the Eilat was on a routine patrol of the Sinai coastline, which took her some 15 miles (25 km) from the Egyptian city of Port Said, when she suddenly came under attack from an Egyptian Komarclass missile boat. The boat fired a Russian-built SS-N-2 Styx anti-ship missile that struck the Eilat, destroying her communications and powerplant. The Eilat was attacked again 90 minutes later, receiving another missile strike that caused her magazine to detonate. The crew abandoned ship, but many were wounded in the water when one of the ship's depth charges exploded. A total of 47 Israeli sailors were killed.

The Eilat was the first ship to be sunk in battle by a ship-launched anti-ship missile. It was a huge blow to the Israeli navy and led to a major review of Israeli naval strategy. The resulting focus on fast, missile-armed boats and missile countermeasures would reap major benefits for the Israeli navy six years later at Latakia.

7.6. Symonds, *The Battle of Midway*, Editor's Note, p. xi:

In a matter of eight minutes on the morning of June 4, 1942, three of the four aircraft carriers in Japan's principal striking force were mortally wounded by American dive bombers. The fourth would follow later that day. The Japanese Navy never recovered from this blow. These pivotal minutes—the most dramatic of World War II, indeed perhaps in all of American history—reversed the seemingly irresistible momentum toward Japanese victory and started the long comeback of American forces from the disasters at Pearl Harbor and the Philippines six months earlier.

7.7. From the US Fish & Wildlife Service website, http://www.fws.gov/midway:

Midway, part of the Papahānaumokuākea Marine National Monument, is one of the world's most spectacular wildlife experiences. Nearly three million birds call it home for much of each year, including the world's largest population of Laysan Albatrosses, or "gooney birds." Hawaiian monk seals, green sea turtles and spinner dolphins frequent Midway's crystal blue lagoon.

Midway became an "overlay" refuge in 1988, while still under the primary jurisdiction of the Navy. With the closure of Naval Air Facility Midway Island in 1993, there began a transition from bullets to birds, a change in mission from national defense to wildlife conservation. Midway is one of the most remote coral atolls on earth. Yet, it is much, much more!

- the last link in a global telegraph system, inaugurated by a message from President   Teddy Roosevelt on the Fourth of July, 1903
- a landing site for Pan Am Clippers en route across the Pacific Ocean in the late 1930s
- the focus of a 1942 battle that changed the tide of war in the Pacific
- from July 1942 to the end of hostilities, Midway served as a submarine base that aided   in bringing the war to a close
- naval air facility that played a pivotal role in support of the Korean War, the Cold War and the Vietnam War

7.8: For the origin of this quote go to http://quoteinvestigator.com/2010/11/21/collision-at-sea.

7.9. See: http://hawgheadtoo.tripod.com/DIARY-1.html,

Quartermaster W. F. "Bill" Mackey's 1968 WESTPAC diary

7.10. See http://hawgheadtoo.tripod.com/LHIST-5.html:

On 18 May, as *FURSE* made her approach on LOWRY for a personnel transfer, *FURSE* experienced a steering casualty and a collision occurred. The *FURSE*'s starboard anchor and bow caused considerable damage to the bulwark on LOWRY's port side from frame 75 to frame 110; superficial damage from that point (frame 110) aft to the screwguard. The shipfitters made temporary repairs to the bulwark while the torpedomen and sonar technicians freed a warshot Mk 37 torpedo from a twisted Mk 25 torpedo tube damaged in the collision. That torpedo and two suspect Mk 46 warshots from the triple Mk 32 tubes were transferred to NavMag, Subic Bay on arrival.

7.11. Marolda, p. 263.

7.12. Marolda, p.137:

Throughout this period, the Seventh Fleet's gunfire support ships off South Vietnam formed the Cruiser-Destroyer Group (Task Group 70.8). The subordinate Naval Gunfire Support Unit (Task Unit 70.8.9), in coordination with MACV [Military Assistance Command], actually directed operations along the coast. Ships were assigned to the group from the fleet's cruiser-destroyer command and from the Royal Australian Navy, but were also temporarily attached from carrier escort units, from Sea Dragon force steaming off North Vietnam, and from the amphibious force. U.S. Navy and U.S. Coast Guard combat craft conducted inshore coastal and river patrols which also provided gunfire support for allied operations. Typically, one cruiser, four destroyers, one inshore fire support (IFS), and two medium rocket landing ships (LSMR) comprised Task Unit 10.8.9. However, the number varied and totaled as many as 2 cruisers, 18 destroyers, and 2 rocket ships during the heavy combat of 1968.

8. Tonkin Gulf Yacht Club (aka Seventh Fleet)

8.1. Kelley, Michael P. *Where We Were: A Comprehensive Guide to the Firebases, Military Installations and Naval Vessels of the Vietnam War, 1945–75* (Central Point, Oregon: Hellgate Press, 2002), pp. 5–557. ISBN 1-55571-625-3.

Yankee Station was a point in the Gulf of Tonkin off the coast of Vietnam used by the U.S. Navy aircraft carriers of Task Force 77 to launch strikes in the Vietnam War. While its official designation was "Point Yankee," it was universally referred to as Yankee Station. Carriers conducting air operations at Yankee Station were said to be "on the line" and statistical summaries were based on days on the line.

8.2. From Wikipedia, based on references including Bowman, John S. *The Vietnam War Almanac* (New York: World Almanac Publications, 1985). ISBN 0-911818-85-5.

PIRAZ originated to protect Yankee station aircraft carriers during the Vietnam war.

The concept originated in the summer of 1966 as Yankee station was established for United States Task Force 77 aircraft carriers launching strikes against North Vietnam. A fixed patrol station within range of land-based aircraft made the stationed aircraft carriers vulnerable to attack. A PIRAZ station was established in the westernmost portion of the Gulf of Tonkin where air search RADAR coverage might extend over North Vietnam and the air-strike routes from Yankee station. This PIRAZ station radio call sign was "Red Crown." The first PIRAZ ships were USS King (DLG-10), USS Mahan (DLG-11), USS Long Beach (CGN-9), and USS Chicago (CG-11). Belknap class cruisers began rotating into PIRAZ station assignments in 1967; and USS Wainwright (CG-28), assisted in the Son Tay Raid on 21 November 1970.

PIRAZ cruisers carried long-range RIM-2 Terrier or RIM-8 Talos surface-to-air missiles to defend their stations. *Chicago* fired RIM-8H

Talos-ARM anti-radar homing missiles against North Vietnamese shore-based radar stations. Each PIRAZ cruiser was accompanied on station by a "shotgun" torpedo boat destroyer with quick-firing guns to defend the PIRAZ cruiser from torpedo boat attack. PIRAZ cruisers provided protective RADAR surveillance of the remotely piloted vehicles performing aerial photo reconnaissance of North Vietnam.

8.3. Account as recorded on the website the Gun Plot, a privately owned site about the Royal Australian Navy (http://www.gunplot.net/vietnam/hobartvietnam.html):

8.4. Conrad, *Heart of Darkness*, p. 18.

8.5. Ibid, p. xi.

8.6. See http://hawgheadtoo.tripod.com/OpSeaD.html.

8.7. Marolda, pp. 76, 78:

Although air power was the cutting edge of Task force 77, surface ships were essential to the interdiction campaign in North Vietnam and Laos. In Operation Sea Dragon, begun in October 1966, cruisers, destroyers, and for one month battleship *New Jersey* (BB 62) ranged the North Vietnamese littoral sinking Communist supply craft, shelling coastal batteries and radar sites, and complementing the aerial interdiction effort by bombarding the infiltration routes ashore. While at first restricted to coastal waters south of 17°31'N, by February 1967 the Sea Dragon force was authorized to operate as far north as 20th parallel. This area was constricted in April 1968 when the bombing halt ended American combat activity north of the 19th parallel.

Steaming generally in pairs, the two to four American and Australian destroyers and one cruiser worked with carrier-based spotter planes, such as the A-1 Skyraider and Grumman S-2 Tracker, to find, identify, and destroy infiltrating vessels and shore targets. Often, North Vietnamese coastal batteries fired back. Although several of the 19 ships that were hit required repairs in shipyards in Japan and the Philippines, no vessel was sunk during the two-year-long Sea Dragon operation.

8.8. See http://www.swiftboats.net and, from Wikipedia:

The PBR was a versatile boat with a fiberglass hull and water jet drive which enabled it to operate in shallow, weed-choked rivers. It drew only two feet of water fully loaded. The drives could be pivoted to reverse direction, turn the boat in its own length, or come to a stop from full speed in a few boat lengths.

8.9. See http://www.ptfnasty.com/ptfHistory.html:

8.10 Full text of letter of April 1969 from Steve Hayes:

It's already late at night and we've been up since 4 this morning, but I've got to write something about today—while it's still fresh in my mind.

5 boats underway at 0500 with Chinese mercenaries on board. Entered the Cua Lon just at dawn—full moon, reddening sky, the river was a river of glass. Up into the canal at the junction of the Bo-De and the Cua Lon.

Inserted troops and UDT on both sides of the canal—canal 75' wide—foliage very thick—mangroves. The troops were in mud up to their knees. Both banks were lined with punji stakes and "Tu Dig" [check spelling] signs—3 boats in the canal staying in the "pocket."

100 meters in—left bank ran across booby traps—grenades and claymores (homemade) troops detonated them intentionally—no injuries. Pushed on—going very

slow—mud too thick—troops extracted (on board) then inserted again further up.

And then it happened: on the left bank the VC fired into a claymore detonating it. Two Chinese injured—head injuries. VC opened up with small arms about 150' from us and from the troops. Troops fired—we opened up with both 50s. We were beached on the right bank firing diagonally up and across. A few rounds splattered the mud bank next to us. One more WIA (a round through the leg) stumbled out of the foliage—the interpreter.

We backed off—cast, and beached on the right bank—UDT corpsman jumped off the boat to the bank—helped WIA's on board—WIA's not serious

Suppressed fire

WIA's out the Bo De on 23 & 67 boats

We re-inserted UDT right bank—10' from a set fish stakes—later discovered a home-made claymore rigged to the stake—good god!!!—it could have killed us!

But that's another story....

Troopers detonated more booby traps, burned more hootches, and on and on...

1500-operation completed; out the Bo De and into the wonderful, fresh, safe, ocean-spray kicking up over the bow; wonderful spray washing away the caked-on mud—washing away the tension. The radio went on; people went to sleep—on the deck, in the cabin, in the gun tub, everywhere.

The breeze and sun and water were all so fresh and sweet—and we steamed around the point into the Gulf of Thailand—steaming, laughing and sleeping, I think, on borrowed time.

8.11. From http://www.olive-drab.com/od_history_vietnam_french.php:

A French offensive around Hoa Binh in 1951 ended with French withdrawal, after losses of about 900 French and ten times the number of Vietminh. Giap counterattacked French garrisons and drew them into repeated attempts to seize control of the war, all of which failed with high French casualties. In April 1953, the Vietminh upped the ante by invading Laos, further increasing the burdens on the French attempts to defend the region. The French countermoves attempted to draw the Vietminh into conventional battles at strong points, culminating at Dien Bien Phu, a long valley near the Laotian border. Giap destroyed the French at Dien Bien Phu by moving artillery into the surrounding hills, a position the French had discounted as impossible. While the French held out in a battle of attrition until May 1954, they lost over 7,000 soldiers there and had 11,000 taken prisoner, most of those never repatriated.

8.12. See Conrad, *Heart of Darkness*, p. 20:

Once, I remember, we came upon a man-of-war anchored off the coast. There wasn't even a shed there and she was shelling the bush. It appears the French had one of the wars going on thereabouts. Her ensign dropped limp like a rag; the muzzles of the long six-inch guns stuck out all over the low hull; the greasy, slimy swell swung her up lazily and let her down, swaying her thin masts. In the empty immensity of earth, sky, and water, there she was, incomprehensible, firing at the continent. Pop, would go one of the six inch guns, a small flame would dart and vanish, little white smoke would disappear, a tiny projectile would give a feeble screech-nothing happened. Nothing could happen. There was a touch of insanity in the proceeding, a sense of lugubrious drollery in the sight; and it was not dissipated by somebody on board assuring me earnestly there was a camp of natives—he called them enemies!-hidden out of sight somewhere.

9. Ship's Company

9.1. Wikipedia, from references including William H. McMichael, *The Mother of All Hooks: The Story of the U.S. Navy's Tailhook Scandal* (New Brunswick, NJ: Transaction Publishers, 1997), p. 273.

In September 1991, the 35th annual symposium in Las Vegas featured a two-day debrief on Navy and Marine Corps aviation in Operation Desert Storm. It was the largest such meeting yet held, with some 4,000 attendees: active, reserve, and retired personnel.

According to a Department of Defense (DoD) report, 83 women and 7 men stated that they had been victims of sexual assault and harassment during the meeting. Several participants later stated that a number of flag officers attending the meetings were aware of the sexual assaults, but did nothing to stop them.

The issues were never quite settled, and as late as 2002, the Tailhook chairman spoke of "the alleged misconduct that occurred in 1991."

Frontline on PBS reported:

Ultimately the careers of fourteen admirals and almost 300 naval aviators were scuttled or damaged by Tailhook. For example Secretary of the Navy H. Lawrence Garrett III and CNO Admiral Frank Kelso were both at Tailhook '91. Garrett ultimately resigned and Kelso retired early two years after the convention.

Author Jean Zimmerman developed the thesis that the scandal underscored the shifting status of women in the military and particularly the role of women in combat. As such, Tailhook can be seen as part of the evolution of the armed forces that continued through the losses of female soldiers in Iraq.

9.2. See "Ship Commander Under Fire For Lewd Videos He Filmed,",http://gantdaily.com/2011/01/02/ship-commander-under-fire-for-lewd-videos-he-filmed/).

9.3 From Nathaniel Bowditch, *The American Practical Navigator*, 1802, as excerpted in *Halsey's Typhoon*, Drury and Clavin, p. 63:

A tropical cyclone is a cyclone originating in the tropics or sub-tropics. Although it generally resembles the extratropical cyclone of higher latitudes, there are important differences, the principal one being the concentration of a large amount of energy into a relatively small area. Tropical cyclones are infrequent in comparison to middle and high latitude storms, but they have a record of destruction far exceeding that of any other type of storm. Because of their fury, and because they are primarily oceanic, they merit special attention by mariners. A tropical storm may have a deceptively small size, and beautiful weather may be experienced only a few hundred miles from the center. The rapidity with which the weather can deteriorate with the approach of the storm, and the violence of the fully developed tropical cyclone, are difficult to imagine if they have not been experienced.

9.4 See *Halsey's Typhoon*, Drury and Clavin, where three destroyers were lost in a typhoon off of the west coast of Luzon Island in the Philippines in December 1944.

9.5 *Knight's Modern Seamanship*, pp. 552–553.

10. A Ship Has No Brakes

10.1. Stavridis, *Destroyer Captain*, p. 67.

10.2. *Watch Officer's Guide*, 9th edition, page 83.

10.3. See http://www.minihelicopter.net/AH1HueyCobra/index.htm for a description of the AH-1 Huey Cobra.

11. Battlewagon and Battle Stations

11.1. See http://en.wikipedia.org/wiki/USS_New_Jersey_(BB-62) and http://www.ussnewjersey.org/1968_narrative.htm.

11.2. See http://www.naval-technology.com/projects/dd21.

11.3. See http://www.history.navy.mil/danfs/n4/new_jersey-ii.htm

New Jersey, then the world's only active battleship, departed Philadelphia 16 May, calling at Norfolk and transiting the Panama Canal 4 June before arriving at her new home port of Long Beach, California, 11 June. Further training off Southern California followed. On 24 July *New Jersey* received 16 inch shells and powder tanks from *Mount Katmai* by conventional highline transfer and by helicopter lift, the first time heavy battleship ammunition had been transferred by helicopter at sea.[2]

Reactivated once more in the 1980s as part of the 600-ship Navy program, *New Jersey* was modernized to carry missiles and recommissioned for service. In 1983, she participated in U.S. operations during the Lebanese Civil War.

11.4: From the *Lowry*'s website, http://hawgheadtoo.tripod.com/LHIST-5.html:

While carrying out their duties 66 Sea Dragon ships were fired upon by coastal defense batteries in 169 incidents, with 38 ships receiving enemy fire on three or more occasions (for Sumner it was 12 times). Of these, 29 warships were hit, with three ships hit twice. Despite improved accuracy of shore-based artillery, Sea Dragon forces suffered only light casualties—five sailors killed and 26 wounded. Communist gunners failed to put any ship out of commission, although 19 ships withdrew to Japan or the Philippines for repairs.

12. Back to the Future

12.1: *Back to the Future* is a 1985 American science-fiction comedy film. It is a classic time machine film where the protagonist is transported instantaneously to and from the past in a souped up car which goes through a time warp when it reaches high speed..

13. Into the Sunrise

13.1: Coleridge, "Rime of the Ancient Mariner"

A more extended version is:
'At length did cross an Albatross,
Thorough the fog it came;
As it had been a Christian soul,
We hail'd it in God's name.

It ate the food it ne'er had eat,
And round and round it flew.
The ice did split with a thunder-fit;
The helmsman steered us through!

And a good south wind sprung up behind;
The Albatross did follow,
And every day, for food or play,
Came to the mariner's hollo!

In mist or cloud, on mast or shroud,
It perched for vespers nine;
Whiles all the night, through fog-smoke white,
Glimmer'd the white moonshine.'

"God save thee, ancient Mariner,
From the fiends that plague thee thus! -
Why look'st thou so?' -"With my crossbow
I shot the Albatross."

Part II

'The sun now rose upon the right:
Out of the sea came he,
Still hid in mist, and on the left
Went down into the sea.

And the good south wind still blew behind,
But no sweet bird did follow,
Nor any day for food or play
Came to the mariners' hollo!

And I had done a hellish thing,
And it would work 'em woe:
For all averr'd I had kill'd the bird
That made the breeze to blow.
Ah wretch! said they, the bird to slay,
That made the breeze to blow!

13.2. from: http://www.islandnet.com/~see/weather/elements/stelmo.htm

The appearance of St. Elmo's Fire was regarded as a good omen, for it tended to occur in the dissipating stages of severe thunderstorms when the most violent surface winds and seas were abating. Thus, it was interpreted as the answer to the sailors' prayers for heavenly intervention. Its appearance preceding a storm or during fair weather portended that the guiding hand of St. Elmo would be present.

written by Keith C. Heidorn, PhD, THE WEATHER DOCTOR, May 30, 1998

13.3. from: http://airandspace.si.edu/collections/imagery/apollo/as11/a11.htm:

Apollo 11 was the first manned mission to land on the Moon. The first steps by humans on another planetary body were taken by Neil Armstrong and Buzz Aldrin on July 20, 1969. The astronauts also returned to Earth the first samples from another planetary body. Apollo 11 achieved its primary mission - to perform a manned lunar landing and return the mission safely to Earth - and paved the way for the Apollo lunar landing missions to follow. 13.4. For a fuller historical explanation see: http://www.goatlocker.org/resources/nav/crossline.pdf.

13.5. Wikipedia, Angola:

Angola was a Portuguese colony from the 16th century to 1975. After independence, Angola was the scene of an intense civil war from 1975 to 2002. The country has vast mineral and petroleum reserves; however, its life expectancy and infant mortality rates are both among the worst-ranked in the world.

13.6. Wikipedia, Cape of Good Hope:

When following the western side of the African coastline from the equator...the Cape of Good Hope marks the point where a ship begins to travel more eastward than southward. Thus the first rounding of the cape in 1488 by Portuguese explorer Bartolomeu Dias was a milestone in the attempts by the Portuguese to establish direct trade relations with the Far East. Dias called the cape *Cabo das Tormentas.* "Cape of Tempests" was the original name of the "Cape of Good Hope."

As one of the great capes of the South Atlantic Ocean, the Cape of Good Hope has been of special significance to sailors for many years and is widely referred to by them simply as "the Cape." It is a waypoint on the clipper route followed by clipper ships to the Far East and Australia, and still followed by several offshore yacht races.

14. The World

14.1 The full text of Walter Cronkite's statement can be found at :

Source: *Reporting Vietnam: Part One: American Journalism 1959–1969* (1998), pp. 581–582

14.2: Wikipedia from references including:

Stephen E. Ambrose, "The Christmas Bombing", *MHQ: The Quarterly Journal of Military History* 4 (Winter 1992), pp. 8-17.

Dr. Albert Atkins, *We Won: And Then There Was Linebacker II: Strategic and Political Issues Surrounding the Bombing Campaign.* Bloomington, IN: AuthorHouse, 2009. (237 pp?).

Operation *Linebacker II* was a US Seventh Air Force and US Navy Task Force 77 aerial bombing campaign, conducted against targets in the Democratic Republic of Vietnam (North Vietnam) during the final period of US involvement in the Vietnam War. The operation was conducted from 18–29 December 1972, leading to several of informal names such as "The December Raids" and "The Christmas Bombings." It saw the largest heavy bomber strikes launched by the US Air Force since the end of World War II. *Linebacker II* was a resumption of the Operation Linebacker bombings conducted from May to October, with the emphasis of the new campaign shifted to attacks by B-52 Stratofortress bombers rather than tactical fighter aircraft. 1,600 civilians died in Hanoi and Haiphong in the raids.

See also Marolda, "Linebacker," p. 333.

INDEX

ABOUT THE AUTHOR

Hank Abernathy is an architect practicing and living in New York with his wife, Pam. He enjoys running, sketching, and being with his family.

52532330R00207

Made in the USA
Lexington, KY
16 September 2019